THE NVIDIA WAY

THE
NVIDIA
WAY

Jensen Huang and the Making of a Tech Giant

TAE KIM

W. W. NORTON & COMPANY

Independent Publishers Since 1923

For information about permission to reproduce selections from this book, write to
Permissions, W. W. Norton & Company, Inc., 500 Fifth Avenue, New York, NY 10110

For information about special discounts for bulk purchases, please contact
W. W. Norton Special Sales at specialsales@wwnorton.com or 800-233-4830

Manufacturing by Lakeside Book Company
Book design by Beth Steidle
Production manager: Lauren Abbate

ISBN 978-1-324-08671-0

W. W. Norton & Company, Inc.
500 Fifth Avenue, New York, NY 10110
www.wwnorton.com

W. W. Norton & Company Ltd.
15 Carlisle Street, London W1D 3BS

10 9 8 7 6 5 4 3 2 1

To Helena and Noah

CONTENTS

PART IV
INTO THE FUTURE
(2013–PRESENT)

THE NVIDIA WAY

INTRODUCTION

IN ANOTHER LIFE, JENSEN HUANG MIGHT HAVE BEEN A teacher. His preferred medium is the whiteboard: at many of the meetings he attends at Nvidia, where he has been the CEO since he cofounded the company in 1993, he will leap up, his favorite chisel-tip, dry-erase marker in hand, and diagram a problem or sketch out an idea—even if someone else is speaking or whiteboarding themselves at the same time. In fact, he alternates between teacher and student, fostering a collaborative ethos among his employees to develop their thinking and solve the issues they face. His sketches are so precise that they could be turned into usable schematics for technical documents; colleagues call him "Professor Jensen" for his ability to explain complicated concepts on the whiteboard in a way just about anyone can understand.

At Nvidia, the whiteboard is more than the primary form of communication at meetings. It represents both possibility and ephemerality—the belief that a successful idea, no matter how brilliant, must eventually be erased, and a new one must take its place. Every conference room in the company's two headquarters buildings in Santa Clara, California, has a whiteboard, signaling that each day and each meeting is a new opportunity, and that innovation is a necessity, not an option. Whiteboarding also requires active thinking and inevitably reveals how well (or not) any employee, including an executive, knows the material. Employees must demonstrate their thought process in real time, in front of an audience; there's no hiding behind neatly formatted slides or slick marketing videos.

The whiteboard is perhaps the ultimate symbol of the unique culture at Nvidia—the microchip designer that has grown from humble beginnings in the 1990s, when it was one of dozens of computer graphics chip companies and known mainly by hardcore gamers seeking the best performance for the first-person shooter *Quake* and other games, into the premiere supplier of advanced processors for our age of artificial intelligence (AI). The architecture of the company's processors is well suited for AI workloads because of its ability to perform mathematical calculations simultaneously—essential for training and running advanced large-language AI models. Nvidia's early recognition of the significance of AI and its forward-thinking investments over the course of more than a decade—including enhancement of hardware capabilities, development of AI software tools, and optimization of networking performance—made the company's technology platform perfectly positioned to capitalize on and become the primary beneficiary of the current AI wave. AI use cases are now plentiful. Companies are harnessing Nvidia-powered AI servers to boost programmer productivity by generating lower-level code that developers find tedious to write, automating repetitive customer-service tasks, and empowering designers to create and alter images on the basis of text prompts, enabling the faster iteration of ideas.

Nvidia's reinvention has paid off: on June 18, 2024, the company surpassed Microsoft to become the world's most valuable company, at a market capitalization of $3.3 trillion. It reached that milestone on the back of the immense demand for its AI chips; the company's stock price had tripled over the previous twelve months. To call Nvidia's stock a historically good investment is to understate things. Between its IPO in early 1999 and the end of 2023, Nvidia investors enjoyed the highest annualized compound return for any U.S. stock in history through a compound annual growth rate (CAGR) of more than 33 percent.[1] If an investor had purchased $10,000 of Nvidia stock when it made its market debut on January 22, 1999, that stock would have been worth $13.2 million on December 31, 2023.

Nvidia's culture starts with Jen-Hsun Huang, who is known simply as "Jensen" to his friends, employees, suppliers, competitors, investors, and admirers. (This is how I refer to him throughout the book.) He had already found a modicum of fame before the AI boom, having been named to *Time* magazine's list of the one hundred most influential people in the world in 2021. But as Nvidia's value reached $1 trillion, then $2 trillion and $3 trillion, his profile has grown commensurately. It is now common to see his trademark leather jacket and shock of silver hair, always combed into a simple side part, in articles and video clips, many of which described Jensen as the "genius you've never heard of."

To those of us who have covered the semiconductor industry, Jensen has been a known quantity for some time. He has run Nvidia for its entire three-decade history, the longest tenure of any current technology CEO. He has driven the company not only to survive, but to surpass all of its competitors in the unforgiving and volatile chip sector, and to surpass just about every other company on Earth, as well. I have been following Nvidia in a professional capacity for much of my career—first as an equity analyst and now as a journalist—and I have seen how his guidance and strategic vision have shaped the company over the years. Even so, my view has remained that of the outside observer, dependent as much on interpretation as on concrete fact. To learn the secrets of Nvidia's success, I would have to talk with many people, inside and outside the company. I would also have to speak with Jensen himself: to become his student, much like his employees do.

I GOT MY CHANCE JUST four days before Nvidia became the most valuable company in the world. Nvidia knew I was writing a book, and, in early June 2024, a representative offered to arrange a meeting with Jensen to occur immediately after his commencement address to the California Institute of Technology's graduating class of 2024. I agreed, and a few minutes before 10:00 a.m. on Friday, June 14, I found myself in front of a stage, waiting for Jensen to appear. It was a perfect California day, clear blue sky and warm sunshine. The students and their families took their seats under a large white tent. David Thompson, the chair of Caltech's Board of Trustees, introduced Jensen and joked that the Nvidia CEO had drawn so much attention earlier in the day, as the two made their way around campus, that it felt like he had been walking alongside Elvis.

During his speech, Jensen suggested to the students that their graduation from Caltech would mark one of the peaks of their lives. He mentioned that he knew something about peaks, too. "We are both at the peaks of our career," he said. "For all of you who have been paying attention to Nvidia and myself, you know what I mean. It's just that in your case, you'll have many, many more peaks to go. I just hope that today is not my peak. Not the peak." He vowed to work as hard as ever to ensure that there would be even more peaks ahead for Nvidia, implying that the new graduates should follow his example.

After Jensen concluded, I was whisked over to the Keck Center for Space Studies and led into a wood-paneled conference room with black-and-white photos of pilots, astronauts, and presidents on the walls, where he was waiting for me. We chatted a bit before I got to my prepared questions. I explained that I was a PC gaming nerd who had been building my own computers since the 1990s. I first encountered Nvidia while researching graphics cards and invariably chose their products. And I mentioned that earlier in my career, at a Wall Street fund, an investment in Nvidia became my first big winner.

"Good for you," Jensen deadpanned. "Nvidia is my first big winner too."

We launched into a wide-ranging discussion of the company's history. Jensen knows that many of his former employees look back on Nvidia's beginnings with nostalgia. But he resists overly positive accounts of Nvidia's start-up period—and his own missteps.

"When we were younger, Tae, we sucked at a lot of things. Nvidia wasn't a great company on day one. We made it great over thirty-one years. It didn't come out great," he said. "You didn't build NV1 because you were great. You didn't build NV2 because you were great," he said, referring to the company's first two chip designs, both of which were flops that nearly killed Nvidia. "We survived ourselves. We were our own worst enemy."

There were several more near-death experiences. But each time, amid the stress and the pressure, the company learned from its mistakes. It retained a core of die-hard employees, many of whom remain in the fold to this day. Of course, there were also people who didn't stay, requiring the company to integrate new hires. "Every single time, somebody left, and every single time we picked ourselves up. We healed the company into existence," he said.

He slipped into the third person. "If Jensen wasn't even involved in the first fifteen years of our company, I would really like that," he laughed, meaning he wasn't proud of how the company was managed then or of his own naïveté and lack of strategic thinking.

I was put in the unusual position of defending Nvidia's past to its founder. I pointed out that the early decisions—about which I had learned a great deal by this point in my research process—weren't all bad ones. While mistakes were made, some of the misfires were tied to factors that were unpredictable or out of his or the company's control. With hindsight, many of them appeared to have been unavoidable.

"Yeah, that's fine," said Jensen. "I don't love talking about our past."

I FOUND THIS TO BE A pervasive attitude within Nvidia: that the culture of the place discourages looking back, whether at errors or successes, in favor of focusing on the future—the blank whiteboard of opportunity. But you cannot understand what Nvidia is today without understanding how it got to this point. This book is the first to tell the story of Nvidia—the full story, not just Jensen Huang's, although he is at the center of everything. It explores the founding of Nvidia by Jensen, Curtis Priem, and Chris Malachowsky, in a back booth at a Denny's all the way back in 1993—many lifetimes ago, to anyone working in technology. Nvidia would never have come into existence without the contributions of all three men. Jensen's business acumen and hard-driving management style were critical to Nvidia's early success, but Priem's chip architecture prowess and Malachowsky's manufacturing expertise were essential, too.

It is a thirty-year story, so far, and to tell it I interviewed more than one hundred people. Many of them are current or former Nvidia employees and know the company's inner workings intimately—this group includes Jensen, his two cofounders, and most of the early and current senior management team. Others include the two original venture capitalists who invested in Nvidia; technology industry CEOs; the partners who have helped Nvidia manufacture and sell its chips; and those at other semiconductor companies who competed with, and almost invariably lost to, Nvidia.

Through these interviews, I began to understand what makes Nvidia special. Its defining characteristic is not its technological prowess, which is more a consequence than a root cause. It is not the financial resources and the new opportunities that come from a high market valuation. It is not a mystical ability to see the future. It is not luck. Rather, it is a unique organizational design and work culture that I have come to call "the Nvidia Way." This culture combines unusual independence for each employee with the highest possible standards; it encourages maximum speed while demanding maximum quality; it allows Jensen to act as strategist and enforcer with a direct line of sight to everyone and everything at the company. Above all, it demands an almost superhuman level of effort and mental resilience from everyone. It's not just that working at Nvidia is intense, though it certainly is; it's that Jensen's management style is unlike anything else in corporate America.

Jensen runs the company in the way he does because he believes that Nvidia's worst enemy is not the competition, but itself—more specifically, the complacency that grips any successful company, particularly one with a long and impressive track record such as Nvidia. In my work as a journalist, I have seen that companies tend to become dysfunctional as they succeed and grow, largely because of internal politics, with employees focused not on driving innovation or serving customers but on advancing their bosses' careers. This jockeying distracts them from doing their best work and leaves them constantly looking over their shoulder for the threat from the next office over. It is something that Jensen has structured Nvidia to eliminate.

"Over the years, I realized what was happening, how people protect their turf and they protect their ideas. I created a much flatter organization," Jensen said. His antidote to the backstabbing, to the gaming of metrics, and to political infighting is public accountability and, if needed, public embarrassment. "If we have leaders who are not fighting for other people to be successful and [who are] depriving opportunities to others, I'll just say it out loud," he said. "I've got no trouble calling people out. You do that once or twice, nobody's going to go near that again."

Nvidia's unique culture might sound strange or unusually grueling, even for the tech industry. But among all the former Nvidia employees I talked to, it was hard to find a dissenter. They all reported that the company was largely free from the internal politics and indecisiveness typical in large organizations. They mentioned how difficult it was to adjust to working at other companies where direct, blunt communication is rare and there's far less urgency to get things done. And they described how Nvidia not only empowered them, but also *required* them to fulfill their professional calling, as a necessary condition of employment.

In a sense, that is the Nvidia Way in its purest form. It is the unwavering belief that there is tremendous reward in doing your job the best you can. It is the drive to persevere amid adversity. Or, as Jensen put it when looking directly into my eyes: the secret to his company's success is nothing more than "sheer will."

MORE PRECISELY, IT IS JENSEN'S personal will that has shaped Nvidia. He has personally made the most consequential decisions in its history. His ability to place the right major bets on emerging technologies stems from his deep technical knowledge—a founder with an engineering background. I have tried in this book to distill the Nvidia Way down to a set of principles that anyone can learn from, if not use. But behind them all lurks a question: Can you really separate Nvidia from its CEO?

As of this writing, Jensen is sixty-one years old. He has run the company for thirty-one years—more than half his life. Nvidia is bigger, more profitable, and more crucial to the global economy than ever before. Yet it still relies on Jensen, as a business leader and a tone setter. Apple survived the ouster of Steve Jobs in 1985 and his death in 2011; Amazon, Microsoft, and Google all did well after Jeff Bezos, Bill

Gates, and Larry Page and Sergey Brin wanted to move on. Someday, Nvidia will have to face a similar transition. It is not quite clear what the company might look like post-Jensen—whether its culture will survive, whether it will maintain its momentum.

After all, a whiteboard is only as useful as the person who holds the marker. It can reflect genius, but it cannot create it.

PART I

THE EARLY YEARS

(PRE-1993)

CHAPTER 1

Pain and Suffering

WHEN JENSEN HUANG WAS FOUR YEARS OLD, HIS FATHER visited New York City and fell in love with America. From that point on, his parents had one goal: to find a way to raise him and his older brother in the land of opportunity.

It would not be an easy task. Jensen was born in Taiwan on February 17, 1963, to Taiwanese parents. They were not wealthy and moved around based on the needs of his father's work. They ended up in Thailand for an extended period. Jensen's mother taught her two boys English, each day selecting ten words at random in the dictionary and asking them to spell the words and memorize their definitions.[1]

After a wave of political unrest hit Thailand, Jensen's parents decided to send him and his brother to Tacoma, Washington, to live with their aunt and uncle. Tacoma was once called the "City of Destiny," because it sat at the end of the Northern Pacific Railroad, but by the 1970s it was about as far from the dynamism of New York City as it was possible to get: damp, dreary, and smelling of sulfur thanks to the paper pulping and processing plants that lay on the outskirts of town. Jensen's aunt and uncle were recent immigrants to the United States themselves and did the best they could to help their nephews adjust to their new country while they waited for Jensen's parents to follow them across the Pacific.

The two boys were difficult to handle. "We could never sit still," Jensen said. "We were eating all the candy in the cupboard, jumping off the roof, climbing out the windows, tracking mud into the house, forgetting to close the shower curtain, and flooding the bathroom floor."[2]

Even though they had not yet made the move to the United States themselves, his parents wanted to send their children to an American boarding school so they could get a good education. They found one called Oneida Baptist Institute, which was located in eastern Kentucky and accepted international students. They could afford the tuition only by selling nearly all of their possessions.

Jensen remembers the initial drive through the mountains of Kentucky, past the single building that was the town of Oneida's only gas station, grocery store, and post office all at once. The boarding school had around three hundred students, evenly split between boys and girls. But it was not a prep school as Jensen's family originally thought. Oneida Baptist Institute was, instead, a reform school for troubled young people. It had been founded in the 1890s to remove children from feuding families in the state and thus keep them from killing each other.

As befit its original purpose, the school held its students to a strict routine. Each morning, Jensen would cross the Red Bird River on a worn-out swing bridge to attend his classes. He joined the swim team, played soccer, and discovered new foods such as Jell-O, sausage, biscuits, and gravy. He went to church twice a week and watched ABC's Sunday Night Movie on the weekends. Some evenings, he would play chess with the school custodian. On others, he would help him fill the vending machines and get a free soda in return. The occasional trip to town gave him an opportunity to buy fudgesicles at the grocery store; otherwise, he would content himself eating apples off of the tree outside his dorm room window.

Above all, there were the chores. Every student was required to work every day. Already strong enough for extended manual labor, Jensen's brother was assigned to work at a nearby tobacco farm. For his part, Jensen was on janitorial duty for his three-story dorm. "I had to clean the bathrooms," he said. "You can't unsee that kind of stuff."[3]

Jensen's relative youth, and likely his different ethnicity as well, made him a target of bullies. Even though the school was ostensibly designed to reform its pupils, in practice oversight could be lax, and Jensen was beaten up often in his first months on campus. Even his roommate was intimidating: he was eight years older than Jensen, and his whole body was covered in tattoos and scars from stab wounds. Eventually, Jensen learned to overcome his fear. He befriended his roommate and taught him how to read, and in exchange the other boy introduced Jensen to weightlifting. Jensen took to it, and it gave him not only strength but confidence—the ability and desire to stand up for himself.

Later in his life, Jensen's executives would say he had developed his tough, street-fighter mentality during his days in Kentucky. "Maybe this is a bit of my early schooling, I will never start a fight, but I will never walk away from one. So, if someone is going to pick on me, they'd better think twice," Jensen himself said.[4]

After a few years, Jensen's parents moved from Thailand to Beaverton, Oregon, a city on the outskirts of the Portland metropolitan area. They withdrew the boys from the "boarding school" in Kentucky and enrolled them in public school. Although Jensen was happy to be back with his parents, he looked back on his time at Oneida Baptist as formative.

"I don't get scared often. I don't worry about going places I haven't gone before. I can tolerate a lot of discomfort."[5]

ON THE FOURTH FLOOR OF the Elks Club building in downtown Portland, inside an ornate ballroom with chandeliers and carved ceilings, a man named Lou Bochenski had started a table-tennis club called the Paddle Palace. It was open every day from 10:00 a.m. to 10:00 p.m. and had a thriving juniors program for young enthusiasts. After school, Jensen would often end up at the Paddle Palace, where he discovered both a talent and a passion for the sport. He would also once again find himself doing janitorial work, now to make some extra money—Bochenski paid him to scrub the Paddle Palace's floors.

This was not just charity on Bochenski's part. His daughter, Judy Hoarfrost, was a member of the "ping-pong diplomacy" team that visited China in 1971. In fact, Hoarfrost and her eight teammates were the first group of Americans to make a state-sponsored visit to China since the Communist Revolution in 1949. Although they lost most of their matches, their trip signaled a thawing in U.S.-Chinese relations— and helped increase the profile of table tennis in the United States. Bochenski considered it his duty to help discover promising young table-tennis players and develop them into national-level talents.

Both Hoarfrost and Bochenski were impressed by Jensen's skills and work ethic,[6] so much so that in 1978, Bochenski wrote a letter to *Sports Illustrated* magazine that praised Jensen as the "most promising junior" ever to emerge in the Pacific Northwest. He pointedly said that, unlike other teenagers written up in the magazine whose families spent $10,000 annually on traveling to tournaments, Jensen earned his own travel money.

"He is a straight-A student and very hungry to become a table-tennis champion. He has played only three months, but I suggest you watch out for him in another year," Bochenski wrote.[7] At the time, Jensen was only fourteen.

At one point, he went to Las Vegas for a national table-tennis tournament. But the lights and sounds of the city were too alluring for him. Instead of resting up before his matches, he stayed up all night walking up and down the Strip. He lost badly—and never forgot the sting of his own failure.

"When you're thirteen or fourteen years old and you go to Las Vegas for the first time, it's hard to focus on the match," he said three decades later.[8] "To this day, I regret not being more focused on the tournament."

When he was fifteen, he entered the U.S. Open Junior Doubles tournament. This time, he knew better than to let himself get distracted and came in third place overall.

JENSEN WAS ALWAYS A GOOD student. Learning how to interact socially with other people, though, was more challenging.

"I was very introverted. I was incredibly shy," he said. "The one experience that pulled me out of my shell was waiting tables at Denny's."

When Jensen was fifteen, his brother helped him get a job at a

Denny's in Portland. He would work at the twenty-four-hour diner for several summers in high school and college. Jensen started where he always had, doing the dirty work of washing dishes and cleaning bathrooms. "I did more bathrooms than any CEO in the history of CEOs," he would recall.[9] He then became a busboy and later waited tables.

He believed that Denny's equipped him with a number of significant life skills, including how to navigate chaos, work under time pressure, communicate with customers, and handle mistakes (in this case, from the kitchen). It also taught him to find satisfaction in the quality of his work, no matter how minor the task, and to fulfill each according to the highest possible standards. It didn't matter if he was cleaning the same toilet for the hundredth time or interacting with a new customer who had never been to a Denny's before and didn't know what to order. He recalls pushing himself to do the best he could, even if it meant chasing an absurd goal such as being able to carry more cups of coffee at a time than anyone else on staff. He learned to take pride in daily toil.

"I'm certain I was the best dishwasher, busboy, and waiter they've ever had," he said.

Except when it came to one common order. "I hated shakes because I hated making them," he said; it took a long time to prepare a single shake and an even longer time to clean up afterward. He would try to nudge customers to order Coke instead, and if they persisted, he would ask, "Are you sure?"[10] Already, he was learning another fact of working life: the trade-off between having high standards and being efficient with one's time.

JENSEN ATTENDED ALOHA HIGH SCHOOL in Beaverton, Oregon, where he made friends in the math, computer, and science clubs. He spent all his free moments programming BASIC on the Apple II and playing games on teletype terminals, which looked like electric typewriters, and which were connected to a larger mainframe computer.

He "fell in love" with video games, in particular the *Star Trek* mainframe game, which was based on the classic Hasbro board game *Battleship*.[11] He also spent a good deal of time playing Atari and Konami games at the arcade, including *Asteroids*, *Centipede*, and *Galaxian*.[12] He didn't have a computer at home, so he had to go elsewhere to get his gaming fix. "We had no money," he said.[13]

The precocious Jensen had skipped a grade at his elementary school in Thailand and again at Oneida Baptist Institute in Kentucky. He graduated from Aloha High School at the age of sixteen and decided to attend Oregon State University in Corvallis, both because of the low in-state tuition and because his best friend, Dean Verheiden, was going there too. Together, Jensen and Verheiden chose electrical engineering as their major and took many of the same classes. Hoping to gain relevant work experience, Jensen applied repeatedly for an internship at a local technology company called Techtronic Industries but was rejected every time.

During his sophomore year, Jensen met Lori Mills, one of only three girls in an electrical engineering class of two hundred fifty students. "I was the youngest kid in the class. I was tiny. I was skinny. But I had a great pickup line," Jensen said, who by this point had grown out of his awkward phase and had sharpened his social skills. "Do you want to see my homework?"[14]

The line worked. He and Mills began dating, and they got married shortly after they both graduated in 1984. Jensen was invited to interview with some of the largest semiconductor and chip makers in the country. He first had his eye on Texas Instruments, whose offices spanned multiple zip codes, but his interview went poorly, and he didn't get an offer. He next interviewed with two companies based in California. The first was Advanced Micro Devices, or AMD, a company that Jensen had idolized ever since he saw a poster of one of their microprocessors at Oregon State. The second was LSI Logic, which made customizable microchips called application-specific integrated circuits, or ASICs, for technical and scientific uses.

He received offers from both companies and chose AMD, because he was more familiar with its reputation. By day, he designed microchips; at night and on the weekends, he took courses at Stanford so that he could get his master's in electrical engineering. On top of his work and his continuing studies, he and Lori had a son, Spencer, and daughter, Madison. Because he couldn't take many classes at once, completing the master's degree was a long, arduous process; he finally finished after eight years. "I have a very long-term horizon," he said. "I can be impatient about certain things, but infinitely patient about others. I plug away."[15]

Between his job, his master's, and his family, Jensen had achieved the dream of so many immigrant parents, who make huge sacrifices to move to the United States in order to give their children the chance for a better life.

"My father's dream and my mom's aspirations for our success are what ultimately put us here," Jensen said nearly thirty years later, when asked to reflect on his past. "I owe them a great deal."[16]

Yet Jensen's well of ambition ran deeper still. The drive to do every job to perfection and, at the same time, as efficiently as it could possibly be done now led him to question his own work designing microprocessors. Although he was good at designing microchips for AMD, he found it tedious; at the time, it was still done manually, by hand.

One of his office mates had left for LSI and wanted Jensen to come with him to the company. And Jensen, like most people in the chip-making industry, had heard that LSI was now pioneering new software tools that promised to make the process of chip design much faster and easier. The idea intrigued him. Although he knew it would mean taking a risk, he felt a need to work at a company that, to him, seemed to have a clear grasp on the future of the chip industry. It was an early sign of his restless, forward-thinking nature, which would lead him to pursue the cutting edge even if it meant leaving safety and security behind.

He took the plunge and joined LSI. There, he was given a technical role working with customers. He was assigned to a start-up called Sun Microsystems, where he met two engineers, Curtis Priem and Chris Malachowsky, who were working on a secret project that promised to revolutionize how people used workstation computers—high-performance computers built to perform specialized technical or scientific tasks, such as three-dimensional modeling or industrial design.

Luck had clearly played a part in bringing Jensen to this new opportunity. So had his own talent and skills. But as he saw it, the biggest single factor that propelled him from scrubbing toilets to managing entire divisions of a microchip company was his willingness, and ability, to put in more effort, and tolerate more suffering, than anyone else.

"People with very high expectations have very low resilience. Unfortunately, resilience matters in success," he later said. "Greatness is not intelligence. Greatness comes from character."[17] And character, in his view, can only be the result of overcoming setbacks and adversity. To Jensen, the struggle to persevere in the face of bad, and often overwhelming, odds is simply what work is.

It is why, whenever someone asks him for advice on how to achieve success, his answer has been consistent over the years: "I wish upon you ample doses of pain and suffering."

CHAPTER 2

The Graphics Revolution

AS A TEENAGER, CURTIS PRIEM TAUGHT HIMSELF HOW TO program by writing games in the computer lab of his high school in Fairview Park, Ohio, just outside of Cleveland. The school had a Teletype Model 33 ASR Coupler terminal, which connected to a mainframe computer located about ten miles away and transmitted data over a phone line at a speed of about 10 characters per second. He wrote in BASIC, transferred his instructions onto punched paper tape, and fed the tape into the Teletype's tape reader in order to run his programs remotely on the mainframe.

Priem's most ambitious project was a billiards game. The program would show a layout of balls on a billiards table by using text characters, and players would take turns specifying the angle and speed at which they would strike the cue ball. The mainframe would then calculate the collisions and the resulting positions of the billiard balls. The program was massive; its punched tape roll measured nearly nine inches in diameter and took almost an hour to print every time Priem wrote a new version of the game. When he submitted it as an entry in a local science fair, he won first prize.

Priem's programming exploits brought him to the attention of Elmer Kress, the chair of Fairview Park's math department. Kress became Priem's mentor and allowed him to access the school's lone mainframe terminal as often as he wanted, once the other students had their chance to use it for schoolwork. As Priem became more proficient at programming, he learned how to digitize images by hand by use of a monochrome wheel, and he wrote a program that could manipulate those digitized images on the computer. Priem's journey into computer graphics began with the simple act of scaling and rotating a digitized photo of Kress.

WHEN CONSIDERING COLLEGES, PRIEM FOCUSED on three schools: the Massachusetts Institute of Technology, Case Western Reserve University, and Rensselaer Polytechnic Institute (RPI). Two factors led him to favor the last: at RPI, professors, not teaching assistants, taught freshman classes, and the school had recently announced that it would be acquiring an advanced IBM 3033 mainframe computer, which would be made accessible even to incoming freshmen. Although Priem was accepted at all three schools, there was never any question where he would end up once he heard about the new IBM.

At RPI, Priem immersed himself in computers. He hand-built his own multibus computer, linking an Intel 8080 processor to two eight-inch floppy disk drives and a monitor. And, of course, he spent plenty of time with the university's IBM 3033—a room-sized mainframe that was housed inside RPI's Voorhees Computer Center and which generated enough heat to warm the entire building during the winter.

But Priem's trajectory seemed to change during his sophomore year, after his father lost his job. Without a steady income, his parents could no longer afford to pay for his education. They asked RPI for assistance, but the college didn't offer any direct aid beyond a job at a campus engineering lab; the wages Priem would earn there wouldn't be nearly enough to cover tuition. To fund his last two years at RPI, Priem enrolled in a work-experience program sponsored by General Motors, which sought to fast-track promising engineers into management positions. Each summer, Priem and his GM Scholar cohort would work on a number of projects at various assembly plants. During one stint, Priem programmed the machines that produced compression-molded body panels for the Pontiac Fiero.

When Priem received his degree in electrical engineering in 1982, General Motors offered him a full scholarship to continue his graduate studies, provided that he take a job with the company afterward. RPI also invited him to continue on as a graduate-level researcher in graphics.

Priem had other ideas. Two years earlier, a pair of entrepreneurs in California named Steve Jobs and Steve Wozniak had led their personal computer start-up to a blockbuster IPO—and had earned themselves a more than $100 million payday each in the process. Apple's revenues had reached nearly $300 million on the sales of the Apple II computer, making it the fastest-growing company in history. The Apple II proved that there was a huge market for personal computers that were smaller, cheaper, and better, for both productivity and entertainment, than mainframes and minicomputers. The emergence of the personal computer gave engineers such as Priem opportunities not only to do what they loved, which was to make cutting-edge graphics chips, but to do it in a setting that could earn them a huge payday.

Priem decided to accept a job offer from Vermont Microsystems, a hardware start-up that appeared to be on the cusp of its big break. It was located in an old textile mill just outside of Burlington, about a three-hour drive north of RPI's campus. Vermont Microsystems made its own plug-in boards, including graphics cards, for computer manufacturers. At a trade show in Chicago, an IBM representative visited the company's booth and asked whether Vermont Microsystems could make a graphics card specifically for the IBM PC. In true start-up fashion, the representatives at the booth said absolutely. What they didn't say was that they had precisely one person on staff with the necessary knowledge and skills to make such a card, and that person was the newly graduated, newly hired, twenty-three-year-old Curtis Priem.

Overnight, Priem went from staff engineer to principal design architect for the card that became the IBM Professional Graphics Controller, or PGC, which was released in 1984. The PGC represented a significant upgrade over the graphical capabilities of graphics cards of earlier IBM PCs. The first PCs used a Monochrome Display Adapter

(MDA) card, which could render only green text on a black background that was eighty characters wide and twenty-five characters tall. Subsequent models used Color Graphics Adapter (CGA) cards, which gave PCs the ability to manipulate individual picture elements (pixels) at a resolution of up to 640 × 200 and a depth of up to sixteen colors. But engineers wanted more space to do their work and grew tired of the limited range of purples, blues, and reds that the cards could render.

Priem's PGC offered more colors and at higher resolutions than any other IBM PC graphics card on the market: it could render up to 256 colors at once at resolutions up to 640 × 480 pixels. The card could also run graphics routines independently of the main central processing unit (CPU), leading to faster rendering times. Priem had the card boot in CGA compatibility mode and only activate its advanced features when needed.

Despite his initial excitement over the job and the significant responsibilities swiftly granted to him, Vermont Microsystems ended up being nothing like Apple. The company had difficulty hiring other qualified engineers, partly because it refused to offer any employee stock options or equity—a tool that many start-ups use to attract and retain workers and keep them motivated while living under the inherent risk and pressure of a company whose money could run out. No matter how hard Priem worked, no matter the quality of the graphics cards he made, he would never become as rich as Steve Jobs if he stayed where he was.

So he started looking west, to Silicon Valley. He booked a vacation to northern California that was, in reality, a job search. Once he arrived, he headed not to the beach but to a newsstand, where he bought a copy of the *San Jose Mercury News* and turned straight to its Help Wanted section. Amid the many openings at start-ups, one in particular caught his eye: a hardware engineer role at a company called GenRad, which was at the time one of the world's leading manufacturers of testing equipment for circuit boards and microprocessors. That meant the company had access to early versions of the latest chips by most major manufacturers—a prospect that would be hard for Priem to turn down.[1] He interviewed at GenRad and received an offer.

When he got back in Vermont, Priem submitted his resignation.

He had worked at Vermont Microsystems for only two years, and in that time he managed to design one of its highest-profile products to date. He left on the very day that the company shipped its first cards to IBM. As the launch party started, Priem was ushered into his exit interview, after which he was walked to the exit.

He didn't know it, but GenRad was a company in crisis by the time he joined. Despite its successful 1978 IPO and its command of nearly 30 percent of the electronics-testing market—a share that put it comfortably ahead of rivals Teradyne and Hewlett-Packard (HP)[2]—a series of management missteps saw the company's very existence come into question. Its executives had spent lavishly to break into the testing market for semiconductors, only to have their operation fall flat. In order to build a competitive moat around the business, executives began to insist that manufacturers completely outsource their chip-testing functions to GenRad, which caused friction with the company's largest clients such as IBM and Honeywell. And a failed merger with a company called LTX led to a crisis of confidence in GenRad's senior leadership, followed by an exodus of talent that strengthened its rivals. Shortly after Priem arrived, GenRad entered a nose dive from which the company would never fully recover. After two years of corporate turbulence, Priem asked a tech industry headhunter to find him a role somewhere else.

A man named Wayne Rosing offered Priem an interview at Sun Microsystems. Sun was an early pioneer in high-end UNIX computer workstations, which it sold for thousands or even tens of thousands of dollars. It was founded by three Stanford graduate students—Scott McNealy, Andy Bechtolsheim, and Vinod Khosla—in 1982.

Rosing was a former Apple employee who had run the engineering team behind the Lisa desktop computer that was released in 1983, around the same time that Priem was making PGC cards for IBM. Lisa was supposed to change desktop computing forever: it would be the first mass-market personal computer to feature a graphical user interface (GUI) instead of a text-only command line and the first to feature five megabytes of hard-drive storage in an era when most other computers had none at all. But a lack of software that would make it competitive with similarly priced workstations and its lofty price tag of nearly $10,000 doomed the Lisa even before it launched. After disappointing sales, Apple hired a company to take its remaining inventory of unsold units and bury them in a Utah landfill. Rosing left Apple shortly thereafter.

During the development of Lisa, Rosing spent a considerable amount of time assessing the capabilities of competing machines. The one graphics card that he envied was Priem's PGC. It was the sort of card that Rosing wanted but could not make work for the Lisa, which shipped with basic graphics that could support only a monochrome display at a resolution of 720 × 364 pixels, nowhere near the performance of PGC-powered IBM machines. After joining Sun Microsystems, Rosing vowed to take advantage of the increasing technical ability to render fast, beautiful, color graphics. To do that, he needed someone who could design powerful graphics chips. Hence his interest in Curtis Priem.

In Priem's interview, when Rosing asked the young engineer whether he could make a graphics card like the PGC at Sun, the reply was brief: "Yes."

IT WAS EXACTLY THE OPPOSITE of what Sun's executives wanted Rosing to do. At the time, the company was focused on launching a new line of computers called the SPARCstation series. These were UNIX-based workstations designed for specific scientific and technical applications, in particular computer-aided design (CAD) and computer-aided manufacturing (CAM) programs that could be used to design complex physical objects, from bridges to airplanes to mechanical parts. Sun believed that CAD and CAM tools would make industrial design far faster, cheaper, and more accurate than hand-drafting. And the company wanted the SPARCstation to lead the way.

Bernie Lacroute, Sun's vice president of engineering and Rosing's immediate boss, believed that the SPARCstation could dominate the market on CPU power alone. He directed the SPARCstation team to focus on improving the device's main processor and to not do any work on its graphics capabilities. He was satisfied with the graphics solution from the previous generation of Sun workstations, in which most of the rendering took place within the CPU.

Rosing disagreed vehemently. His experience with Apple's Lisa taught him the importance of speedy graphics. For the typical workstation user, fast computation or extensive storage wouldn't compensate for laggy graphics. He thought the SPARCstation should have state-of-the-art displays that could render a million pixels and hundreds of colors. To achieve that, however, he would need to move graphics processing out of the CPU and onto separate graphics-accelerator chips—like the PGC from Vermont Microsystems. And he would have to do it behind his boss's back.

So when Priem asked for clarification from Rosing, the answer was almost completely open-ended.

"Curtis, do anything you want. Just fit it in the same size frame buffer as the last workstation," Rosing said. "As long as it fits in that area, you'll have a spot on the motherboard."[3]

This was as close to carte blanche as Priem—or any engineer—could reasonably expect to get on any project. Priem could design and build whatever he could dream up, so long as it could work within the data-throughput constraints of the "frame buffer"—the memory that the SPARCstation dedicated to graphics processing.

Priem realized he couldn't tackle the project alone; he needed help. It would come soon from another engineer, Chris Malachowsky, whom Sun Microsystems had hired from Hewlett-Packard. The two men would share an office and become known as the "closet graphics" team. They worked in secret on the one thing that their boss's boss did not want anyone working on.

UNLIKE HIS OFFICE MATE, CHRIS MALACHOWSKY had come late to the world of computers. Born in Allentown, Pennsylvania, in May 1959, the son of an obstetrician and an occupational therapist turned homemaker, he grew up in Ocean Township, New Jersey. As a teen, he loved carpentry and considered becoming a cabinetmaker, but his parents pushed him toward medicine. At that point, he had never considered electronics or technology as a possible career path.

He graduated from high school at seventeen and enrolled at the University of Florida, which was well known both for its medical school and its school of construction management, and about as far away from cold New Jersey winters as Malachowsky could get. In addition, the school's pre-med program had a unique philosophy: it wanted to give future doctors a broad foundation of knowledge and thus made them take classes beyond the life sciences. To fulfill his non-life-sciences requirement, Malachowsky took a physics class and earned an A in the electrical section of the course. He found that engineering came naturally to him.

He didn't think too much of it until the lunch break between his MCAT medical school entrance exam sessions. While Malachowsky laid down on a picnic table and stared up at the Florida sun, he contemplated life as a doctor and following in his father's footsteps. Is that what he wanted to do for the rest of his life? Be on call at all hours, working four-to-five-day stretches with little to no sleep? He wondered, "Do I really want to know what all the names on drug bottles mean?"

"No," he realized. "I like this engineering stuff. I'd rather be an engineer."

After finishing the MCAT exam, he headed back to his rental house, stopping only to pick up a case of beer at a 7-Eleven on the way, and called his parents as soon as he got home.

"Mom, Dad, I've got good news and bad news," he told them. "The good news is the test wasn't that hard. The bad news is, I don't want to be a doctor anymore."

He waited for a response, sure that his parents would be upset. But they expressed relief.

"Good," said his mother. "You never read directions anyway. We didn't think you'd be a good one. We thought you were doing it for your father."

Malachowsky went on to major in electrical engineering and parlayed his good grades into a job at Hewlett-Packard in California. He ended up working in the manufacturing department, responsible for the production of a new 16-bit minicomputer that HP was developing in its research and development lab.

"It turned out to be great for me because it gave me a chance to learn about how real computers were built," he said.

While many people knew how to design a computer chip in principle, few could design one that could be manufactured in large volumes, and at a profit. When Malachowsky first arrived at HP, he saw that hands-on experience in its manufacturing department could give him a practical perspective on the industry that few others seemed to possess. On top of that, HP had a reputation for molding young engineers into disciplined veterans through its mentorship and training programs. Malachowsky knew that his time at the company would prepare him for whatever opportunity came next.

It was after his stint on the HP manufacturing floor that he was invited to join the company's research lab to develop new chips. He worked on the HP-1000 Minicomputer product line and learned how to write embedded control software for its communication peripherals. Later, he led the team that would make the HP-1000's CPU, which would be manufactured in the same building where he started his career at HP.

While working every day on the most crucial element of the HP-1000, he also pursued a master's degree in computer science from nearby Santa Clara University. Once both projects—the chip and the degree—were finished, he and his wife, Melody, whom he married a year after college, began to think about where they could start a family.

At first, they considered transferring to HP's satellite office in Bristol, England, but his wife didn't like the idea of moving so far away. They then considered the East Coast. Her family was in Northern Florida, while his parents were in New Jersey. Halfway in between was North Carolina's Research Triangle, home to both world-class universities in Duke and UNC and the offices of tech behemoths IBM and Digital Equipment Corporation, or DEC.

Before making the transcontinental move, however, Malachowsky decided to apply for jobs at other companies, solely for the purpose of getting some practice interviewing. His first invitation came from the nascent supercomputer division at Evans and Sutherland, a graphics company otherwise known for making high-end flight simulators for military training. He was rejected right away; his interviewers thought he questioned the status quo too much and felt that he would be a poor fit at the company. (Malachowsky believed their feedback didn't bode well for the company's future. He was right. Evans and Sutherland's first supercomputer later failed to sell, and the looming end of the Cold War meant that simulator demand from the military was already drying up.)

The second practice interview was at Sun Microsystems, where he had applied for an unspecified position making graphics chips. Although Malachowsky had no prior graphics experience, his curiosity got the better of him, and he agreed to interview with the lead engineer, Curtis Priem. What started out as a mere prep session ended up changing the course of Malachowsky's life—and the course of the entire tech industry.

"CURTIS WAS THE ONE WHO understood graphics," Malachowsky later recalled. "I turned out to be the build-it guy. Tell me what to do, what needs to be done, and I'll go figure out how to do it."

In order to produce the high-quality graphics that Rosing wanted (but that Rosing's boss didn't), Priem had designed a monstrosity of a graphics accelerator. It would contain two dedicated ASICs: the frame buffer controller, or FBC, which rendered high-resolution images at fast speeds; and the transformation engine and cursor, or TEC, which could quickly calculate the motion and orientation of objects as a user manipulated them. Instead of relying on the CPU to perform all of these tasks, as earlier Sun workstations had done, Priem's accelerator would handle up to 80 percent of the computational workload on its own—meaning the dedicated graphics chips would do the limited set of functions that they did best, and the CPU would be freed up to handle the myriad other tasks that it did better.

It was a good design, in theory, but now it was up to Malachowsky to figure out how to make it a reality. Unlike HP, Sun did not make its own chips. Instead, Malachowsky would rely on LSI Logic, headquartered in nearby Santa Clara, which was then the global leader in fabricating custom ASICs for hardware manufacturers. Malachowsky's timing was fortuitous: LSI had just introduced a new chip architecture called "sea-of-gates," through which they could fit more than ten thousand gate arrays onto a single chip, a feat that no other manufacturer had been able to accomplish. Although LSI's own prototypes were impressive, Priem's chip designs would need to be larger still in order to produce sufficient processing power for the SPARCstation. LSI's executives recognized the potential to turn Sun Microsystems into a big customer and agreed to take the contract—even though, as Malachowsky later noted, they seemed nervous about their ability to deliver.

To make sure that Priem and Malachowsky got the chip they had drawn up, LSI assigned one of its rising stars to manage the Sun account—a relatively new hire named Jensen Huang.

"This young kid had just joined them from AMD who had worked on microprocessors," Malachowsky said. "Curtis knew what he wanted, I could design it, and Jensen helped us figure out how we were going to build it."

Together, the three of them worked out the manufacturing process that would make Priem's design ready for fabrication. As problems arose, each man worked within his own area of expertise to solve them. But a small team laboring on a high-pressure project could create tension.

"Curtis is so bright. He thinks so fast," said Malachowsky. "He starts with an idea and jumps to a solution and there are no breadcrumbs between the two. I really felt that my biggest contribution was helping him articulate [his ideas] for other people in a way that they could get behind. My communication skills turned out to be equally important as my engineering skills."

Sometimes, communication turned into outright conflict.

"Chris and I would have these knock-down, drag-out fights. Not physically, but we'd be yelling, screaming at each other," Priem recalled. "He was trying to get something out of me about a decision on a chip. Then when I told him what he wanted, I would just keep going because I couldn't settle down. Chris would then say, 'No, no, we're done. You gave me the answer.' "

Priem would then storm out of the office, while the rest of his team—which at this point consisted of two hardware engineers named Tom Webber and Vitus Leung—would look at Malachowsky with alarm. Eventually, someone would ask if the team would now be disbanded.

"We're good," Malachowsky would always reply.

Jensen saw more promise than peril in these explosive fights, too. He called them examples of "honing the sword." Just as a sword only becomes sharper when it meets grinding resistance, the best ideas always seemed to come from spirited debate and argument, even if the back-and-forth could get uncomfortable. Already, he was learning to embrace conflict rather than shy away from it—a lesson that would eventually come to define his philosophy at Nvidia.

"We broke every tool that LSI Logic had in their standard port-folio," recalled Malachowsky. "Jensen was bright enough and savvy enough to say, 'Look, I'll fix these problems at the back end. You can ignore them. These you'd better fix because I don't know if I can handle those.' "

In 1989, the three men finalized the specifications for Sun's new graphics accelerator. The FBC would require 43,000 gates and 170,000 transistors in order to do its job properly; the TEC, 25,000 gates and 212,000 transistors. They would sit together on a single graphics accelerator, which was packaged as the "GX graphics engine"—or just GX for short.

The "closet graphics" team got one more boost just as they were ready to release the new chips. Bernie Lacroute, the executive who had shown such antipathy toward graphics chips just a few years earlier, had recently asked Wayne Rosing if he had followed his order not to put any effort toward improving the SPARCstation's graphics capabilities. Rosing replied in the negative.

"Good," said Lacroute.[4]

GX STARTED AS AN OPTIONAL add-on, for which Sun up-charged customers $2,000. GX made everything on the display work faster: two-dimensional geometry, three-dimensional wireframing, even the mundane task of scrolling through lines of text was quicker and better with GX accelerators than without them.

"For the first time, probably in history, the scrolling of the text in a windowing system was faster than you could see," said Priem. "It allowed you to scroll up and down a large document without actually seeing the FBC painting."

But the best showcase for GX graphics was a game that Priem had been working on in his spare time. Back at Vermont Microsystems, he had started making a flight-simulator game featuring the A-10 Warthog. A squadron of Warthogs was stationed at the nearby Vermont Air National Guard Base in Burlington. After work, he would park his car at the end of the base's runway and watch the jets take off. His simulator program was meant to get him even closer; it was supposed to let him fly the A-10 in its intended role as a "tank buster" during an imagined Cold War conflict. But his personal computer, an Atari 800, didn't have enough graphical processing power to render the complex physics of an A-10 in flight. He never finished the game. In fact, no card then on the market could bring to life the game that Priem had imagined.

Until the GX-enabled SPARCstation. For the first time, a realistic flight simulator became possible. Priem bought a workstation for his own personal use with his 60 percent employee discount, which shaved thousands of dollars off of the price. After he spent sixty hours a week at his day job, he would go home and get back to laboring on his new simulator program that would take full advantage of the new GX chips. Finally, he was able to realize his vision and complete the game, which he called *Aviator*.

Aviator placed users in the cockpit not of the A-10 but of the high-performance F/A-18 fighter jet and pitted them against other F/A-18s in an aerial dogfight. The game fully modeled the F/A-18's weapons, including Sidewinder missiles, guns, and bombs. Priem rendered *Aviator*'s battlefields realistically, purchasing satellite data to get elevations and land contours right, and adding texture-mapped graphics. He even designed a hardware device adapter to enable PC-compatible joysticks to work with Sun's workstations, so that players wouldn't have to use the keyboard to control their virtual aircraft.

Priem had a business partner for the game: Bruce Factor, who worked in Sun's marketing department and agreed to handle sales and marketing. Factor quickly realized that *Aviator* could do more than just pass the time—it could also help Sun move workstations. The game was a fantastic means to demonstrate the GX's graphical capabilities, running at a high resolution (1,280 × 1,024 pixels) and at 256 colors, at a time when most other PC games could only manage resolutions up to 320 × 200 pixels. *Aviator* also allowed clients with multiple networked Sun workstations to play against each other in real time, using Sun's new "multicasting" protocol—a kind of rudimentary local area network (LAN) that presaged the LAN party craze of the 1990s and 2000s.

Priem and Factor gave out free copies of *Aviator* to every sales office at Sun Microsystems. The company's reps used it as a way to show off the computer's capabilities and would often buy more copies to present as gifts to their workstation customers.

"I was getting every last bit of performance out of the hardware," Priem said. "*Aviator* became pretty serious. It was the best demo the Sun Microsystems sales force used to show off the performance of a standard workstation."

Aviator was officially released to the public in 1991. It was demonstrated at the annual conference of the Special Interest Group on Computer Graphics and Interactive Techniques (SIGGRAPH). At the show, Priem and Factor set up a network of eleven workstations so attendees could try dogfighting against each other.

The process of developing *Aviator* taught Priem some important lessons beyond game design. The game was hacked by a Sun employee within two days of release, enabling people to play without paying for a copy of their own. To prevent future hacks, Priem released a new version that could disable itself if it detected any changes to the code and which would e-mail him the details of the users trying to pirate the software. Later, Priem would incorporate similar private-key encryption technology into his first Nvidia chip design.

After a few years of torrid sales as an add-on option, the GX chips became standard on every Sun workstation. Its success boosted the careers of Priem and Malachowsky, who became graphic architects and were given their own team, called the Low End Graphics Option group. Meanwhile, LSI's gamble on the chip had paid off handsomely. The company's revenues grew from $262 million in 1987 to $656 million in 1990, driven partially by GX sales, even as it reduced the list price of each unit from nearly $375 for the initial two-chip run to around $105 for the later one-chip version. Jensen was promoted to director of LSI's

CoreWare division, which made custom chips for third-party hardware vendors by using a library of reusable intellectual property and designs.

IRONICALLY, GX'S SUCCESS HAD THE opposite effect on Sun Microsystems. By the early 1990s, it had shifted away from the agile, start-up-like environment that gave people such as Rosing, Priem, and Malachowsky the independence to follow their instincts and display their technical virtuosity. The culture was now becoming more bureaucratic, more controlled, and thus slower. Project teams no longer competed to come up with the most innovative ideas; they competed to create PowerPoint presentations that would win over the most executives. In short, Sun Microsystems had become political.

It was not an environment where Malachowsky or Priem wanted to be. Priem, in particular, was bothered by a culture where "it was easier to sabotage or get the other project killed than to come up with better technology." He just wanted to make good graphics chips and had no interest in corporate infighting.

New chip design releases at Sun ground to a halt as cycle after cycle of new proposals—many of which looked good on a slide but were either technically or economically unviable—were approved one quarter, then wound down the next.

"For two years, nothing exited the building," Malachowsky said. "My assessment was they had been so successful leading up to this time that they were more concerned with protecting success than driving for it. It was getting caught up in fear of failure. They stopped being very aggressive."

Worse still, Sun actually tried to undo much of the progress that Priem and Malachowsky had made with GX. During one pitch cycle, Priem's team proposed a new generation of graphics accelerators that would incorporate cutting-edge video-memory technology from the Korean chip manufacturer Samsung. But Priem lost out to a rival named Timothy Van Hook, who believed that the best way to push the graphical envelope for Sun workstations was to task the CPU with more high-end 3-D graphics functions rather than rely on a dedicated graphics chip.[5] Priem was convinced that the idea wouldn't work, from a technical perspective. But it didn't matter because Van Hook had one advantage that Priem didn't: the ear of one of Sun's cofounders, Andy Bechtolsheim. Without an internal champion of that stature, Priem knew that he and his group had no chance.

"Andy came and told me that our product line was a dead end," Priem said.

He soon realized that his days at Sun were numbered. Rumors swirled that Sun leadership wanted to disband his team, fire him, and move Malachowsky onto another chip project. Having worked side-by-side with Priem for the past six years, Malachowsky was angry over the treatment of his friend and one of the company's most talented engineers.

"Chris knew every single struggle I went through, taking all the hits from Sun management," Priem said. "He respected me taking all the arrows in the back. There were times I was so chastised by the VP of graphics that I'd be out with HR walking around the buildings in the park crying. It was just brutal."

Bechtolsheim choosing Van Hook's idea was the last straw for both men, whose success with GX now meant little in what they saw as in increasingly dysfunctional company.

"We realized our time was limited and neither of us wanted to work at Sun," Priem said. They already had a new project in mind: resurrecting the next-generation accelerator chip that Sun leadership had passed on.

"Why don't we just go build Samsung a demonstration chip?" Priem asked Malachowsky. "We'll just be consultants and show them the value of this new memory device they are committing to build."

Malachowsky thought it sounded like fun. They knew how to build chips, and they knew that they had a plan for a good one. But this advantage could just as easily become a liability too: in the high-stakes, multibillion-dollar world of semiconductors, no company would think twice about stealing an idea from a pair of engineers if it would give them even the slightest competitive edge. Unless they had a partner with business savvy to match their technical brilliance, they might as well not even bother.

Then another idea hit Malachowsky.

"We knew a guy!" he recalled later. "We knew a guy who we were good friends with who had moved into technology licensing and building systems on a chip for other people. So, we reached out to Jensen."

Malachowsky and Priem asked Jensen Huang for help writing a contract to work with Samsung. The three started meeting to devise a business strategy to deal with the Korean company. Then one day Jensen said, "Why are we doing this for them?"[6]

CHAPTER 3

The Birth of Nvidia

CURTIS PRIEM AND CHRIS MALACHOWSKY'S IDEA FOR A graphics-chip venture was perfectly timed. In 1992, two major developments—one in hardware, one in software—accelerated the demand for better graphics cards. The first was the computer industry's adoption of the Peripheral Component Interconnect (PCI) bus, a type of hardware connection that transferred data among the expansion cards (such as graphics accelerators), the motherboard, and the CPU at a much higher bandwidth than that available from the prior Industry Standard Architecture (ISA) bus. The process of designing higher-performance cards would be easier, and there would be a far larger market for the resulting products.

The second development was Microsoft's release of Windows 3.1, which was intended to showcase the very latest in computer-graphics capabilities. It introduced TrueType fonts, which rendered pixel-perfect text across all Microsoft programs, and it supported high-quality video playback with its new Audio Video Interleave (AVI) video-encoding format. Importantly, it did not hide these developments under the hood. With garish screensavers, user-customizable interfaces, and the constant nudges to use Windows Media Player, the operating system wasn't shy about showing off its graphical prowess. In its first three months after its release on April 6, 1992, Windows 3.1 sold nearly three million copies and proved that there was strong demand for programs that could take advantage of the PC's improving graphics.

Priem and Malachowsky decided the PC market, rather than the workstation market, represented the best opportunity for their start-up. They were thinking, in part, of Priem's flight simulator, which they planned to make available to any gamer who had a personal computer—instead of restricting it only to those who had access to Sun Microsystems hardware at their place of employment. As they had at Sun, Priem and Malachowsky would not manufacture the chips or circuit boards themselves, to keep costs down. Instead, they would focus on designing the best chip possible and would outsource production to semiconductor firms that already had the expensive production infrastructure in place.

Still, Priem had little idea how they would stack up against the competition. "I knew Chris and I were good, but I didn't know if we were good compared to the rest of the world," he said.

Sun machines had always had a Windows-like graphics interface, and PCs running Windows would soon need to support a similar multi-window operating system environment, a feature Priem and Malachowsky had already created. They knew their skill set would be valuable in the PC market.

"You have to do all sorts of security protections and abstractions with ten windows open," said Malachowsky. "These were the kinds of things the PC hadn't had to deal with because they had a DOS environment that basically owned the whole screen."

In late 1992, Priem, Malachowsky, and Jensen met frequently at a Denny's at the corner of Capitol and Berryessa in East San Jose to figure out how to turn their idea into a business plan.

"We'd show up, we'd order one bottomless cup of coffee. And then, you know, work for four hours," Malachowsky said.[1]

Priem remembers eating plenty of Denny's pies and the Grand Slam breakfasts—two buttermilk pancakes served with eggs, bacon, and sausages. Jensen doesn't recall his typical order, but he thinks it was likely the Super Bird sandwich—turkey, melted Swiss cheese, tomato, and his favorite addition, bacon.[2]

Jensen still needed to be convinced to leave his job. Between bites, he peppered Curtis and Chris with questions about the size of the opportunity.

"How big is the PC market?" Jensen asked.

"It's big," they replied, which was true—but obviously not detailed enough to satisfy Jensen.

"Chris and I were just sitting there watching Jensen," Priem said. He kept working through his analysis of the PC market and the potential competition. There was a place for their start-up, he believed, but he didn't want to leave his current job until he felt like the business model made sense. He was grateful that Chris and Curtis had somehow decided he was essential, even though he remembers thinking, "I love my job, you hate your job. I'm doing well, you're doing crap. For what reason do I leave with you?"

He told them that he would join them if they could prove that the start-up could eventually generate $50 million in annual sales.

Jensen reminisces fondly about the long conversations at Denny's. "Chris and Curtis were the two brightest engineers, computer scientists that I have ever met," he said.[3] "Luck has a lot to do with success, and my luck was having met them."

Eventually, Jensen decided that $50 million in revenue was possible. He was confident, as a gamer himself, that the gaming market was going to grow considerably.

"We grew up in the video-game generation," he said.[4] "The entertainment value of video games and computer games was very obvious to me."

The question then turned to who was going to make the first move. Priem was ready for it to be him—the way things were going at Sun, he would have to leave the company in a few months, anyway. But Jensen's wife, Lori, didn't want him to leave LSI until Malachowsky also left Sun—and Malachowsky's wife, Melody, didn't want him to leave Sun until Jensen committed.

In December of 1992, Priem forced their hand. He submitted his letter of resignation to Sun Microsystems, effective December 31. The following day, alone in his house, he founded the new venture, "just by declaring that this was started," he later recalled.

Even this was a bit of an overstatement. Priem had no name for his company. He had no funding. He had no employees. He didn't even have Malachowsky or Jensen aboard just yet. All he had was an idea—and some leverage over his friends.

"I put pressure on both of them that we can't let Curtis flail alone," Priem said, adding that he almost guilt-tripped them. "I think they joined together and said because Curtis quit, they have to quit. Because they quit simultaneously, they solved the problem with their wives, making sure we were a team."

Malachowsky agreed to stay at Sun Microsystems long enough to sign off on his last project, a new upgrade to the GX lineup. Once his engineers verified that the chip was 100 percent perfect, he was comfortable declaring that his final day would be in early March of 1993.

"A good engineer doesn't walk away from their responsibilities," he said.

A good engineer doesn't walk away without his tools, either. Before he left, Malachowsky asked to take his Sun workstations with him to the new start-up. Wayne Rosing, who was still his boss, agreed, and in his last days on campus, Malachowsky made sure to upgrade as many components in his devices as he could.

"They got upgraded by the maximum memory, maximum disk drives, and maximum monitor size," Priem said.

Jensen, too, wanted to leave LSI on good terms. He spent the first six weeks of 1993 distributing his projects to other leaders within the company. He officially joined Priem on February 17, which happened to be Jensen's thirtieth birthday.

ROSING THOUGHT THAT PRIEM, HIS protégé, was making a big mistake. In January, while Priem was still "flailing alone," Rosing invited his now-former engineer to an off-site location where several Sun employees were working on a secret project. After getting Priem to sign a nondisclosure agreement, Rosing revealed that Sun was creating a new general-purpose programming language that would eventually become Java. Although the project was off to a promising start, Rosing believed that it ran too slowly to be useful. He asked if Priem would be interested in designing a new chip that could take some of the processing load off of the CPU and accelerate the execution of the new language.

Priem was tempted, especially as he wasn't yet sure whether Jensen and Malachowsky were going to follow through on their promises to join him in the new venture. "If I had said yes, it would have taken my career down a totally different path."

Although he seriously considered Rosing's proposition, he had no real interest in designing CPUs and was far too excited by the prospect of designing his own graphics chips with his friends, even if it entailed huge risk. He passed on Rosing's offer.

Undeterred, Rosing tried again in February. This time, he didn't try to peel one of them away from the others. He tried to get all three at once. He offered to license Sun's entire portfolio of patents to their start-up, including all of Priem's and Malachowsky's old GX chip designs. In exchange, they would agree to make their new chips compatible with both Sun's GX graphics and IBM PCs.

After hearing Rosing's pitch, the three men retreated to the parking lot of Sun's campus to debate the decision. Priem considered all the implications of the proposal and declared it "interesting." The partnership would give them a large, brand-name customer right off the bat and would protect them from any copyright-infringement claims from their former employer. But the downside was that the agreement would force them to spend less time and resources on the PC market, which was, in their view, where the real opportunity lay. They weren't even sure whether they could make a single chip work for both the Sun and the PC platforms. They agreed to decline Rosing's proposal and go it alone.

During the parking-lot discussion, Priem revealed that he already had basic specifications in mind for a new PC-based graphics accelerator. It would have more colors and work with a larger frame buffer than that of the GX chips he and Malachowsky had made at Sun. In many ways, it would be an evolution of the GX chip they had worked on for six years. He pointed out that Microsoft named their new operating system Windows NT, with "NT" meaning "next technology." That's why, he said, he wanted to call the chip the "GX Next Version," or GXNV.

It sounded like "GX envy," a phenomenon that was common among Sun's workstation competitors. Priem had heard stories about rivals, such as Digital Equipment Corporation, who had lost customers to Sun's sales teams armed with GX graphics and copies of *Aviator*. The name indicated their resolve to do it again—and to do it on their own terms, this time.

To emphasize the clean break with their past (and, likely, to prevent even the faintest whiff of possible copyright infringement), Jensen told Priem to "drop the GX." Their new chip would be called the NV1.

THE THREE COFOUNDERS STARTED WORKING out of Priem's townhouse in the San Jose suburb of Fremont with little more than a vision and Malachowsky's Sun workstations. Priem cleared every room except his bedroom and moved all of the furniture into his garage, setting up large folding tables for all of their equipment. The first few weeks, there wasn't much to do. The three of them would get together each day and talk about food.

"What did you do last night? What did you have for dinner?" Jensen recalled them asking each other. The day's big event would be the decision on what to eat for lunch. "It sounds pathetic, but it's true."

After a time, they decided to make their first official hardware purchase, ordering an IBM-compatible PC made by Gateway 2000, the mail-order computer manufacturer that famously shipped its devices in black-and-white cow-print boxes. Upon arrival, the machine utterly confused Priem and Malachowsky, whose professional lives up to that point had been focused on Sun Microsystems hardware and software.

"We were not PC people," said Malachowsky. "It was funny. We were going to take over the world, but we didn't know anything about PCs."

Fortunately, they would not be on their own for long. Once news of the three cofounders' new venture spread, several senior engineers at Sun Microsystems quit and joined the fledgling start-up. Two crucial early hires were Bruce McIntyre, a software programmer on the GX team, and David Rosenthal, a chip architect who became the start-up's chief scientist.

"I can't believe how many amazing people joined us. We had a dozen people working without a salary," Priem said. "We didn't pay them until I think June, when we first got our funding."

McIntyre and Priem took a Sun GX graphics chip and attached it to a board that could plug into their Gateway. The hardware interface was easy; the software integration was much harder. The Sun hardware processed instructions in a manner that Microsoft's operating system could not understand. It took a full month of work to remap the GX's graphics registers to work with Windows 3.1, but eventually the team solved the problem. Naturally, the first game they ported over to Windows was the latest version of Priem's *Aviator*, which they renamed *Zone5*.

Now, the start-up had a staff. It had a viable demonstration product. It only needed an official name, so that it could be legally incorporated. Priem had already written down a list of potential options. One early leader was "Primal Graphics," which sounded cool and combined the first few letters of two of the cofounders' last names: PRIem and MALachowsky. Others liked it, but the whole team felt that in order to be fair it had to include Jensen's name as well. Unfortunately, this made it impossible to come up with a name that sounded remotely appealing. The other contenders included Huaprimal, Prihuamal, and Malhuapri. The name-combination idea was dropped.

Most of the other possibilities on Priem's list incorporated "NV" as a reference to their first planned chip design. These names included iNVention, eNVironment, and iNVision—the kinds of everyday words that other companies had already co-opted for their own brands, such as a toilet paper company that had trademarked the name "Envision" for its environmentally sustainable product line. Another name was too similar to the brand of a computer-controlled toilet. "These names were all stinky," Priem said.

The last remaining option was "Invidia," which Priem found by looking up the Latin word for envy—in a sense, another callback to their work on the GX, when he and Malachowsky believed that their rivals, both within and beyond Sun, had envied their success.

"We dropped the 'I' and went with NVidia to honor the NV1 chip we were developing," said Priem, "and secretly hoped that someday Nvidia would be something that would be envied."

With a name in hand, Jensen sought out a lawyer and chose James Gaither, who worked at the law firm of Cooley Godward. Gaither's firm was midsized, with fewer than fifty attorneys on staff. Even so, it had carved out a niche for itself as the go-to firm for early-stage Silicon Valley start-ups. During their first meeting, Gaither asked Jensen how much money he had in his pocket. Jensen said $200.

"Hand it over," said Gaither. He then told Jensen he now owned a large equity stake in Nvidia.

Nvidia's incorporation documents gave each of the cofounders equal ownership. Jensen returned to the townhouse and asked his cofounders to each invest $200 of their own to "buy" their shares of the company.

"It was a good deal," Jensen later observed, with typical dryness.

On April 5, 1993, Nvidia was officially born. That same day, Priem drove to the Department of Motor Vehicles to order a vanity license plate: NVIDIA.

THE FIRST TEST OF NVIDIA'S viability—the search for funding—loomed. The world of venture capital (VC) was much smaller in 1993 than it is today. Silicon Valley VC firms, most of which—then as now—were headquartered on Sand Hill Road in Palo Alto, only accounted for about 20 percent of the nation's total venture investments and competed with firms based in Boston and New York. The entire VC industry was really a niche in the economy, making just over a billion dollars in outlays per year (close to $2 billion in today's dollars).[5] Today, Bay Area VC firms now dominate the industry, investing more than half of the $170 billion in funding that gets distributed every year.

Two things have remained constant about venture capital, however. The first is that founders whose start-ups already produce revenue are far more successful with their pitches than start-ups that have no products in the market—and this was especially true in the early '90s, when venture interest in early-stage companies was at a ten-year low. The second is that, as with many things in the business world, success depends as much on who one knows as it does on how strong one's business is. In Nvidia's case, the founders' connections were extensive enough to make up for the company's nonexistent revenue stream.

Jensen's decision to ease his way out of LSI Logic turned out to pay immediate dividends during Nvidia's fund-raising process. When he submitted his resignation, his manager had immediately taken him to LSI's CEO, Wilfred Corrigan, a British engineer who pioneered several semiconductor manufacturing processes and design principles that are still in use today. Jensen's manager wanted "Wilf," as he was known throughout the company, to talk the young engineer out of leaving LSI altogether. But when Corrigan heard about Jensen's vision for a new generation of graphics chips, he asked him a question: "Can I invest?"[6]

Corrigan grilled Jensen on the start-up's addressable market and strategic positioning: "Who plays games?" "Give me an example of a gaming company." Jensen responded that if they built the technology, more game companies would be founded. Existing companies in the space, such as S3 and Matrox, typically made 2-D accelerated-graphics cards, and games with 3-D graphics were only beginning to take off.

Still, Corrigan remained skeptical that Jensen's business would be viable.

"You'll be back soon," Corrigan told him. "I'll hold your desk."

Nevertheless, Corrigan promised to introduce Jensen to Don Valentine at Sequoia Capital. Valentine had invested in LSI Logic back in 1982, which earned him a handsome payout when the company went public a year later. He had hit it even bigger in other investments in tech companies such as Atari, Cisco, and Apple. By the early '90s he was considered "the best venture capitalist in the world."[7]

Although Corrigan may have had doubts about Nvidia's potential, he had none about Jensen himself. When he called Valentine after his conversation with the young, departing engineer, he didn't pitch Jensen's start-up idea; he pitched Jensen.

"Hey Don," he said, "we've got this kid who is going to leave LSI Logic. He wants to start his own company. He's really smart. He's really good. You guys should take a look at him."[8] Valentine agreed to meet with Jensen, Priem, and Malachowsky and had a junior partner set an appointment for the end of May. In the meantime, they would be free to pitch other potential investors.

In mid-April, just weeks after Nvidia's incorporation, the three cofounders visited Apple's headquarters to discuss the graphics needs for the Macintosh line. Nothing came of the meeting.

Three weeks later, they visited the offices of Kleiner Perkins Caufield & Byers, another venture capital firm that, like Sequoia, got its start in the 1970s and had made its own series of home-run investments. These included America Online, Genentech, and Sun Microsystems—the last being how the VC firm came to the Nvidia cofounders' attention. At the meeting, one of the Kleiner partners fixated on the topic of circuit boards, insisting that Nvidia needed to bring board manufacturing in-house. Nvidia's plans were to design the graphics chip, have it manufactured by someone else, and then sell the chip to a board partner, who would mount it on a graphics card and sell that card to PC makers.

The partner's insistence made no sense to Malachowsky. "Why would we compete on pennies on a resistor?" he asked. "I mean, we have no special expertise there. We'll stick to what we're good at, and if that's not for you, it's not for you."

Part of this was the typical, if not necessary, bravado of a start-up founder, but part of it was Malachowsky's practical nature shining through once again. For all their ambition to take over the PC graphics market, Nvidia had to focus its resources on the single best opportunity rather than spread themselves thin chasing all possible ones. This was why they had declined Wayne Rosing's offer to make chips that could run on both Sun workstations and IBM-compatible PCs. Now, it meant walking away from the conversation with Kleiner Perkins, too.

The next meeting they took, with Sutter Hill Ventures, went more smoothly. Once again, the cofounders' prior connections meant that they were not going in completely cold. Sutter Hill had also invested in LSI Logic and had contacted Wilf Corrigan to ask about

Jensen. Corrigan gave the same enthusiastic endorsement he had given Don Valentine. But Sutter Hill had already made some investments in graphics companies, and the firm doubted whether a new start-up could really differentiate itself in a market that they considered extremely competitive and highly commoditized already. The only partner excited about Nvidia was Tench Coxe, who had joined the firm a few years prior.

"It was a controversial deal," Coxe recalled. "I was the young guy at Sutter in a partnership of five guys."

Coxe was impressed by the three cofounders. He already had Corrigan's endorsement of Jensen. In the meeting, he probed Priem's and Malachowsky's expertise and was surprised by their depth of knowledge about 3-D graphics and computer operating systems.

The positive meeting with Sutter Hill seemed to bode well for the big test two days later: their pitch to Don Valentine at Sequoia. Although Nvidia still didn't have its own proprietary chip to show off yet, they could present the Sun GX graphics card that they had hacked to work with their Gateway 2000 PC as a proof-of-concept. The chip was four years old at this point, but it was still far more capable than any other Windows graphics card on the market. To demonstrate that, they would play a twenty-minute session of *Zone5*, electing to run the demo not on a standard monitor but through an early virtual-reality headset made by another start-up. They believed that the dazzling graphics alone would make their pitch successful.

What the Nvidia team didn't know was that Valentine *hated* product demos. The Sequoia founder had sat through enough pitches to know that entrepreneurs loved showing off their technology and would always present well. He believed, however, that even more important than a flashy product was a real understanding of the product's potential market and competitive position. The Nvidia cofounders were walking into a trap of their own making.

The three cofounders were met at Sequoia's offices on Sand Hill Road by Mark Stevens, a newly promoted junior partner who had previously worked at Intel and was now the firm's semiconductor specialist. He led them to a dark, wood-paneled conference room, where they set up the demo. After it concluded, Valentine switched over to his preferred style of evaluating a start-up: a rapid-fire series of questions designed not only to test the founders' expertise but also to see how they would perform under pressure. Malachowsky later referred to it as Valentine "holding court."

"What *are* you?" Valentine asked the three cofounders. "Are you a gaming-console company? Are you a graphics company? Are you an audio company? You have to be one."

Priem froze for an instant. Then he blurted out an answer. "We're all of them."

He went on a long and deeply technical explanation of how they could integrate all the features Valentine asked about into their one proposed chip. Although Priem didn't say anything untrue about the NV1's potential, his flustered response was so dense that only an engineer could understand it. To Priem, the plan was a sign of their ambition and expertise: they could develop a single chip that could address multiple different markets at once, expanding the potential of the chip without increasing its engineering complexity all that much. To Valentine, it sounded like Priem was being indecisive.

"Pick one," he snapped. "Otherwise, you're going to fail because you don't know who you are."

Valentine then asked where Nvidia would be in ten years. Priem responded, "We're going to own I/O architecture." It was another engineer's reply to a business question. What Priem meant was that he saw future generations of Nvidia chips accelerating not just graphics, but other computer-board operations such as sound, game ports, and networking. Once again, however, his answer was impenetrable to everyone on the Sequoia side. According to Malachowsky, it even confused his cofounders.

Stevens stepped in to bring the conversation down to a more practical level. Who, he asked, did Nvidia expect to actually manufacture their chips? The cofounders replied that they planned to use SGS-Thomson, a European semiconductor firm that had only recently avoided bankruptcy through deep cost cuts and by outsourcing production to Singapore and Malaysia. After hearing this, Valentine and Stevens looked at each other and shook their heads. They wanted Nvidia to work with the Taiwan Semiconductor Manufacturing Company (TSMC), which had a better reputation.

Jensen attempted to steer the conversation back toward Valentine's preferred topics of market position and strategy, but by now even he was flustered by the barrage of questions and the fact that the Nvidia team seemed unable to produce a satisfying answer to any of them. The meeting ended without a commitment from Sequoia.

"I did a horrible job with the pitch," Jensen said, taking responsibility for the entire performance. "I had a hard time explaining what I was building, who I was building it for, and why I was going to be successful."

After the meeting, Valentine and Stevens discussed what they had just heard. They agreed that the three cofounders were bright and that the vision to bring 3-D graphics to the PC platform had promise. Although they themselves were not gamers, Sequoia had invested in Electronic Arts, the publisher of software computer games that had recently gone public and made Sequoia money. They were also invested in S3, the company that primarily produced 2-D graphics-accelerator chips and which the Nvidia cofounders thought they could beat, so they knew the market was viable. Additionally, Valentine regretted passing on Silicon Graphics, which now dominated the market for high-end graphics workstations.

Sequoia met with Nvidia's cofounders two more times in mid-June. At the last meeting, they decided to invest.

"Wilf says to give you money. Against my better judgment, based on what you just told me, I'm going to give you money. But if you lose my money, I will kill you," Valentine told the Nvidia team.

Nvidia secured $2 million of Series A funding from Sequoia Capital and Sutter Hill Ventures—$1 million apiece—at the end of the month.

Nvidia now had enough money to fund the development of its first chip and to start paying its employees. It was a humbling moment for Jensen, Priem, and Malachowsky: they had succeeded on the strength of their reputation, not their business plan or their demo. It was a lesson Jensen would never forget. "Your reputation will precede you even if your business plan writing skills are inadequate," he said.

Chris Malachowsky and Jensen Huang in 1994. (NVIDIA)

PART II

NEAR-DEATH
EXPERIENCES

(1993–2003)

CHAPTER 4

All In

FINALLY, NVIDIA COULD STOP MERELY TALKING ABOUT ITS first chip and start building it. The first order of business was moving the company out of Priem's townhouse and into a real office. With the money from Sutter Hill and Sequoia, Nvidia could afford to rent a suite of offices inside a single-story building that was located just off Arques Avenue in Sunnyvale. The location was less than ideal—a nearby Wells Fargo bank would be robbed several times during the company's lease period—but it gave Nvidia's employees a sense of legitimacy.

For the first time, the company could also afford to pay its staff. Before fund-raising, Nvidia had only a handful of employees, and they worked without salaries, with the promise that at some point the money would flow. Now, Nvidia went on a hiring spree, bringing twenty new people aboard to fill both engineering and operations roles.

One such hire was Jeff Fisher, who was lured away from a graphics chip maker called Weitek to run Nvidia's sales department. During the interview process he was impressed by each one of Nvidia's cofounders.

"Great guys. All very different, but super smart," he recalled. "Jensen is an engineer at his core, but he could wear many hats. Curtis is an architect, determined to solve the forward-backward compatibility unified architecture. Chris could sling transistors like there's no other."

Robert Csongor and Jensen Huang in front of
Nvidia's first office. (ROBERT CSONGOR)

Robert Csongor, another of Nvidia's earliest employees, was so
excited about his first day that he convinced Jensen to take a photo with
him in front of the Nvidia sign on the front door of the office.

"One day we'll be big and famous," insisted Csongor, "and this picture will be cool."

Before Nvidia increased its headcount, the three cofounders established a chain of command. Priem and Malachowsky wanted to maintain the same working relationship they had had at Sun: Priem would
handle chip architecture and products as the company's chief technical
officer, and Malachowsky would run the engineering and implementation teams. They simply assumed that Jensen Huang would make the
business decisions.

"We basically deferred to Jensen on day one," Priem said, telling
him, "you're in charge of running the company—all the stuff Chris and
I don't know how to do."

Huang remembers Priem being even more direct: "Jensen, you're
the CEO, right? Done."[1]

With roles defined and project teams fully staffed, Priem launched into the design for the NV1 chip. In the world of PC graphics, the constraints were even harsher than on the Sun SPARCstation. Intel's current generation of CPUs, which powered most PCs, had difficulty performing the high-precision "floating-point" math calculations that were helpful for graphics rendering. Manufacturing capacity for chip designers was scarce and not very advanced, which limited the number of transistors Nvidia could fit on a single chip. And prices for semiconductor memory chips, which the graphics accelerators needed to perform their increasingly complex operations, were extremely high, at nearly $50 per megabyte, as a result of rising demand for PCs.

Priem and his team planned to build a chip that could display graphics at a resolution of 640 × 480 pixels, with high-quality textures and fast rendering speeds. But they would have to invent their way around the PC's limitations. The biggest hurdle involved the cost of memory. If they used standard chip-design methods on the NV1, the chip would need four megabytes of onboard memory, at cost of $200. This alone was enough to make any graphics card that used the chip unaffordable to most gamers, who were used to much cheaper prices. Before this first era of powerful 3-D PC chips, most 2-D-focused graphics chips cost under $10 and used limited amounts of memory.

Priem attempted to solve the problem with a new software process for handling textures, which was called forward texture mapping. The NV1 would render 3-D polygons by using quadrilateral shapes instead of the traditional inverse texturing, which was based on triangles. The shift to quadrilaterals would require less computational power and therefore lower memory requirements. The only downside was a significant one: software developers would have to completely rework their games in order for them to take advantage of Priem's forward texture mapping. If the NV1 tried to run a game that was built around the older inverse texturing process, the result would be slow rendering and poor graphical quality. However, Priem was confident that in the fragmented world of PC video-game graphics, where there was not yet a single dominant standard, Nvidia's technically efficient process would eventually win out.

As if inventing an entirely new texture-rendering process wasn't enough, Priem also wanted the NV1 to improve the audio capability of games. At the time, the market leader in audio was the SoundBlaster sound card, which to Priem's ears produced unrealistic, tinny music. He added high-quality wavetable synthesis to the NV1, which re-created digitized sound from recordings of actual instruments, whereas the SoundBlaster's audio samples were completely synthetic.

This alternative audio standard was another risky decision. Combining graphics and audio in one card was an unusual move, as most computers came with separate cards for each function. Yet Priem believed that this meant there was a market inefficiency waiting to be corrected by a technically superior multifunction card. The adoption of the new format was not guaranteed: with such a strong incumbent in SoundBlaster, Priem was banking on software makers switching from an inferior but widely adopted standard in favor of a proprietary one that produced better audio but that required more work to implement.

While Priem was working on the design, Jensen focused on convincing Intel to support his new card. His contact at Intel was a young executive named Pat Gelsinger, who was responsible for managing revisions to the Peripheral Component Interconnect (PCI) expansion-slot standard for PCs that all forthcoming graphics cards would use. Jensen wanted PCI to add different types of throughput modes for the NV1 to take advantage of; Gelsinger was resistant.

"I can remember vicious conversations that Jensen and I had on different architectural points," Gelsinger recalls.[2]

In the end, Jensen prevailed. Intel went with a more open standard, one with better capabilities and that encouraged innovation. It was a victory not only for Nvidia but also for the graphics industry as a whole—with an open standard, peripheral card makers could dictate the pace of technological improvements without having to wait for Intel to catch up. According to Gelsinger, Nvidia owed its future success to "the open PCI platform that enabled his graphics devices to really race ahead of everybody else."

As the NV1's design came into focus, Jensen and Malachowsky finalized their partnership with the foundry that would be manufacturing all of their chips, SGS-Thomson in Europe. Although Don Valentine and Mark Stevens had been critical of SGS-Thomson's suitability as a partner, Nvidia was able to use the European chip-maker's relative weakness as bargaining leverage. Their agreement gave SGS-Thomson the exclusive license to manufacture the NV1 chip for Nvidia and also to create a stripped-down version of the NV1 that the foundry could resell as a mid-tier chip under its own white-label brand. In exchange, the manufacturer would pay Nvidia around $1 million per year to write regular software and driver updates for all major Windows operating systems. SGS-Thomson essentially agreed to fund Nvidia's entire software division of around a dozen people in order to secure the privilege of manufacturing the NV1 chip.[3]

In the fall of 1994, SGS and Nvidia presented the NV1 at COMDEX in Las Vegas, one of the largest computer trade shows in the world. They prepared three working prototypes installed in PCs. Right before the convention opened, Priem and another engineer were still debugging the software drivers and brought one prototype back to a hotel room to continue to work on it. They decided to keep the other two machines at their booth. A security guard strolling by recommended that the company hire someone to guard their equipment overnight. The Nvidia team declined.

When they returned the next day to set up, they found that everything was gone. The doors to the exhibition floor had been left unlocked, and someone had walked in overnight and stolen their prototypes. Fortunately, they still had one chip back in the hotel, and the NV1 made its official debut as the conference opened.[4]

Amid the busyness of the trade show, the Nvidia team managed to secure an introduction to representatives from the Japanese video-game and console maker Sega.[5] Impressed with the NV1 demonstration, Sega agreed to begin working with Nvidia as it planned its next console. On December 11, 1994, Jensen and Curtis Priem flew to Tokyo to suggest a chip-development deal to Sega management.[6]

It was the first step in what should have been a long and beneficial relationship between the two companies. In May 1995, Sega and Nvidia signed a five-year partnership, where Nvidia agreed to build its next-generation chip, the NV2, exclusively for Sega's next gaming console. In return, Sega agreed to boost the NV1's launch on PC by porting several games originally developed for their current-generation console, the Sega Saturn, and rewriting them to support the NV1's forward texturing process. Sega also purchased $5 million worth of Nvidia preferred stock.

When the commercial terms were settled, Curtis Priem took over as Nvidia's main point person with Sega, given the technology collaboration the deal required. He would travel to Japan six times in 1995 to manage the two companies' joint projects. He oversaw the design specifications for the NV2-based console, including how it would read game cartridges and perform color compression. He also helped Sega understand the nuances of porting their Saturn-based games to the PC.

The NV1 had all the ingredients for a successful launch. It had a unique marketing angle, as a single-chip multimedia accelerator with several new texturing and rendering features. It had significant initial sales, including a 250,000-chip order from Nvidia's primary board partner, a company called Diamond Multimedia that packaged the chip in a $300 graphics card under the "Edge 3D" brand. And it had a splashy launch partner in Sega, which not only agreed to support the current chip but also had committed in advance to Nvidia's next one. The chip was officially announced in May 1995, and the entire company expected it to be a runaway success.

BUT NVIDIA HAD GRAVELY MISJUDGED the market. For one, over the previous two years, memory prices had plummeted from $50 per megabyte to $5 per megabyte, which meant that the NV1's stinginess with onboard memory was no longer much of a competitive advantage. As a result, few game developers saw the need to rewrite their software to support Nvidia's new graphics standard. Sega's PC ports, which included *Virtua Fighter* and *Daytona USA*, ended up being some of the only titles specifically designed to run on the NV1. Just about every other game ran poorly on Nvidia's new chip, which used an intermediate software wrapper to perform inverse texturing and thus was prone to slow rendering.

It was a single game, the first-person shooter *DOOM*, that sealed the NV1's fate. At the time of the chip's launch, *DOOM* was the most popular game in the world: its kinetic visuals and gruesome, fast-paced combat were unlike any other gaming experience ever produced. This was in large part due to the technical wizardry of John Carmack, the game's designer and cofounder of its publisher, id Software. Carmack built the game using the 2-D Video Graphics Array (VGA) standard and leveraged every hardware-level trick he knew for maximum visual impact. Priem had been sure that most game designers would switch to the NV1's 3-D accelerated graphics and leave VGA behind. So the NV1 chip only partially supported VGA graphics and relied on a software emulator to supplement its VGA capabilities—which resulted in slow performance for gamers playing *DOOM*.

Even *DOOM*'s iconic soundtrack and sound design didn't work properly on the NV1. The chip's proprietary audio format, which Priem had included more as a flourish than a strict necessity, was not compatible with the industry-standard SoundBlaster format made by sound-card maker Creative Labs. However, most PC manufacturers required their peripherals to be SoundBlaster compatible, and that wasn't changing as quickly as Priem had expected. To work around this, Priem wrote yet another emulator, this one designed to produce sound rather than visuals. But it would break every time Creative Labs updated its proprietary format and would stay broken until Nvidia could follow up with a patch. NV1 users would have to endure long periods where the sound on their games didn't work properly.

It was a hard lesson in the value of backwards compatibility and the dangers of innovating for innovation's sake. Nvidia's new card, which was supposed to push the boundaries of the graphics industry, could not keep up with the world's most popular game. It was sunk by a lack of truly compatible games and the ongoing support from most game makers for inferior, though widely adopted, technical standards.

"We thought we had built great technology and a great product," Malachowsky said. "It turns out we only built great technology. It wasn't a great product."

Sales were dismal, and most of the units sold during the holiday season were returned. By the spring of 1996, Diamond Multimedia had returned nearly all of the 250,000 chips it had ordered.

Jensen realized Nvidia had made several critical mistakes with the NV1, from positioning to product strategy. They had overdesigned the card, stuffing it with features no one cared about. Ultimately, the market simply wanted the fastest graphics performance for the best games at a decent price—and nothing else. Computer manufacturers also told Nvidia that combining video and audio functionality onto one chip made it harder for Nvidia to win a contract.

"The irony was that the thing that killed NV1 wasn't the most important thing, which was the graphics," said Michael Hara, Nvidia's director of marketing at the time.[7] "It was the audio. Games back then needed SoundBlaster compatibility, and NV1 didn't have it."

"We really like your graphics technology, so if you guys ever want to get rid of the audio, come back and see us," Hara recalled being told several times.

The NV1 could simply not stack up against other cards that were more narrowly designed. Nvidia saw that it couldn't again build things customers would not pay extra for.

"We were diluted across too many different areas," Jensen recalled.[8] "We learned it was better to do fewer things well than to do too many things even though it looked good on a PowerPoint slide. Nobody goes to the store to buy a Swiss Army knife. It's something you get for Christmas."[9]

Nvidia had spent nearly $15 million to develop the NV1. That money had come from the initial investment from Sutter Hill and Sequoia, as well as from SGS-Thomson and Sega.[10] The company was counting on strong sales of the NV1 to recoup most of its development costs, so that it could move on to the next chip. The bad result, however, meant that Nvidia was now facing a cash crisis. Jensen, Priem, and Malachowsky needed to secure more money, and soon, or else their dream would come to an abrupt, and self-inflicted, end.

DURING ONE OF NVIDIA'S VERY FIRST board meetings, director Harvey Jones, a former CEO of a leading chip-design-software company called Synopsys, asked Jensen about the NV1: "How would you position this?"

At the time, Jensen didn't realize that Jones was not merely asking about the NV1's feature set or product specifications. He was asking him to consider how Nvidia would sell the new chip in a highly competitive industry. He knew that products had to be presented in the clearest, most precise terms in order to stand out.

"He asked me a simple question. I had no idea how simple it was. It was impossible for me to answer because I didn't understand it," Jensen remembered.[11] "The answer is supremely deep. You'll spend your whole career answering that question."

In the aftermath of the NV1's failure, Jensen regretted not taking Jones's question a little more seriously. It frustrated him that he and the Nvidia team had put in so much effort for so little reward, and he believed that it came down to his own shortcomings as the leader of a new company.

"We were just bad at our jobs," he said. "The first five years of our company. We had really talented people, working super, super hard, but building a company is a new skill."

Jensen vowed that he would absorb as much as he could about leading a business to prevent himself, and his fledgling company, from ever making the same mistakes again. In his search for answers to Jones's question, he gravitated to the book *Positioning: The Battle for Your Mind* by Al Ries and Jack Trout. In it, Ries and Trout argue that positioning is not about the product itself but rather about the mind of the customer, which is shaped by prior knowledge and experience. People tend to reject and filter out anything that doesn't align with their existing worldview, which makes it hard to change their minds with reason and logic. But emotions can change quickly, and a skillful marketer can manipulate people to feel a certain way about a product, if a company uses the right message. According to the two authors, potential buyers didn't want to be persuaded. They wanted to be seduced.

But seduction requires a simple message, and Nvidia's message with the NV1 was far too complicated. It wasn't superior to the competition in any obvious way, and it was actually inferior under some circumstances.

"The customer's always thinking of alternatives," Jensen said.

And in the customer's mind, the alternatives could do what the NV1 could not—they could play *DOOM*. No amount of complaints about how the game used older graphics standards, or didn't to take advantage of the NV1's performance-boosting capabilities, would offset that one, easy-to-understand, negative message. No matter how many times Nvidia pointed to the NV1's innovative audio and graphical capabilities, it could not counteract what gamers saw with their own eyes and heard—or didn't hear—with their own ears.

THE NV1 DISASTER JEOPARDIZED THE company's relationship with Sega. The Japanese company had commissioned Nvidia to build the NV2 for its next console after the Saturn and be a follow-up to the successful, earlier Genesis console. The code name for the NV2 within Nvidia was "Mutara," after the location of the climactic space battle in *Star Trek II: The Wrath of Khan*—during which the Genesis device fires, collapsing the Mutara Nebula into a new, life-bearing planet. In the same way, Nvidia now needed its NV2 chip to breathe new life into the struggling company.

From the start, things did not look promising. In spite of Priem's direct involvement and his several trips to Japan, Sega's programmers increasingly soured on Nvidia's proprietary graphics-rendering technology. In 1996, Sega informed Nvidia that the company would no longer be using the NV2 in its next console. But Jensen had deftly worked into the initial contract a clause for a $1 million payment from Sega if Nvidia was able to produce a working prototype of a chip that could be installed onto a self-contained motherboard that was about the same size as the older Sega Genesis/Mega Drive motherboard.

Priem assigned a lone engineer, Wayne Kogachi, to build the NV2 prototype. It was an isolating and thankless job. Kogachi had only a single chip and a motherboard to play with, and Priem had assigned the rest of the engineering team to the company's next chip, which was then called NV3. The few interactions Kogachi had with his colleagues often involved juvenile, late-night shenanigans, such as the time when the entire engineering division started measuring and recording the circumference of everyone's head, a sort of jocular phrenology.

"Wayne had the largest circumference of anyone at Nvidia at the time," Priem remembered, with a laugh.

After about a year spent on the project, Kogachi was able to get an NV2 prototype working within Sega's specifications. The milestone triggered the $1 million payout, money that was a key lifeline during a time of crisis. Still, it did not solve all of Nvidia's woes. The majority of the $1 million was immediately put into research and development on the NV3, and there was not enough left over to pay for the many employees who had been hired in anticipation of selling huge amounts of NV1s and NV2s, and who had nothing to do now that both chip projects were essentially dead. To conserve the company's remaining cash, Huang elected to lay off the majority of the staff: Nvidia went from more than one hundred employees to forty.[12]

"We had a marketing team, we had a sales team, and all of a sudden we had a road map that was no longer viable," said Dwight Diercks, a software engineer who survived the culling.

While Nvidia reeled from its missteps with the NV1 and NV2 and was pivoting to focus on the NV3, a formidable new competitor had emerged in the PC graphics market. Three alumni of Silicon Graphics, Scott Sellers, Ross Smith, and Gary Tarolli, founded the company 3dfx in 1994, just one year after Nvidia's incorporation. In the 1990s, Silicon Graphics, or SGI, was best known as a manufacturer of high-end graphics workstations used for computer-generated movie effects, including the dinosaurs in Steven Spielberg's *Jurassic Park*. The founders of 3dfx intended to bring that same level of performance to the PC market at a price gamers could afford. In the fall of 1996, after two years of development, the company announced that it was ready to launch its first graphics chip, branded as "Voodoo Graphics."

3dfx decided to unveil Voodoo Graphics at a conference held by the tech-focused investment bank Hambrecht & Quist in San Francisco. There, an executive named Gordon Campbell planned a session that would demonstrate how 3dfx's chip could produce high-end, enterprise-grade graphics on low-end, consumer-grade equipment. The centerpiece of his demo was a 3-D cube, rendered with such precision that it could have passed for something made by an SGI workstation.

"I was down in the basement in a little tiny room with a PC, a projector, and our first chip on a card," Campbell said.[13]

The 3dfx session was scheduled to take place at the same time as a keynote session that featured Silicon Graphics' CEO, Edward McCracken. Initially, Campbell's demonstration was sparsely attended, as most people who might have been interested were listening to McCracken walk through SGI's corporate history. But partway through his presentation, McCracken's SGI workstation, which retailed for $85,000, crashed and brought the keynote to a complete halt. As the crowd grew restless, word began to trickle in that the downstairs session was more compelling—that a small start-up had managed to engineer 3-D graphics on par with SGI's machines, but on a consumer PC card.

"People were kind of blown away," said Campbell. "There were all going *you got to see this* and dragging people in."

The dueling sessions not only became part of 3dfx corporate lore but also informed the marketing message for Voodoo Graphics, which went on sale in October 1996. 3dfx pitched itself as the only start-up that could bring SGI-level performance to personal computers, at a fraction of the cost. These themes were reinforced everywhere in the launch materials for Voodoo Graphics, such as a quote that Ross Smith, 3dfx's head of marketing, provided to a company called Orchid that featured the Voodoo Graphics chip on their Righteous 3D graphics card.

> Last year at Comdex [*sic*], Bill Gates played *The Valley of Ra* in the Orchid booth on a quarter of a million dollar SGI Reality Engine-based Voodoo Graphics simulator. That same real-time 3D graphics performance is now available to PC consumers for $299 from Orchid. That's Righteous![14]

Knowingly or not, 3dfx followed the exact principles laid down by Al Ries and Jack Trout in *Positioning*. The company pitched its product as a clear alternative to the other cards in the marketplace and appealed to its customers' emotions—the feeling of "beating the system" by getting outsized performance at a great price—rather than try to convince them with facts and performance statistics.

3dfx was offering more than just marketing puffery. In June of 1996, id Software launched the title game in its new series of first-person shooters, *Quake*. Just like *DOOM* had done three years prior with 2-D cards, the original version of *Quake* pushed the capabilities of 3-D graphics cards to their limits, in this case by rendering everything in real-time 3-D. In January of 1997, id Software released an updated version of *Quake*, dubbed *GLQuake*, which added support for 3-D graphics hardware acceleration—the very feature that the Voodoo Graphics chip excelled at.

"Our sales just went crazy," 3dfx's chief engineer, Scott Sellers, recalled.[15]

The company's revenues exploded, from $4 million in the 1996 fiscal year, to $44 million in 1997, to $203 million in fiscal 1998 after the release of the upgraded Voodoo2 graphics card. The vast majority of this demand came from *Quake* gamers; it was the killer app that motivated buyers to upgrade their hardware so that they could get better graphics performance and quality, all to make their gaming experience more immersive.

3dfx's executives knew that Nvidia was under significant financial strain and considered making an acquisition play for their fading rival. Even though its first two chips had failed to gain traction, Nvidia still had some of the best graphics engineers in Silicon Valley on its payroll. In the end, however, 3dfx executives opted not to make a move. Its executives believed that Nvidia's bankruptcy was inevitable, and that it would be cheaper to wait until Nvidia collapsed so that they could pick up its talent and assets for a bargain.

"The mistake that we made at 3dfx is we should have killed them when they were down," said Ross Smith. "That was a huge tactical error on our part, not buying them. We had them on the ropes."

"We were very aware if the RIVA 128 chip had come back and there were any bugs in it, they would be dead," said Sellers, referring to the chip that started as the NV3 and would later be sold as the RIVA series. "They had no time. We were betting that if we just waited a little bit, they were going to implode on their own."

They did make one attempt to push Nvidia over the edge. Sellers had previously worked with Dwight Diercks at another small start-up and knew that the Nvidia engineer was exceptionally skilled at programming software drivers for graphics chips, which are critical to a card's success. Sellers aggressively courted Diercks, trying to convince him to abandon the sinking Nvidia and join the ascendant 3dfx.

"We were so close to getting him," Sellers later said, with more than a hint of regret in his voice.[16]

Diercks, for his part, seriously considered the opportunity.[17] But he remained at Nvidia for two reasons. One was curiosity: he wanted to see the RIVA 128 through to production before he considered leaving. The other was Jensen, who talked with Diercks and convinced him to stay. To this day, Jensen claims that he "saved" Diercks; in turn, Diercks likes to joke that if he had left, 3dfx would have bought Nvidia outright. Diercks is still at Nvidia three decades later, overseeing the company's software engineering.

JUST AS *QUAKE* WAS PUSHING 3dfx to new heights, Jensen Huang and Nvidia counted their dwindling reserve of cash and wondered whether it was enough to see their next chip through to production. With $3 million left in the bank, the company could afford to operate for nine more months.[18] To survive, it had to do more than just create an above-average or merely good chip. It had to create the fastest graphics chip possible with the manufacturing and memory technology available—something that could win against 3dfx's excellent Voodoo line.

To beat such a formidable competitor, Nvidia would have to rethink its entire approach to chip development. The NV1 had been designed to do what Nvidia engineers wanted rather than what the market wanted. The proprietary standards that Curtis Priem had included on the chip showcased his technical acumen but ended up alienating manufacturers. In June 1996, Microsoft made it even harder for new graphical standards to gain traction when it released Direct3D, an application programming interface (API) for graphical texturing that used the traditional inverse triangle approach. Within a few months, game developers almost universally abandoned small-scale proprietary graphics standards such as Nvidia's in favor of one of the two big and well-supported alternatives, Microsoft's Direct3D and OpenGL.

Jensen saw where the industry was headed and demanded that Nvidia's engineers follow the market rather than fight it.

"Guys, it's time to quit polishing the turd," he told his remaining employees.[19] "At this point it is clear we're doing it the wrong way and nobody's going to support our architecture."[20]

Malachowsky agreed with the new approach. "Instead of trying to be smarter than the competition with a different technology like NV1, we just had to out-engineer everybody else using the same basic tactics," he said.

Jensen's message inspired Priem to go big, literally, with the NV3. In order to make a much faster chip, the team wanted to use a wide 128-bit memory bus and design a graphics pipeline that would be able to generate pixels at record-breaking speeds. Nvidia would have to produce a chip that was physically larger than any that had ever been successfully manufactured.

Priem cornered Jensen in a hallway in the Nvidia offices to ask for his approval, despite the technical challenges involved.

"Let me think about it," Jensen answered. He took the next two days to map out the schedule, pricing, manufacturing plans, and business model for the revised NV3. In the end, he not only approved the larger-sized chip; he also wanted Priem and his engineers to add another 100,000 gates, or about an extra 400,000 transistors—for a total of 3.5 million transistors on the entire chip.[21]

"Jensen gave us the green light to fill up the chip with even more functionality," Priem said.

"I wasn't worried about my cost," Jensen said years later, when asked to explain his decision-making process. "I built a chip that physically was as large as anyone could build at the time. We just wanted to make sure this is the most powerful chip the world's ever seen."

As a nod to Nvidia's ambitions—and, perhaps, as a way to signal a clean break with its past design philosophy—the company decided to give the NV3 an external brand that was different than its internal code name and dubbed it the RIVA 128, which encapsulated the chip's ultimate purpose: RIVA stood for Real-time Interactive Video and Animation Accelerator, and "128" was a nod to the 128-bit bus, which would be the largest ever included on a single chip—another first for the consumer PC industry.

Given its financial position, Nvidia would have to make the RIVA 128 in record time, and without the safety net of multiple quality-assurance runs. Standard chip development usually spans two years, involving multiple revisions to identify and fix bugs after a chip "tapeout," when a finalized chip design is sent for prototype manufacturing. The NV1, for example, had three or four physical tape-outs. Nvidia could afford just one physical tape-out for the NV3 before the company had to send it to production.

To shorten the timeline, Nvidia would have to shorten the testing cycle. Jensen had heard about a small company, Ikos, that made refrigerator-sized chip-emulation machines. The massive machines enabled engineers to run games and tests on digital chip prototypes, bypassing the need to make an actual chip for testing and fixing bugs, and thus saving time and resources. An Ikos machine wasn't cheap: a single one cost $1 million and thus would cut Nvidia's payroll runway from nine to six months—but Jensen realized it would speed up the testing process by significantly *more* time. He argued the point with the company's other executives, who wanted as much time as possible by raising more money. The CEO stood firm.

"We're not going to find more money," he said. Venture capitalists had "ninety other companies to believe in. Why believe in us? We got to do it this way."

Jensen won the argument and bought an emulator from Ikos. As soon as it arrived, Diercks and his software team began running tests on the digital RIVA 128 in order to identify and fix issues with the chip. Diercks remembered that the first conversation between his team and the hardware engineers was a disaster.

"Hey guys, we can emulate for the first time for our chip," he said. "It's just booted DOS, very slow."[22]

One of the hardware guys said, "Yeah, look at that. It's already got an error. The C colon was off by two pixels."

Normally, chips don't error out so quickly after boot up or on something so basic. As a result, the hardware team assumed that the emulator wasn't working properly and that Jensen and Diercks had just wasted three months of payroll cushion for no good reason.

"But it was actually the first bug we found in our hardware," Diercks said.

Working with the Ikos machine was an arduous process. The setup consisted of two large boxes connected to a motherboard that was exposed to the open air. Instead of a chip, wires were plugged into the socket to transmit the data that, with a physical chip, would be sent from the chip to the CPU. The software-emulated chip was much slower than a real hardware chip.

"It took fifteen minutes to load Windows. I remember moving the mouse just a tiny bit and having to wait for the screens to refresh frame by frame," tester Henry Levin said. "Trying to click a button was a nightmare because if you moved it slightly, it would overshoot."[23]

Levin drew a map on his desk so he would know where to place the mouse to access specific parts of the screen without needing to wait for the emulator to refresh every frame. The testers would run basic utilities, such as drawing a triangle or circle. The running of benchmarks often meant leaving the machine on overnight and returning the next morning to see whether it had finished.

The emulator did not produce any bug reports automatically. Instead, when a program froze, all Levin could do was take a screenshot and call over one of the hardware engineers to figure out what happened or where the corruption occurred. If it was a significant problem, the engineers would go back to redesign a part of the chip.

One engineer recalled that the team attempted to run a longer benchmark over a weekend. Somehow, an overnight cleaning crew gained access to the testing lab and unplugged the emulator in order to plug in a vacuum cleaner. The engineers returned to find their benchmark test completely ruined; they would have to run it again from the start, which cost time. The cleaning crew didn't even need to be in there, as the lab did not have a carpet.

Unnecessary janitorial services were not the only challenge the team faced. Nvidia didn't have the time to start from a completely clean-sheet design. So Priem, Malachowsky, and chip architect David Rosenthal figured out a way to reuse parts of the NV1 but add support for multiple new features, including inverse texturing, better math capabilities, and a very wide memory bus. Even if Nvidia wanted to make a clean break from its first chips, the DNA of those early designs would persist in the RIVA 128.

"We got it to work," Malachowsky said.[24]

The company also now knew that its chips needed to have 100 percent hardware support for the old VGA standard. The NV1 had tried to get by with a solution that was half hardware, half software emulator, but this approach caused significant issues in many DOS-based games, including *DOOM*. Nvidia couldn't afford to fall short on VGA once again.

But the company didn't have anyone on staff with the expertise to design a VGA core in-house. Incredibly, Jensen was able to source and license a VGA core design from one of Nvidia's competitors, a company called Weitek.

"Jensen is the best deal cutter in the world. Hands down," Priem said. "Somehow Jensen is able to come up with these amazing business deals for Nvidia that save the company again and again."

Not only did Jensen sign a licensing agreement with Weitek—he was also able to poach its VGA chip designer, Gopal Solanki, who became a project manager and one of the CEO's top lieutenants. A former Nvidia employee said that they worked like "business soulmates." Solanki was known for being extremely tough and demanding—and for delivering. Jensen, for his part, gave Solanki credit for saving the company.

"Gopal is really important," Jensen said nearly thirty years later. "If not for Gopal, we'd be out of business now."[25]

"You always had a good feeling when Gopal was assigned to the next generation of NV chips. You would know things would turn out okay," Priem agreed.

Nvidia unveiled the RIVA 128 in April at the 1997 Computer Game Developers Conference. The conference was where hardware companies showcased their latest products, in hopes of securing orders from PC manufacturers and retailers. Nvidia's timelines were so tight that it was uncertain whether the chips would arrive in time for the conference—or whether they would be in good enough shape to show-case. The samples from the factory came only a few days before the event, and Nvidia engineers worked feverishly to troubleshoot any software bugs that remained. Their goal was to ensure the chips could run the Direct3D graphics benchmark that hardware manufacturers would use to evaluate their quality. Mere hours before the show started, the engineers managed to get the chips stable enough to work without crashing at unpredictable moments.

"Our dirty little secret was the RIVA 128 would only run that particular test once and it did so tenuously," said Eric Christenson, a regional sales manager for Nvidia who attended the 1997 conference.[26] "You had to treat it with the utmost care and respect. It would just as likely lock up the system mid-test if you looked at it the wrong way."

Representatives from rival graphics-card manufacturers visited Nvidia's booth, mainly for an opportunity to heckle the company about its NV1 failure.

"Oh, you guys are still around?" one 3dfx employee said.

But enough people saw Nvidia's benchmark tests—and were impressed enough by the results—that RIVA 128 began to attract buzz. The industry collectively understood that it might be something special. Near the day's end, 3dfx cofounder and head of engineering, Scott Sellers, approached the booth and asked for a demonstration.

"In order to give the best experience, I'm going to power-down this system to let you see a clean run," said Christenson. "We'll just re-boot the system, open the app, and run the demo."

Although he tried to sound as matter-of-fact as possible, Christenson was taking a gamble in order to impress his rival. The chips were especially prone to crashes after a reboot, so he couldn't be sure that the device would come back up. At the same time, if he ran a test without rebooting the device, Sellers could claim that the benchmarks were less accurate than they would have been otherwise.

Christenson held his breath while the device restarted. It came back online without crashing. He ran the benchmark test. The results appeared on the PC display. Sellers didn't—couldn't—believe them. They were not only better than 3dfx's benchmarks but also higher than anything Sellers had ever seen from a consumer graphics card. Christenson assured him that the test results were unassailable. Sellers realized the implications of the test. First, the RIVA 128 could outperform 3dfx's best cards; and second, the company that 3dfx had left for dead was instead about to come roaring back into the 3-D graphics market.

Walt Donovan, the chief architect at another 3-D graphics start-up, called Rendition, also came over and looked at the RIVA 128's test results. He asked Nvidia's relatively new chief scientist, David Kirk, a series of questions about the chip and its performance. Listening to Kirk's answers, all Donovan could say was, "That's amazing." None of Donovan's projects would ever come close to the performance of the RIVA 128. In the span of a single benchmarking test, his company had gone from competitive to failed.

Once he processed the situation, Donovan asked one more question. "Can I have a job at Nvidia?" He was hired shortly thereafter.

WITH A WORKING PROTOTYPE CHIP that produced strong performance numbers, Jensen now had leverage to raise more money.

"We did not want Sutter Hill's or Sequoia's money early," Priem said. If Jensen had gone back right after the NV1 or NV2 fiascos, when Nvidia had no clear path forward, he would have faced a skeptical audience demanding unfavorable investment terms—if they agreed to invest any additional money at all. Now, however, the venture capital firms were highly motivated to keep the company going just when it was on the verge of possible success. Jensen asked for another investment round so that he could buy chips from the fabs. Both funds agreed to invest again, with Sutter Hill committing $1.8 million on August 8, 1997.[27] (I have not been able to determine how much Sequoia invested in this round, only that it did. Sequoia did not offer the information after requests.)

In late summer, Jensen gathered the whole company in the office cafeteria. He pulled a piece of paper from his pocket and read off some dollar figures, down to cents. He folded the paper back into his pocket and said, "That's how much money we have in the bank."

The room fell silent. The number was not very large at all—barely enough to pay everyone's salary for a few more weeks. One recent hire remembered being brought to the verge of panic. "My God," he thought, "we're almost out of cash."

Jensen then pulled out another piece of paper from his pocket. He opened it up and read, "One purchase order from STB Systems for 30,000 units of RIVA 128." It was the chip's first major order. The cafeteria erupted in cheers. Jensen had indulged in a bit of showmanship for dramatic effect.

The RIVA 128 was the company's first big hit. The stellar reviews it received upon release more than erased the bad memories from the NV1 launch.

"Whoever is a die-hard gamer will have to buy this card," *Tom's Hardware*, a leading tech enthusiast website, said. It is "the fastest 3D chip for PCs currently available."

Within four months of the chip's release, Nvidia had shipped more than a million units and captured a fifth of the PC graphics market. *PC Magazine* named the RIVA 128 an Editors' Choice product, and *PC Computing* named it the Product of the Year for 1997.[28] Large PC manufacturers, including Dell Computer, Gateway 2000, Micron Electronics, and NEC, all incorporated the chip into their computers for the holiday season. The torrid pace of sales allowed Nvidia to turn a $1.4 million profit in the fourth quarter of 1997—the company's first profitable quarter since its founding four years earlier.

Jensen's flair for the dramatic was apparent again at a company meeting near the end of the year. In those days, he still preferred to wear sport coats and jeans; he had yet to start donning his signature black leather jackets. From his front coat pocket he produced a thick envelope that was stuffed full of crisp new $1 bills. He walked around the room, giving each employee a single bill from the envelope, as a symbol of the financial lifeline that the RIVA orders had given them—and a reminder that their situation was still too precarious for a lavish celebration.

Then, he went back to a woman named Kathleen Buffington, who worked in operations and was responsible for packing graphics chips and shipping them out to customers. He had already given her one dollar; now, he gave her a second. He said to the whole company that she had worked so hard to get all the chips out the door that she deserved a double bonus.

Jensen's distribution of dollar bills was a much-needed moment of levity and celebration for a company that had been operating on the brink of failure for years. "The RIVA 128 was a miracle," Jensen said. "When our backs were against the wall, Curtis, Chris, Gopal, and David Kirk built it. They made really good decisions."[29]

CHAPTER 5

Ultra-Aggressive

THE RIVA 128 DID MORE THAN ENSURE NVIDIA'S SURVIVAL.
It also served as a magnet for talent, drawing people from across the relatively insular world of computer graphics to a small office park in Sunnyvale, where they believed they would get a chance to work on something extraordinary.

Caroline Landry was a chip designer for the Canadian company Matrox Graphics when she first heard about Nvidia's new chip. "I was in my late twenties. I wasn't completely up-to-date on all the industry trends, but I knew Nvidia had released the first RIVA, which had taken the industry by storm. It was way ahead of a product I was working on at Matrox that wasn't even close to taping out," she said.[1]

Her boyfriend had recently found a job in the Bay Area, but Landry wasn't sure if she wanted to join him. Until, that is, a headhunter put her in touch with Nvidia, and she flew down for a full day of interviews. She was offered a job right away and accepted it just as quickly, solely on the strength of Nvidia's reputation. She was the company's first female engineer.

When she started, she had trouble adjusting to Nvidia's intense culture. She would often work until eleven at night during the week, and she would put in full days nearly every weekend, too. She recalls that one time an executive checked in on a late Friday afternoon to ask about her work objectives for that weekend. "Canada was a good place to recruit from because engineers there were paid much less than engineers in the U.S.," she said. "But quality of life is generally more important to Canadians."

Landry mentioned to Jensen that some employees were griping about the long work hours. His response was typically direct.

"People who train for the Olympics grumble about training early in the morning, too."

Jensen was sending a message: long hours were a necessary prerequisite for excellence. To this day, he has not deviated from that view or altered Nvidia's expectation that employees adopt extreme work habits.

Landry also noticed Nvidia's managers were quick to recognize special talent. She joined Nvidia around the same time as Jonah Alben, a young engineer barely out of school who was, as she put it, obviously "brilliant." Jensen saw Alben's potential early, saying at a company meeting, "in 20 years I expect I'll be working for Jonah." Initially, Landry felt a bit jealous about the attention her colleague was receiving but got over it. "At Nvidia, you embrace your smart colleagues and don't feel threatened. This is not about your ego. This is about whether we make it or not. Be grateful that you have people like that to work with," she said. Alben would later rise through the ranks to become the head of graphics processing unit (GPU) engineering.

Jensen insisted that new hires should know exactly what they were getting into the moment they walked in the door.[2] He tasked Michael Hara, Nvidia's director of marketing, with giving a frank talk at every orientation session. As Hara recalls, his speech was intended to encourage new arrivals to not be afraid of speaking up and to offer fresh perspectives and new ideas at every opportunity.

"We're ultra-aggressive," he told the new employees. "We don't waste time finding excuses for why things don't work. We move on. If you came here thinking you can just hide in the back, collect your paycheck, and go home at five, you're mistaken. If that's what you think, you should resign today."

Hara remembers that the human resources employee who was

handling the new-hire class looked aghast. He continued his speech, undeterred.

"We don't do things like anybody else. If you come here and say, 'This is how we did it before,' we don't care. We're about doing things differently and better. When we were just twenty-five people, Jensen taught us to come here, take risks, do things outside the box, and make mistakes. I encourage you to do all three. But don't make the same mistake twice, because we will fire you in a heartbeat."

Hara meant it, too. John McSorley, Nvidia's former head of human resources, said that the company had a policy of hiring quickly—but also of firing fast if a new employee wasn't working out. Jensen's primary guidance to all of his hiring managers was simple: "Hire someone smarter than yourself." However, as Nvidia grew and began adding new employees at a pace of more than one hundred a month, executives understood that they would occasionally make the wrong decision. Better to correct those mistakes as soon as possible than to let them fester and harm Nvidia's culture.

In Nvidia's early years, even the longer-tenured employees could never feel totally secure because the company had adopted an "up or out" approach, with people either getting promoted on a regular cadence or getting pushed out to make room for someone with greater potential. The company handled personnel in the same uncompromising way that it approached chip design.

SINCE NVIDIA'S FOUNDING, JENSEN HAS insisted that all Nvidia employees work at the "Speed of Light."[3] He wants their work to be constrained only by the laws of physics—not by internal politics or financial concerns. Each project must be broken down into its component tasks, and each task must have a target time-to-completion that assumes no delays, queues, or downtime. This sets the theoretical maximum: the "Speed of Light" that it is physically impossible to exceed.

"Speed of Light gets you into the market faster and makes it really, really hard, if not impossible, for your competitors to do better," a former Nvidia executive said. "How fast can you do it, and why aren't you doing it that fast?"

It was not just a rhetorical question—Jensen used this measure to gauge the performance of his employees. He would reprimand subordinates who set goals that referred to what the company had already done before or what the competitors were doing in that moment. As he saw it, he needed to prevent the kind of internal rot that he observed at other companies, where employees often manipulated their projects to provide steady and sustainable growth that would advance their individual careers, when in reality they were making only incremental improvements that actually *hurt* the company in the long term. The "Speed of Light" notion ensured that Nvidia would never tolerate such sandbagging.

"The theoretical limit of what you could do—that's what Speed of Light is. That's the only thing we were allowed to measure against," remembered former executive Robert Csongor.

The RIVA 128 was a prime example of "Speed of Light" project planning. Jensen had confronted two facts: most graphics chips take two years to get from concept to market, and Nvidia had only nine months. During the planning phase, Jensen had asked software engineer Dwight Diercks, "What's the main limiting factor in getting a graphics card to market?"

Diercks responded that software drivers—the specialized programs that enable the operating system and PC applications to interface with and use the graphics hardware—were the primary obstacle, because they needed to be completely ready by the time the chip was prepared for mass production. In traditional production processes, the first step was to build a physical prototype of the chip. Once it was complete, software engineers could begin work on the drivers and fix any bugs they encountered. Then the chip's design was optimized at least one more time to accommodate the new driver.

To save time, Jensen decreed that Nvidia would have to develop the driver software for the RIVA 128 *before* the prototype chip was completed—a reversal of the customary process. This would shave nearly a year off of the production timeline, but it would require the company to find a way to bypass the step of testing the software on physical chips. That was why Nvidia invested $1 million in its Ikos emulator, even though every dollar was precious: it would allow them to approach the "Speed of Light."

(Later on, in 2018, Jensen considered replacing "Speed of Light" with a metaphor suggesting something even faster than light—a physical impossibility. He was frustrated with the increasing slowness across the organization as it grew in size. He yelled at his executive staff that they had to move faster than light, and then turned to Robert Csongor. "Rob, what's the *Star Trek: Discovery* propulsion system that allows them to instantaneously travel somewhere?"

"Well, Warp Drive is faster than the speed of light, but I think you're referring to the Mycelium Spore Drive," Csongor responded.[4]

Both Jensen and Csongor were *Star Trek* nerds. Jensen shouted, "The Spore Drive! We need to be like the Spore Drive." Everyone started laughing. They decided to stick with "Speed of Light" because it was an easier concept to explain than the instantaneous "Mycelium Spore Drive.")

Nvidia pushed against the limits of what was possible with the RIVA 128's development process in other ways, too. The staff created a chip larger than any that had ever been designed and then crammed it full of even more transistors than they originally intended in order to improve performance. They licensed VGA technology from their competitor so that they would not have to build lower-priority components from scratch. Jensen ruthlessly recruited the top engineers from rivals and even Nvidia's partners, including Weitek. All of this happened because Nvidia employees did not let themselves think about what was likely to work or what they could reasonably achieve. They only cared about what would be possible with the maximum amount of effort and minimum amount of wasted time.

Much of what the company learned on the RIVA 128 became standard in its future chip development. From that point on, Nvidia had software drivers ready at the beginning of chip production: the drivers would already have been tested across all the important applications and games and to ensure compatibility with prior Nvidia chips. This approach became a significant competitive advantage for Nvidia, whose rivals had to develop separate drivers for different chip-architecture generations.[5]

Nvidia also decided to handle the maintenance of graphics drivers rather than rely on PC makers and board partners to push out updates on their own schedules. The company distributed new drivers each month. Jeff Fisher, Nvidia's former head of sales and current head of its PC graphics business, explained that a frequent, centralized update process was the best means to guarantee a consistently good user experience, ensuring that gamers always had optimal performance for the latest software released by developers and other companies. "Graphics drivers are perhaps the most challenging piece of software in the PC after the operating system," he said. "Every app touches it, and every app release or update can potentially break it."

WHEN GEOFF RIBAR WAS HIRED away in December of 1997 from Advanced Micro Devices to serve as Nvidia's CFO, he found that his new boss had two impressive traits: Jensen was extremely persuasive and extremely hardworking.[6]

"There may be people smarter than me," Jensen once told his executive staff, "but no one is ever going to work harder than me."[7]

He was often in the office from 9:00 a.m. to near midnight, and his engineers usually felt obligated to keep similar hours.

"I used to tell people at AMD, Intel, or anywhere else that if they wanted to see how Nvidia was doing, they should visit the company's parking lot on weekends. It was always busy," said Ribar.

Even for the marketing department, working sixty to eighty hours a week, including every Saturday, was the norm. Andrew Logan, Nvidia's director of corporate marketing, remembers leaving the office to take his wife to a 9:30 p.m. showing of the movie *Titanic*. On his way out, his coworker shouted, "Oh, half day, Andy?"[8]

Tester Henry Levin recalls that whenever he found himself working late, he was never the only one there. Even when he stayed to 10:00 p.m. or later, Nvidia's graphics architects would still be at the whiteboard, passionately discussing chip optimization and rendering techniques. His contemporary, Director of Materials Ian Siu, has imprinted on his memory the image of colleagues spending the night at the office, even over the weekends, after bringing sleeping bags to work. Employees would also bring their kids to the office so that they could spend time with their families without leaving their workplace.

"We worked our asses off all the time," Siu said. He had fond memories of the camaraderie in the office and of close relationships with his coworkers.

Ribar rarely worked until midnight, but he would often arrive early in the morning. He quickly learned that one big disadvantage to sitting near the CEO at the office was that he was often the first person Jensen saw in the morning. And Jensen was known to unload on the first person he encountered, whoever it was.

"Jensen would often stew with his thoughts on something overnight about products or marketing," Ribar said. "It was almost never a finance issue but it didn't matter. If I saw him first, I would get the first blast from him."

As the day went on, no place in Nvidia headquarters was safe from a drive-by grilling from Jensen. Kenneth Hurley, a technical marketing engineer, was at a urinal when Jensen walked up to the one next to him.

"I'm not the kind of guy who likes to talk in the bathroom," Hurley said.[9]

Jensen had other ideas. "Hey, what's up?" he asked.

Hurley replied with a noncommittal "not much," which earned him a sidelong glance from the CEO. Hurley panicked, thinking, "I'm going to get fired because he thinks I'm not doing anything. He's probably wondering what I'm doing at Nvidia."

To save face, Hurley proceeded to list twenty things he was working on, from convincing developers to buy Nvidia's latest graphics card to teaching those developers how to program new features on them.

"Okay," Jensen replied, apparently satisfied with the engineer's answer.

FEAR AND ANXIETY BECAME JENSEN'S favorite motivational tools. At each monthly company meeting, he would say, "We're thirty days from going out of business."

It was hyperbole, on one level. The tense, high-stakes RIVA 128 process was not a complete outlier—as we'll see—but it certainly wasn't a regular occurrence. Yet Jensen didn't want to allow any complacency to creep in, even in successful periods. And he wanted to confront new hires with the kind of pressure they would face going forward. If they didn't have what it took, they needed to self-select out sooner rather than later.

But on another level, the line "We're thirty days from going out of business" was true. In the technology industry, a single bad decision or product launch could be fatal. Nvidia had gotten lucky twice before, barely surviving the disasters of the NV1 and the NV2 before succeeding—with only months to spare—with the RIVA 128. That luck would not hold forever. But a good corporate culture would fortify the company against the dire consequences of most mistakes. And a mistake or downturn in the market was inevitable.

Still, as Dwight Diercks said, "It always felt like we were at zero. And the reason is that no matter how much money we had in the bank, Jensen could explain why we were going to be at zero with three things happening. He would say, 'Let me tell you how. This could happen, this could happen, this could happen, and all that money goes to zero.'"

Jeff Fisher pointed out that fear can be clarifying. Even today, although Nvidia is no longer thirty days away from going out of business, the company could easily be thirty days from starting down a path that will lead to its destruction. "You're always trying to look around corners and see what we're missing," Fisher said.

That paranoia came to a head in late 1997. Intel had always been both an important partner for Nvidia and a potential competitive threat. Nvidia's graphics chips all had to be compatible with Intel's processors, because Intel was the primary CPU maker for the PC market. But that fall, Intel started telling industry partners it had its own graphics chip coming, which threatened to take business away from Nvidia and other companies in the space.

Just months after the RIVA 128 launched to great fanfare, Intel announced its own chip, the i740. It was a direct challenge to Nvidia—its new chip and its very existence. Unlike the RIVA 128, which had a four-megabyte frame buffer, Intel's i740 had an eight-megabyte buffer—twice the size of the one on Nvidia's chip—that the company was trying to set as the new standard in the industry. Intel had the ear of every PC maker in the world, as it supplied the vast majority of their CPUs. After Intel's i740 announcement, "our sales pipeline started to dry up," one Nvidia executive said. If Intel could force adoption of the eight-megabyte buffer, the RIVA 128 would quickly be rendered obsolete.

"Make no mistake. Intel is out to get us and put us out of business," Jensen declared at an all-company meeting. "They have told their employees, and they have internalized this. They are going to put us out of business. Our job is to go kill them before they put us out of business. We need to go *kill Intel*."[10]

Caroline Landry and the rest of the Nvidia team worked even harder to fight off the new competitor, a company that at the time was about 860 times Nvidia's size in terms of revenue. She often worked past midnight, staggering home and falling asleep for a few hours before waking back up to do it again.

"I'm super tired. I need to get up. It's hard," she told herself. "But we need to kill Intel. Must kill Intel."

CHRIS MALACHOWSKY SPEARHEADED the response to the Intel threat. Throughout his career at Nvidia, he acted as an ultratalented utility infielder. Jensen would assign him to manage a struggling part of the business, whether operations, manufacturing, or engineering, and Malachowsky would do whatever was necessary to fix the issue. Now, the CEO needed him to go back to his roots as a chip architect and beat the i740.

Even when engrossed in a time-sensitive project that required intense concentration, Malachowsky found himself pulled into a mentorship role, which he embraced. A new hire named Sanford Russell had just joined Nvidia from Silicon Graphics but was having trouble getting up to speed on Nvidia's technology and culture. There was little formal orientation beyond Hara's confrontational pep talks, and few of the company's processes were written down.

One day, Russell noticed that Malachowsky would go home to have dinner with his family and then come back late at night to work on the RIVA 128ZX, an eight-megabyte version of the original chip intended to compete with Intel. He realized that if he showed up at the lab at 10:00 p.m. sharp and pulled up a stool across from Malachowsky, he could ask the Nvidia cofounder whatever he wanted.[11]

Russell would ask him about a deep technical issue, Malachowsky would talk through the topic for a few minutes and then quietly go back to work. Russell sat there until Malachowsky asked him for the next question, at roughly fifteen-minute intervals.

"I did this for weeks, patiently watching him, listening to him mutter, 'Why isn't this working?' as he tried to bring the chip up. The whole company was trying to get the chip working," Russell said. "But Chris still helped me climb the ladder of knowledge of all these chip things because he built them. He was the guy who built the stuff and taught me while he was trying to save the company."

Russell was amazed that Malachowsky could hold the whole chip in his head and work through it until he figured it out. At 2:00 a.m. one morning, everything fell into place. Malachowsky shouted, "I got it! I got it! We're going to live!"

He had internalized Jensen's paranoia and in the sprint to make the original RIVA 128 had helped to future-proof it in one important way: he had left himself some spare capacity in the chip's silicon. Now, he was able to use it to rework the chip so that it had an eight-megabyte frame buffer.

"It was a very elaborate change order, rewiring gates," he recalled. "We were able to make a feature change, on the fly, in metal."

Once he hit on his solution, the company applied focused ion beam (FIB) technology, which can modify chips at the microscale level. The FIB instrument looks like an electron microscope but does not use electrons: it uses ions to modify chip prototypes. The modified chips worked, saving Nvidia's RIVA series from instant obsolescence.

Malachowsky was able to inspire one of his newest employees while doing so. In 2024, when Russell ran into Malachowsky at a conference, he raised the long nights they spent together in the lab.

"You saved me, man," Russell said, thanking him for getting his career at Nvidia—which would last twenty-five years before he moved on—off to a solid start.

Malachowsky demurred. "Nah. You were fine."

"No," said Russell with a chuckle. "No, I wasn't."

IN SOME INSTANCES, NVIDIA'S FOCUS on speed could lead to lapses in quality—at least, relative to the high standards that Jensen set for the company.

Andrew Logan, Nvidia's director of corporate marketing, remembers how one of Nvidia's chips came in second place for a computer magazine awards feature. In his prior job at S3, executives would be happy if their products finished in the top three. Not at Nvidia.

"The first time we came in second place, Jensen sternly told me: Second place is the first loser," Logan said.[12] "I never forgot it. I realized I'm working for a boss who believes we have to win at everything. It was a lot of pressure."

By all measures, the original RIVA 128 was an excellent chip. It could render high-resolution graphics at a much faster frame rate than that of its competitors; even visually demanding games such as *Quake* ran at maximum quality without any slowdown. It was also the largest chip ever manufactured but could still be produced fast enough to meet initial demand. Even so, the Nvidia team had to make some trade-offs to get the chip out in time. On some types of images, the RIVA 128 would apply dithering—a form of intentional noise that was designed to break up or obscure obvious visual irregularities—to certain types of renders, such as smoke or clouds.

Enough gamers had noticed the issue that a major PC magazine decided to publish an exposé on Nvidia's flagship graphics chip. It placed renders from Nvidia's RIVA series and from equivalent current-generation cards from 3dfx and another competitor, Rendition, side-by-side-by-side in a large, detailed image spread. Nvidia's images were blurry and smudged, and the magazine commented that they were the worst of the three—that they "looked terrible."

Upon seeing the article, Jensen called his several executives into his office, where he had the issue spread open on a table. He demanded to know why the RIVA 128's output looked so bad. Chief Scientist David Kirk responded that they had made some image-quality trade-offs in order to get the chip done on time (and save the company). The reply only made Jensen even more agitated. He demanded that Nvidia chips beat the competition not on one metric but on all of them.

The shouting match got so loud that it caught the attention of Walt Donovan. He was the chip architect who had seen the RIVA 128 demo at the Computer Game Developers Conference and who had asked for a job at Nvidia on the spot. He worked on the opposite end of Nvidia's headquarters from Jensen's office, which shielded him from most of the CEO's broadsides. He also had a severe hearing deficiency, wearing hearing aids in each ear. But this time, he couldn't ignore the commotion and invited himself into the argument.

Donovan assured Jensen that Nvidia's next generation of chips, which they were calling the RIVA TNT series, would not only solve the dithering problem; it would also outpace the industry on every possible measure of graphics quality. He pointed to the Rendition image, which the magazine had rated the best of the three.

"That's what RIVA TNT will look like," he said.

It did little to placate Jensen, who at this point wanted to be left alone.

"Get out!" he yelled.

JENSEN'S COMPETITIVENESS OFTEN MOTIVATED his employees to do extraordinary things. But it could also reveal a petty side of the CEO.

Harry Levin, the chip tester who often spent late nights working on the RIVA 128, once challenged Jensen to a game of ping-pong on one of the communal tables inside Nvidia headquarters. He was well aware that Jensen had been a nationally ranked ping-pong player during his teenage years. And he was familiar with the CEO's obsession with winning at business. What Levin didn't realize was that Jensen brought the same level of intensity to any kind of competition, whether professional or recreational. Levin considered himself a good recreational player, but never expected to receive quite the beatdown he got at the hands of his superior.

"He just whooped me," said Levin. "The game was up to twenty-one points, and he let me score only once or twice. It was a very quick match."

Jensen was so competitive that he challenged other employees even when he was at a disadvantage. In high school, CFO Geoff Ribar had ranked among the top fifty chess players in the country. His boss, however, could not accept that someone else was better than him.

"Jensen knew about my chess skills. Being competitive, he was convinced he was smarter than me and could beat me," Ribar said. "There was no way he could have been able to beat me, but he tried."

Jensen attempted to close the gap between his and Ribar's chess skills through brute-force learning. He memorized chess openings and sequences of moves so that he could control the board. Yet Ribar found his playing style predictable. Whenever he saw a standard opening of the type that Jensen had learned, Ribar would counter with an unorthodox move that thwarted his boss's strategy. Every time he lost, Jensen would swipe his arm across the board, knocking over the pieces, and storm away. He would sometimes later insist on a rematch on the ping-pong table. Ribar graciously accepted, knowing Jensen was purposely shifting the competition onto more favorable territory.

"He's good at ping-pong," recalled Ribar. "I'm okay, but he would just kill me to get his revenge. It helped relieve his frustration from losing in chess by beating me in ping-pong."

JENSEN'S CHESS LOSSES WERE NOT the only thing fueling his general frustration. Like other graphics-chip companies, Nvidia only designed and prototyped its products—it did not actually manufacture them at scale. Chip fabrication was instead outsourced to one of the small number of dedicated chip-fabrication companies around the world. These companies invested hundreds of millions of dollars in the clean rooms, specialized equipment, and skilled personnel required to make tiny silicon wafers into advanced computational devices.

Since Nvidia's founding, it had partnered with SGS-Thomson, the European chip conglomerate, to manufacture its chips. As Jensen and his cofounders discovered during their initial meeting with Sequoia,

SGS-Thomson did not have the best reputation, and it had struggled to remain competitive in the face of less expensive labor in East Asia.

Yet now that Nvidia was producing great chips and selling them in massive quantities, SGS-Thomson's weaknesses became far more difficult to ignore. In late 1997, head of sales Jeff Fisher arranged for a team from Gateway 2000 to tour the SGS-Thomson fabrication plant in Grenoble, France. The RIVA 128 had been out for several months and was enjoying robust demand from gamers. The trip was supposed to be a victory lap for Fisher and Nvidia.

During the flight to France, Fisher learned that SGS-Thomson was having yield problems with Nvidia's flagship product. The fabricator estimated that it would be able to fill only about half of Gateway 2000's allocation. As Fisher recalled, "We had to huddle with the SGS guys and discuss how to message it to Gateway."[13]

The disastrous factory tour was just the first warning sign of a full-blown production crisis, which finally exploded over Thanksgiving. Fisher had intended to enjoy a well-deserved break at his mother-in-law's house in northern Indiana. Instead, he spent nearly the entire holiday on the phone, breaking the news to Dell and other computer makers that they would no longer get as many of the winter's hottest graphics cards as they had ordered. In between calls with irate vendors, he talked to Jensen, to pass on the CEO updates from SGS-Thomson.

"We had gotten all these customers signed up, customers that we always dreamed of having, and now we were going to have to get in allocation mode," he said.

Jensen always exhorted his employees to never make the same mistake twice—and he now vowed never to settle for a fabrication partner that couldn't handle the levels of production that Nvidia needed. Fortunately, he had another vendor in mind.

When Nvidia was founded in 1993, Jensen struggled to find chip-manufacturing capacity. He had cold-called Taiwan Semiconductor Manufacturing Company (TSMC)—the best-regarded manufacturer in the world and the one Don Valentine at Sequoia had recommended that Nvidia partner with from the start—multiple times without success. In 1996, he tried a more personal approach. He addressed a letter

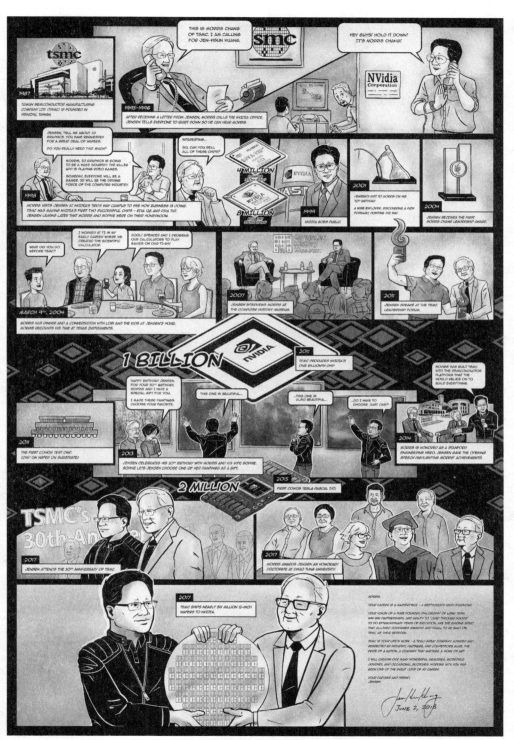

Comic strip about the Nvidia-TSMC partnership. (NVIDIA)

to Morris Chang, TSMC's CEO, asking if the two men could discuss Nvidia's chip needs. This time, Chang called *him*, and the two men arranged for a visit in Sunnyvale.[14]

During the meeting, Jensen outlined Nvidia's future plans, explaining how Nvidia would need larger chip dies for its current generation and even larger ones in the future. He managed to secure some production capacity from TSMC to supplement SGS-Thomson's capabilities, and the relationship seemed to be going well. Chang periodically returned to Sunnyvale to ensure that Nvidia had all the capacity it needed, jotting down notes in a small black book. He even visited during his honeymoon in 1998.

"The biggest joy I get out of this job was to see my customers grow, make money, and succeed," said Chang, and this was especially true for a fast-growing customer such as Nvidia.

The two CEOs and their companies had become so close in such a short period of time—and the relationship between Nvidia and SGS-Thomson had soured almost as fast—that in February of 1998, Nvidia made TSMC its main supplier. The switch occurred just as Nvidia announced its newest chip, the RIVA 128ZX, which debuted just eleven days after the debut of Intel's feared i740 and was positioned by Nvidia as a clear improvement over the competing chip. It offered better performance than the i740 and an eight-megabyte frame buffer, equivalent to the one on the i740, at a cost of $32 per chip, only slightly higher than Intel's $28 list price. It was supposed to ensure Nvidia's continued dominance of the PC market in spite of Intel's attempt to undercut the company.

Yet again, production issues appeared. In the summer of 1998, manufacturing defects plagued TSMC's production of the RIVA 128ZX. The defects, caused by residue called titanium stringers, were scattered randomly across different parts of the chip. As a result, it was impossible to determine which chips were faulty and which were functional; it was clear only that some large proportion of RIVA 128ZX chips was contaminated.

Chris Malachowsky came to the rescue once more.

"Why don't we test every chip and run software on every part?" he asked one day.

"You can't possibly do that," another Nvidia executive replied.

"Why?" asked Malachowsky.[15]

It was, on the face of it, an absurd suggestion. Nvidia would need to ship hundreds of thousands of chips to company headquarters for manual testing—it would have to convert some portion of its messy office and workshop areas into a large chip-testing lab. It would be one of the greatest tests of Jensen's "Speed of Light" maxim.

The company converted one of its buildings into a large testing assembly line with open computer cages, motherboards, and CPUs. "It was a massive operation," said Curtis Priem. "You would go home at 11:00 p.m. and walk by the lab to see dozens of people just putting in chips."[16]

The process was extremely finicky. Priem recalls that they had to redo tests because defective chips would sometimes pass for reasons having nothing to do with the chips themselves, such as if the power wasn't completely disconnected from the testing rig before the next run.

Initially, both Nvidia employees and management pitched in. But soon enough, the strain of such high-volume precision testing began to burn out the engineering team. To take the burden off of his people, Jensen hired hundreds of low-skilled contract laborers, whom Nvidia employees called "bluecoats" because of the color of their lab coats. Soon, bluecoats outnumbered Nvidia engineers in the building. The extra manpower allowed the company to test every chip before it was sent to the customer or trashed.

There was a significant cultural and class divide between Nvidia's employees and the bluecoat testers. Caroline Landry observed the increasing stratification between the less-educated, immigrant bluecoats on one hand and the highly educated engineers on the other.

First, she noticed that no one wanted to sit with the bluecoats at lunch.

"Coming from Canada, we're a little more egalitarian," she said. Ignoring the disapproving looks that followed her around the cafeteria, she "would go sit with the bluecoats and get to know them. I would then get all these remarks from other engineers, like 'You had lunch with the bluecoats? How come?' It was weird. I don't understand the mentality."

The main divide was over food. Nvidia provided generous food perks: breakfast, lunch, and dinner, as well as free snacks, ranging from candy bars and chips to noodles. Seeing this, the bluecoats—who had not normally gotten meal privileges at prior jobs—would come into the cafeteria and load up on food, then empty the drinks and snacks closets after they were restocked on Fridays.

"I came in one weekend and there were a bunch of people with grocery bags full of stuff, carrying it out to their cars," one Nvidia employee said.

"In their mind, it's free. It's not stealing. It's there for the taking, so they take it," Landry said.

Nvidia employees complained so frequently that Jensen sent a company-wide e-mail with the subject line: "Give a bluecoat your pork chop." If the testers wanted the main course from your lunch plate, you should hand it over. Jensen thought Nvidia employees should show gratitude to the bluecoats, as they were instrumental in helping the company navigate a major crisis. Their assistance was far more valuable than the minor inconvenience of running out of free employee snacks.

EVEN WITH HELP FROM THE BLUECOATS, Nvidia could not overcome the production slowdown. Geoff Ribar had been hired as CFO specifically to prepare the company for an initial public offering, which was being underwritten by the investment bank Morgan Stanley. As Nvidia ran out of chips to sell, however, it became significantly less attractive to potential investors. Its quarterly revenue fell by half, from $28.3 million for the quarter ending in April 1998 to $12.1 million in the quarter ending in July 1998. Yet its expenses kept growing, which caused its net losses to balloon from $1 million to $9.7 million quarter to quarter. Only six months earlier, Nvidia had booked its first-ever profitable quarter. Now, it was losing money at an alarming rate.

In a booming economy, Nvidia's deteriorating balance sheet still might have made it appealing to the right buyers. But the financial crisis that had gripped East and Southeast Asia for nearly a year had also tempered enthusiasm for risky IPOs. Morgan Stanley decided to pause the process. The IPO would have given Nvidia a huge infusion of much-needed cash. Instead, Ribar now calculated that at its current burn rate, the company was "within weeks" of becoming insolvent.[17] It was the RIVA 128 situation all over again.

Jensen would have to rely on his persuasiveness and his talent to pull Nvidia through the new crisis. He asked for bridge financing from Nvidia's three largest customers: Diamond Multimedia, STB Systems, and Creative Labs. The companies believed in Nvidia's technological prowess, as they each bought millions of dollars' worth of RIVA chips to use on their high-end graphics cards. Jensen argued that bridge financing would give Nvidia enough additional time and operating cash to recover from the temporary setback. To sweeten the deal, he structured the loans as convertible notes that, when the company introduced its IPO, could convert into equity at 90 percent of the eventual IPO price—which would give Nvidia's potential creditors a far higher potential upside than that of standard loan interest. After two weeks of negotiations, in August of 1998 the three companies agreed to loan Nvidia a total of $11 million. Jensen not only gauged their confidence in Nvidia correctly; he had also managed to turn that confidence into a closer relationship with his biggest customers.

Despite the financial lifeline, Ribar was ready to move on. The pressure "drove my hair gray," he later said. In October 1998, he was recruited by Marvin Burkett, who had mentored Ribar when the two men worked at AMD, to join the Japanese electronics company NEC and help turn around its monitor division. He had lasted at Nvidia less than a year—not enough time even for his first tranche of Nvidia stock to vest.

JENSEN'S RESPONSE TO NVIDIA'S near-death from a production backlog was, paradoxically, to restructure the entire company in order to ship new designs even *faster*. He began to call Michael Hara, Nvidia's head of marketing, into his office to brainstorm strategy. Jensen had observed that no one company ever seemed to have a permanent lead in the industry. Companies that led one year, such as S3, Tseng Labs, and Matrox, were often displaced within one or two chip generations.

"Mike, I don't get it," he said. "If you look at the PC graphics industry, why is it that one company can never hold a lead more than two years?"[18]

Now that Nvidia was one of the market leaders rather than a challenger brand, Jensen became obsessed with the problem. He turned it into a joke: "The only thing that lasts longer than our products is sushi," he would often say to Nvidia employees. Jensen saw that whichever company could solve the problem would build a strong moat around its business.

Hara, who had worked at several of Nvidia's competitors, explained the market dynamics to Jensen. The whole industry moved according to the rhythms of computer manufacturers, who refreshed their product launches twice a year: in spring and fall. The fall cycle was the more critical one, driven by August's back-to-school season and leading into holiday shopping. Computer makers felt compelled to put out updated devices every six months that featured the latest and best-performing chips. They were constantly shopping around for better chips to put in their PCs, readily replacing existing vendors with new ones as faster, higher-quality components became available.

Chip makers, Nvidia included, took eighteen months to design and launch a new chip and typically worked on only one at a time. Yet graphics technology was advancing fast enough that chips were functionally obsolete long before chip makers could come out with a new product.

"That doesn't work. There's got to be a way to solve this problem of the design cycles," Jensen said. The RIVA 128 had revealed that Nvidia could design and launch a new chip in less than a year, although it had taken the threat of imminent bankruptcy to galvanize the company into moving that fast. How could Nvidia do what it had done to produce the RIVA 128, though in a more repeatable and sustainable way?

After a few weeks, Jensen announced to his executive team that he had figured out how to keep Nvidia ahead of the competition—forever. "We're going to fundamentally restructure the engineering department to line up with the refresh cycles," he said.

Nvidia would split the design team into three groups. The first would design a new chip architecture, while the other two worked in parallel to the first to develop faster derivatives based on the new chip. This would allow the company to release a new chip every six months, in line with PC makers' buying cycles.

"We won't lose our sockets because we can go back to the OEM [original equipment manufacturer; the PC maker] and say, 'Here's my next chip that uses the same software. It will have new features and will be faster,'" he explained. Of course, the solution required more than reorganizing Nvidia's design teams. Many technical decisions the company had made earlier would come into play as well.

Early on, Curtis Priem had invented a "virtualized objects" architecture that would be incorporated into all of Nvidia's chips. It became an even bigger advantage for the company once Nvidia adopted the faster cadence of chip releases. Priem's design had a software-based "resource manager," essentially a miniature operating system that sat on top of the hardware itself. The resource manager allowed Nvidia's engineers to emulate certain hardware features that normally needed to be physically printed onto chip circuits. This involved a performance cost but accelerated the pace of innovation, because Nvidia's engineers could take more risks. If the new feature wasn't ready to work in the hardware, Nvidia could emulate it in software. At the same time, the engineers could take hardware features out when there was enough leftover computing power, saving chip die area.

For most of Nvidia's rivals, if a hardware feature on a chip wasn't ready, it would mean a schedule delay. Not, though, at Nvidia, thanks to Priem's innovation. "This was the most brilliant thing on the planet," said Michael Hara. "It was our secret sauce. If we missed a feature or a feature was broken, we could put it in the resource manager and it would work."[19] Jeff Fisher, Nvidia's head of sales, agreed: "Priem's architecture was critical in enabling Nvidia to design and make new products faster."[20]

Nvidia also began emphasizing backwards compatibility for its software drivers, which it had first done with the RIVA 128. But it was a lesson that predated Nvidia: Priem had learned it in his pre-Nvidia days at Sun Microsystems. He had heard about a sales session for a new version of the GX graphics chip, where the sales force had been told that the new chip was compatible with old software drivers. If a customer installed the new GX into an existing Sun workstation, it would just work. There was no need to wait for new software to be installed before a customer could use the newly purchased graphics hardware. The sales team stood up and gave the presenter a standing ovation. When Priem was told about that reaction, he made a mental note that the unified drivers feature solved a pain point for salespeople—and thus for customers.

"We thought, okay, this must be important," he said. "It turned out to be very important to Nvidia."[21]

Jensen saw emulation and backwards-compatible drivers not just as good technical principles but also as competitive advantages. He believed that embracing both would allow the company to implement his new accelerated production schedule, which he called "Three Teams, Two Seasons." He believed Nvidia had a chance of always being ahead of the rest of the industry. Jensen had long insisted that Nvidia chips would always be the best in the market, and they almost always were: that was not going to change. Now, the company would have three times as many chips in the market, none of which was more than six months out of date. Even if a competitor offered a slightly better product, PC makers would have no motivation to switch away from Nvidia, knowing that a faster part would arrive in six months and without the hassle of changing drivers.

Nvidia's rapid iteration meant that "the competition will always be shooting behind the duck," as Jensen described it. Like a hunter who aims at a moving target instead of ahead of it, other graphics-chip makers would lag behind—there would be too many new chips coming out too fast. Nvidia's competitors would simply be overwhelmed.

"The number one feature of any product is the schedule," Jensen later said.[22]

By the end of 1999, Nvidia had reorganized its model for design and production on the "Three Teams, Two Seasons" strategy. It had a philosophy that demanded employees operate at the "Speed of Light," measuring performance against what was physically possible and not what other companies were doing or what Nvidia had accomplished or failed to accomplish in the past. And it had a corporate mantra—"We're thirty days from going out of business"—that served as a warning about complacency and conveyed the expectation that everyone, from the CEO on down, had to work as hard as they possibly could, even if it meant sacrificing their lives outside of Nvidia.

CHAPTER 6

Just Go Win

AS NVIDIA ACCELERATED ITS PRODUCTION SCHEDULES AND methods in order to dominate the graphics-chip market, its competitors fought back. In September of 1998, 3dfx sued for patent infringement, alleging that one of its rendering methods had been stolen by Nvidia. The press release that announced the lawsuit included a link to a page on Nvidia's website about the technology in question. In response, Nvidia's marketing team modified the linked page, so that anyone who clicked through from the press release saw a banner that read, "Welcome to NVIDIA, the greatest 3D graphics company."

Just a year earlier, 3dfx's leaders had been so confident that Nvidia was about to go bankrupt that they didn't even bother making a play for their struggling rival. Now, the situation had been almost turned on its head. Under "Three Teams, Two Seasons," Nvidia was preparing to release three chips in the time it took 3dfx to launch just one. 3dfx's most recent chip, the Voodoo2, had come out in February 1998, and the company was only partway through the development cycle for two next-generation chips, which were code-named in its characteristically over-the-top style: Napalm, scheduled for release in late 1999; and Rampage, scheduled for release in 2001. At its current pace, 3dfx's premium releases would lag Nvidia's by a year or more.

And 3dfx's leaders were not even confident about their slower release schedules. The company's engineers "wanted perfection in every product that we shipped," said Ross Smith, the marketing executive.[1] "There was feature creep in every chip, while Nvidia's mentality was to ship whatever was ready in the chip to meet the deadline and push features out to the next chip."

3dfx had become the victim of its own success in another way, too. Scott Sellers, the cofounder who also served as the company's head of engineering, said that the Voodoo2's brisk sales were making it difficult for the company to manage its distribution channel and relationships with graphics-card partners.

"We had some quality problems where some board manufacturers were not following our design guidelines," he said.[2] "The poor quality was starting to impact our customer satisfaction."

The entire industry was well aware of Nvidia's ability to turn challenges into opportunities. 3dfx now sought to do the same thing. But its approach contrasted sharply with Nvidia's.

First, in an attempt to mimic Nvidia's strategy of getting more chips out into the market, 3dfx announced that it would add several new products to its portfolio. These included the Voodoo Banshee and the Voodoo3, which were designed as combined 2-D–3-D accelerators instead of the kind of purely 3-D chips that 3dfx had produced to date. Unlike Nvidia's product road map, which created efficiencies by making multiple derivative versions of a single chip for a focused area of the market, 3dfx had an overly complicated lineup aimed at too many different customer segments and didn't plan to reuse a common core-chip design.

3dfx then decided to expand into an entirely new part of the graphics industry. In December 1998, it bought the graphics-board manufacturer STB Systems for $141 million. The move made sense on paper. STB was a major board maker, and bringing it under the 3dfx umbrella would give the company more control over its own board supply chain. It would also build brand awareness directly with consumers, as now both the chips and the boards could be sold under the 3dfx brand.

Even more important, from a strategic perspective, was 3dfx's belief that the acquisition would hurt Nvidia. STB had a close relationship with the rival chip maker. It had given Nvidia the very first purchase order for the RIVA 128, the order Jensen had dramatically unveiled at a company all-hands meeting. Since the launch of that chip, it had become Nvidia's leading board partner, and it had loaned Nvidia money as part of the bridge financing round three months earlier. With the purchase, 3dfx forcibly ended that relationship. STB announced that from now on, its boards would carry only 3dfx chips.

"We knew it was a bet-the-company strategy," said Sellers. "We just felt we could do it."

But none of 3dfx's strategic moves and product bets worked. It struggled to make the 2-D side of its mid-tier chips, because it did not have as much in-house expertise as it did for 3-D chips. When STB enacted its 3dfx-only policy, other board makers retaliated by switching over to Nvidia chips, which canceled out that supposed advantage. And Sellers's assumption that 3dfx could effectively manage the new acquisition's business was completely wrong. 3dfx's executives had no prior experience overseeing a retail physical distribution channel or a complicated board-manufacturing supply chain. Once under 3dfx, STB ended up pulling its new parent company's focus away from the core chip-design business.

Most of all, not a single one of these initiatives addressed 3dfx's main problem, which was that it was no longer producing high-performance chips at the necessary speed. Perfectionism, management dysfunction, and distracted leadership had combined to slow output to a crawl. The mid-tier Voodoo3, which had been intended as a stopgap between 3-D chip launches, was delayed until April 1999. Napalm and Rampage slipped even further behind schedule.

"We should have really stuck to our knitting," said Ross Smith. "If 3dfx had brought out Napalm and Rampage on time, Nvidia would have never had a chance."

3dfx soon faced a complete operational meltdown. It failed to manage STB's inventories. Its mid-tier cards failed to sell. It simply ran out of cash. The company's creditors initiated bankruptcy proceedings near the end of 2000. On December 15, Nvidia bought 3dfx's patents and other assets and hired about one hundred of its employees. In October 2002, 3dfx filed for bankruptcy.

When those former 3dfx engineers arrived at Nvidia, they expected to find out that their victorious rival had some kind of unique process or technology that allowed them to make new chips every six months. Dwight Diercks remembers their shock when they found out that the explanation was much simpler.

"Oh my God, we got here and we thought there was going to be a secret sauce," one engineer said.[3] "It turns out it's just really hard work and intense execution on schedules." It was Nvidia's culture, in other words, that made the difference.

PERFECTING THE COMPANY'S OPERATIONS was only one piece of the plan to future-proof Nvidia against institutional dysfunction. The other was bringing the best talent to the company. Nvidia's excellent products attracted high-quality applicants. But often, Nvidia had to lure talented people from its competitors. Rare was the occasion when it could scoop up dozens of engineers from a rival, as it had with the demise of 3dfx. Instead, Jensen and his team learned the fine art of corporate poaching.

In 1997, Jensen asked Michael Hara if he knew anyone good who might want to join Nvidia. Hara floated the name of John Montrym, the chief engineer of Silicon Graphics. Montrym was legendary in the industry for his graphics subsystem work, such as RealityEngine and InfiniteReality. He had some history with Nvidia's cofounder Curtis Priem: the two had worked together back at Vermont Microsystems.

Jensen invited Montrym to lunch at Nvidia's office and went for a direct approach. "John, you should think about coming to Nvidia because ultimately I'm going to put SGI out of business," he said, explaining how SGI could not compete by selling thousands of workstations each year when Nvidia's access to a market of millions of PCs gave it much better economies of scale.[4] Montrym politely declined.

Chris Malachowsky and Nvidia's chief scientist, David Kirk, tried next. Over another lunch, they told Montrym, "All the work you did with SGI's RealityEngine and InfiniteReality, Nvidia is going to put on a single chip for PC, and that will be the end of SGI. Where do you want to be working when that happens?"[5]

Priem also tried to recruit Montrym. The two met at St. James Infirmary Bar & Grill in Mountain View, California. Priem insisted that Silicon Graphics would be a "dead end," and that his old colleague should join him at Nvidia.[6] Once again, Montrym wasn't convinced.

Jensen then decided to try a different tactic—to persuade Montrym with technology, not words. He told his development team to make a graphics demo for their latest chip prototype in the form of a military-themed immersive simulation, mimicking a move that SGI used when it wanted to show off its own new technology. Then, he told Hara to call Montrym up again and invite him over to Nvidia's lab to see the demo in action.

"This time will be more fun," Jensen assured Hara.

When Montrym arrived, Hara presented the new prototype. "Isn't this exactly what InfiniteReality does?" he asked.

The new pitch worked. Of course, Montrym knew that Jensen's assessment of the relative weakness of SGI was correct. His current employer could afford to fund a new chip only every few years, due to its smaller market. Nvidia, by contrast, was releasing a new design every six months. Nvidia's pace of innovation was far beyond what SGI could ever achieve. In time, it would be so far ahead that SGI could no longer catch up. But the demo was still powerful. It showed that Nvidia had so many resources and so much talent at its disposal that in a matter of weeks it could make a graphics engine that had taken Montrym much longer to develop—and that they could do it just for the purpose of recruiting a single person. Montrym resigned from SGI a week later.

Dwight Diercks said Montrym's defection was "a watershed moment, because so many engineers revered John, and they all wanted to come work with John." After Montrym joined Nvidia, every time the company posted a job opening for software developers or chip engineers, résumés and interview requests from Silicon Graphics employees would pour in.[7]

SGI was, understandably, unhappy about losing Montrym and feared losing even more talent to Nvidia. In April 1998, SGI sued Nvidia for patent infringement, alleging that the RIVA family of processors infringed on the company's high-speed texture-mapping technology.

While some Nvidia employees were initially worried about the lawsuit, Andrew Logan, Nvidia's director of corporate marketing, was excited.

"I got a call from the *Wall Street Journal* right now on my voicemail," he told his colleagues after the lawsuit was announced. "This is perfect. We're on the map!"

Jensen agreed. He walked around from office to office, shaking everyone's hand and saying, "Congratulations! We just got sued by the most important graphics company in the world. We're somebody."

The lawsuit went nowhere: in order to succeed, SGI would have to prove financial harm, yet the only evidence the company cited was Nvidia's internal sales projections and forecasts. Nvidia's lawyers argued that these forecasts were inherently volatile, because they were based on broad assumptions about the market that were often wrong, and thus couldn't be relied upon as measures of anything real.

In July 1999, the two companies settled the lawsuit in an agreement that seemed to benefit Nvidia most of all.

"We'd hire fifty of their employees and become a supplier to them of their low-end graphics line. In the end, we gained a partner," Diercks said.[8] Once again, Nvidia won some of the best engineering talent in Silicon Valley.

AS NVIDIA GREW, IT GAINED potential leverage over its supply-chain partners, and it could have pressured companies into helping its own bottom line. Yet Jensen's philosophy of business relationships saw the company maintain good terms with its most crucial suppliers.

Rick Tsai was TSMC's executive vice president of operations when Nvidia first started working with the chip manufacturer. Tsai, who later became CEO of TSMC, was in charge of all manufacturing at the time and served as Nvidia's main point of contact. "I made wafers for Jensen," Tsai said. "His brilliance and charisma were obvious from the beginning."[9]

When TSMC first began to work with Nvidia, the entire industry was working on a smaller scale. Tsai recalled building his first eight-inch-wafer fabrication plant for $395 million, an amount that would be enough to buy only a single chip-making machine today.

Within just a few years, Nvidia's success in graphics made it one of TSMC's top two or three customers. Tsai remembered Jensen would negotiate hard over pricing and would repeatedly cite how the graphics company had only a 38 percent gross margin. One particular dispute prompted Tsai to travel to California and meet with Jensen at a restaurant that wasn't much better than Denny's.

"We tried to resolve the dispute. I forgot the details," Tsai said. "But it really hit me. Jensen taught me his philosophy of doing business called 'rough justice.'" Jensen explained that "rough" meant the relationship was not flat but rather had ups and downs. Justice was the important part. "After a certain period of time, let's say a few years, it would net out to roughly equal."

To Tsai, this was a way of describing a win-win partnership, though one that acknowledged there wouldn't be a win-win every single time. Sometimes one side would get the better of a specific deal or incident, and the next time it would be the other side. As long as it was roughly 50-50

Jensen Huang at his desk in 1999. (NVIDIA)

after a few years—not 60-40 or 40-60—it was a positive relationship. He remembers thinking Jensen's approach made a great deal of sense.

"Those things struck me about Jensen as a person and also a businessman," Tsai said. "Of course, he's not shy in calling me when our wafers were not coming out in time for him. Not shy at all. But together with him, we met and resolved many adversities. If you look at both companies, you cannot find a better partnership over the last three decades."

ON FRIDAY, JANUARY 22, 1999, Nvidia finally went public. With the Asian financial crisis over and the company's finances in solid shape, the stock proved irresistible to investors. The company raised $42 million from its stock sale, and its shares ended the first day of trading up 64 percent at $19.69 per share. At that price, Nvidia was valued at $626 million.[10]

The tone at Nvidia headquarters was muted: instead of exuberance, there was relief. After several quarters when the company had nearly run out of cash, the proceeds from the IPO brought a sense of security, at least for a little while. It was by far the largest single windfall the company had experienced—far larger than the bridge financing or any of the venture rounds.

"We've got some breathing room now," former engineer Kenneth Hurley said, recalling his feelings on IPO day. "We've raised some money. We're not going out of business."[11]

Jensen was more defiant than enthusiastic. "We have had some setbacks, but I'm told I'm the hardest CEO to kill," he told a *Wall Street Journal* reporter when asked for comment about the IPO.[12]

Still, Nvidia's executive team allowed themselves a rare moment to enjoy the accomplishment and to dream about what might come next. During an off-site management meeting, they discussed what each of them would do if the company's stock price ever hit $100 a share. (The share price was $25 at the time.) Head of marketing Dan Vivoli pledged to get a tattoo of the Nvidia logo on his leg. Head of sales Jeff Fisher would get one on his butt cheek. Chief Scientist David Kirk agreed to paint his nails green, and head of human resources John McSorley signed himself up to get a nipple pierced. Two of the three cofounders

Curtis Priem's Nvidia logo hair. (NVIDIA)

went even bigger: Chris Malachowsky would get a mohawk, and Curtis Priem would shave his head *and* get a tattoo of the Nvidia logo on his scalp. Jensen agreed to have his left ear pierced.[13] Vivoli recorded the pledges on a paper placemat and had it framed for display. In that moment, no one thought they would have to follow through on their pledges anytime soon. It was almost impossible to believe that the stock price would quadruple in the near term.

WITH THE MONEY FROM THE IPO, Nvidia pursued ever-larger strategic partnerships. The company had hired Oliver Baltuch, a tech-industry veteran, to manage significant relationships with big companies such as Microsoft, Intel, and AMD. Baltuch was given the authority to spend freely. It was a significant change from his previous roles, where he had to adhere to tight budgets.

One of Baltuch's younger colleagues, Keita Kitahama, was a recent college graduate who had been hired to ensure Nvidia graphics cards worked well with major monitor vendors. Kitahama was naturally shy and didn't know much about the business development process. One day, while Baltuch was drinking his daily cup of tea, Kitahama approached him and asked, "What's the best way to do this?"

Baltuch replied, "You have the industry's hottest commodity. Use it." He was referring to Nvidia's latest graphics cards, called the GeForce. He instructed Kitahama to talk to another product manager, Geoff Ballew, and scour Nvidia's headquarters for as many spare GeForce cards as he could find. Then, he was to "call up every single monitor company and tell them you want to visit them and give them a free GeForce card."

To Kitahama's surprise, the tactic worked. Monitor manufacturers not only took his call—they responded eagerly to his offer. They wanted early access to the company's newest products, no matter how they got them.

Baltuch employed a similar strategy with Intel. At Intel's annual forum for developers, he showed up with a box of fifty Nvidia cards and visited vendors at every single booth, offering to replace the existing cards in their machines with Nvidia's. He knew that Nvidia cards had a significant advantage because they were far easier to swap in and out, thanks to their backwards-compatible software drivers. This ensured developers could play with the newest Nvidia cards with little fear of a clunky installation process, frequent crashes, or poor performance.

Even the biggest tech companies could not resist the allure of free Nvidia graphics cards. Intel was then building several thousand development workstations each year and sending the computers out to software developers around the world. At the time, there was competition among about ten graphics-card manufacturers to get inside the Intel boxes. Nvidia won the contract, both because it had a better product and because its strategy of giving out free cards ensured that Intel already had hands-on experience with Nvidia's chips.

The same strategy was employed with Microsoft, which made the DirectX APIs that developers used to display media and run games on Windows. Like clockwork, Nvidia cards would appear at Microsoft headquarters every time Microsoft updated its API. "We blanketed them through every major release of DirectX," said Baltuch. "You didn't even have to ask for the resources."[14]

Jensen's guidance was direct. "Just go win. The idea was who could run faster to get all the land."

Nvidia still wasn't a large company, with only around 250 employees. And it didn't generate huge revenues; for the fiscal year 1999, it reported $158 million in sales, a fraction of what other tech companies such as Microsoft ($19.8 billion), Apple ($6.1 billion), and Amazon ($1.6 billion) made. But it had spent years sharpening its focus on technical excellence and product execution. Now, that focus was finally paying off in the form of something intangible, yet all-important: industry influence.

The company had stayed away from the gaming-console market since Sega canceled its contract for the NV2 chip. But a few years later, in 1999, Microsoft hinted that it was developing its first console and that it would be based on the DirectX API. Nvidia's existing relationship with Microsoft opened the door for an Nvidia chip to power the console. For several months, the two companies attempted to work out an agreement.

Microsoft soon changed direction, though. In January 2000, the company gave graphics start-up Gigapixel, led by founder and CEO George Haber, a development contract to supply the graphics technology for Microsoft's Xbox console. Microsoft invested $10 million in Gigapixel and an additional $15 million to develop the Xbox chip. Haber moved his thirty-three employees into a Microsoft building in Palo Alto, California.[15]

On March 10, just two months after publicly announcing the Xbox, Bill Gates was scheduled to appear at the Game Developers Conference (GDC) to present the console's specifications and Gigapixel as its graphics supplier. He had invited Haber to attend his speech, a copy of which was provided to Haber for review beforehand. In it, Gates was supposed to say that the relationship between Gigapixel and Microsoft had as much potential to change the industry as an older partnership that saw IBM choose a little-known software start-up named Microsoft to supply the operating system for the original IBM PC. He would tell the world that Microsoft had chosen Gigapixel for one reason: it made the best graphics technology in the world.[16] It was the sort of publicity, and endorsement by a technology legend, that every start-up dreams of.

That dream would not last. Even after the Gigapixel announcement, Nvidia continued to make the case that it was the right partner for the Xbox. Jensen and Chris Diskin, Nvidia's senior director of sales and marketing who managed the relationship with Microsoft, often had weekly meetings with Microsoft during the negotiation process. Jensen and Diskin spent hours on their pitch material, sometimes working until midnight and then starting again at 8:00 a.m. the next day. Both men kept up the same intense work rate that had seen the company through its deepest crises and during the development of the original RIVA 128 and the race to get its derivative, the RIVA 128ZX, out to compete with Intel's i740 chip. This time, they did not have the threat of bankruptcy hanging over their heads. Even so, they pushed themselves just as hard to salvage an opportunity to break into a lucrative new market.

It helped their case that Nvidia's reputation was at a new high.

"We had plenty of advocates inside Microsoft," said Diskin about the Xbox negotiations. "Game developers came out and said, we want Nvidia because it's easier to develop on and less of a risk."[17]

On Friday, March 3, just a week before Gates's GDC speech, Microsoft executives Rick Thompson and Bob McBreen called Diskin and said they wanted to reopen the Xbox contract and work out an agreement. Two days later, they flew down from Seattle to San Jose, California, and spent most of that Sunday in a conference room at Nvidia headquarters. Jensen, Diskin, Thompson, and McBreen agreed that Nvidia would replace Gigapixel as Microsoft's graphics-chip partner. The new console would instead use a new, custom-designed chip from Nvidia, with Jensen and Diskin insisting that Microsoft pay $200 million up front to cover the new chip's research and development, an amount that required personal approval from Bill Gates himself. By ensuring a significant upfront payout and sign-off from Microsoft's CEO, they felt that they had locked down the Xbox job and protected Nvidia against an outcome similar to the one that had just befallen Gigapixel.

On Monday, Microsoft executives informed Haber they had decided to go with Nvidia. He was stunned. The prior week, he had been talking to Wall Street investment bankers about going public in a billion-dollar IPO on the back of the Xbox deal, and even potentially buying 3dfx and other graphics-chip companies; Nvidia executives were, after all, not the only ones who daydreamed about market dominance. Now, he had nothing left except a $15 million development fee that Microsoft had agreed to pay even though the contract was now canceled.

To this day, Haber feels bitter about what happened with Microsoft and the Xbox contract. "Today, I would be running a trillion-dollar company, not Jensen, I presume," Haber said.[18]

In the week of Bill Gates's GDC announcement that Nvidia, in fact, would be the graphics-chip supplier for the Xbox, Nvidia's stock soared above $100 per share. The executive team found itself having to follow through on pledges that seemed like a joke less than a year earlier. But follow through they did: Malachowsky got his mohawk; Fisher, Priem, and Vivoli got their tattoos; Kirk's nails turned green; and McSorley and Jensen got their piercings.

IT WOULD BE ONE OF THE last happy moments at Nvidia for Priem. In the late 1990s, the Nvidia cofounder had started to clash more frequently with the company's engineering staff. During the development of one generation of chips, Priem had found a flaw in the chip architecture. He fixed it and, without telling anyone, pulled down some chip documentation from the communal file server and replaced it with an updated version. This was how he was used to operating in Nvidia's early years, and his colleagues then had accepted it. Now, however, he was part of a much larger organization and found that "the software team went haywire because they were using the original documentation for some of the code in their software." When they learned that he had removed the documents entirely, "they threw a fit."[19]

Priem was adamant that the architecture had to be fixed. The engineers asked Jensen to intervene. In a heated argument, Priem insisted that he could do whatever he wanted because he had personally designed the architecture for Nvidia's chips.

"It was my architecture," he kept repeating.

It was the wrong thing to say to Jensen, who wanted to build a more communal culture. Nvidia as a whole was to be recognized for its achievements—not individuals. After Jensen came back from important business trips, Priem observed that he would always describe his own actions using the plural "we" instead of the singular "I." Priem was initially skeptical, thinking, "What's this 'we' stuff? I don't know anything about negotiating contracts with fabs. But Jensen was right. We all did it together. We all share the credit."

When it came to chip designs, Priem could get possessive. He tended to talk about it as "his" work, "his" architecture. Jensen insisted that Priem do the opposite: that he consider it the collective property of the entire company, which it was. Jensen would reply, "No, it's *our* architecture. You didn't do it. We did it. You don't own those files."

So after learning of Priem's unilateral decision to fix the flaw in the chip architecture, Jensen exercised his authority as CEO and overruled his cofounder. He told Priem to roll back the changes, to restore the original documentation files back to the server, and to never take action on chip documentation again without first informing all of the people whose work might be affected by the change. Using the old documents, the software team was able to finish their code and eventually figured out how to fix the flaw in the chip architecture the following year.

Later on, after Nvidia hired John Montrym and a new generation of 3-D graphics engineers, Priem became more disruptive and began interfering with product development. "I would get in the way of shipping," Priem recalled, because he always wanted a chip to be perfect and to defend it against changes to the architecture he believed he had created.

Priem had started to realize his own deficiencies. He recalls being in an executive meeting with a graphics specialist in anti-aliasing, a technique used to smooth out jagged edges and soften the transitions between an object's line and the background. "Wow. I read his papers to mimic anti-aliasing at Sun," Priem thought, impressed by the presentation. "I give up. How in the world does Curtis live up to all these specialists?"

Priem was now fighting with Jensen so often, and with such intensity, that the company brought in a special workplace consultant to try to resolve their differences. After many arguments, Jensen suggested Priem leave the engineering group to work on defending Nvidia's intellectual property and patents. Priem accepted. "For architectures, my job was really done in the first two years," he said. "I worked on products for five years. I was pulled off products and put on IP. That allowed the other 3-D experts we hired from Silicon Graphics to come in and create better products than I could have done."

In 2003, a few years after his reassignment, Priem took an extended leave of absence to deal with some issues he had with his then-wife. Jensen tried to help Priem by using his connections to help Priem find the best marriage counselors. But after three months, Jensen could no longer dodge employee questions on the whereabouts of the company's cofounder and chief technical officer. He gave Priem a choice and an ultimatum: return to work full-time, transition into a part-time consulting role for Nvidia, or resign. Jensen even suggested a new mobile architecture project that Priem could work on, so that he could oversee one last job before retiring. Priem decided to leave Nvidia. "I was tired,

Nvidia and the Holy Grail. (MICHAEL HARA)

beaten up, and demoralized. I needed to resign," he recalled. "I always wish I could have stayed."

Two decades later, Jensen still seemed pained over the circumstances of Priem's departure. When I explained to him that Curtis felt he didn't have the skills to keep up with other graphics engineers, Jensen offered a stern reply: "Curtis is smart. He could've learned it."

IN EARLY 2000, JENSEN AND Michael Hara, who by this point had moved out of marketing and now ran the investor relations team, embarked on a multi-city road show to meet with bankers, investors, and fund managers to raise capital for Nvidia.

"We're flying from city-to-city with the bankers," recalled Hara. "They kept asking Jensen, 'What things do you watch? What do you find funny?'"[20]

Jensen thought for a moment: *"Monty Python and the Holy Grail."*

The 1975 comedy was the first feature film released by the British comedy troupe Monty Python. Among its many memorable scenes was one set during an outbreak of plague when two peasants pull a cart of dead bodies through a grubby medieval village.

"Bring out your dead!" one of them calls, banging a wooden spoon on a metal triangle to announce himself.

A villager stops the cart to deposit an old man's body, except the old man isn't dead.

"I'm not dead!" he protests.

"Here, he says he's not dead," says the cart master.

"Well . . . he will be soon. He's very ill," says the villager.

"I'm getting better," says the old man.

The three of them banter for several more moments. The old man continues to insist that he's not dead, while the villager and cart master try to persuade him that he really belongs on the cart. Eventually, the cart master strikes the old man on the head, and the villager deposits the man's body.

"Ah, thanks very much!" he says, with apparently sincere gratitude.

Jensen felt that many of the questions from potential investors followed the same grim logic: they thought Nvidia would die.

"Why would we invest in a graphics company?" they asked. "You would be the fortieth one we've backed, and all the others have gone out of business. Why would we do this?"

Investor pessimism became the theme of the road show. Investors demanded more revenue from Nvidia. They assumed Intel would eventually crush the entire graphics industry with a new chip. They expected Nvidia to follow in the footsteps of so many competitors before it: Rendition, Tseng Labs, S3, 3DLabs, Matrox, and others.

This attitude irritated Jensen, who believed Nvidia was nothing like any other graphics company that had ever existed. The company's pitch to investors went like this: its chips were better than anyone else's, it had a strong, defensible position, and its business strategy allowed it to move more quickly and innovate faster than any other chip maker.

But most of all, it had Jensen, who had learned how to manage the company as an extension of himself. Everyone at the company shared his singular focus on the mission. Everyone shared his work ethic. Everyone worked as fast as humanly possible in order to keep Nvidia one step ahead of the competition. And if anyone faltered or doubted, a sharp word from Jensen quickly brought that individual into line.

Some investors did believe in Jensen's future vision for Nvidia and his ability to keep the company trained on that vision. Morgan Stanley ultimately raised $387 million for Nvidia when it made a secondary offering of equity and convertibles in October 2000.

At the conclusion of the round, the Morgan Stanley team presented Michael Hara with a full-color illustration of the road-show team, depicted in a mashup of *Monty Python and the Holy Grail*. Nvidia's deceased competitors are shown as bodies on the plague cart. Investors who asked irrelevant questions are miniature "knights who say Ni." Jensen is the valiant King Arthur, defeating a black knight in single combat.

"I'm better. I'm faster. You can't beat *me*!" he says.

CHAPTER 7

GeForce and the Innovator's Dilemma

IN HIS FAMOUS BOOK *THE INNOVATOR'S DILEMMA,* THE late Harvard Business School professor Clayton Christensen argued that a company's success often contains the seeds of the same company's own failure, and this was especially noticeable in the technology sector. He posited that every industry was shaped not by random chance but by regular and predictable cycles. First, start-ups would release a new, disruptive innovation that was less capable than the market-leading offering from a major company but positioned at the low end of a market. The successful incumbent would ignore the less profitable niche, focusing instead on launching products that sustained and added to its current, robust profit streams. But new-use cases would eventually appear for the disruptive innovation, and the start-ups that capitalized on it would usually be able to iterate and innovate faster than the established corporation. Eventually, the start-ups would have far more capable products, and by the time the incumbent realized it was in trouble, it was too late. For instance, Christensen wrote about how Control Data, the market leader for fourteen-inch mainframe disk drives, failed to achieve even a 1 percent share of the subsequent market for eight-inch minicomputer disk drives. Analogous shifts happened to makers of 8-inch drives when the smaller 5.25-inch and 3.5-inch drives came out. Each time, the cycle began again, and a new wave of incumbents fell to the start-ups.[1]

The Innovator's Dilemma is one of Jensen's favorite books, and he was determined not to let such a fate befall Nvidia. He knew it would be hard for a rival to surpass Nvidia's high-quality chips, because competing at the top of the market required massive investments in capital and engineering talent. Influenced by Christensen, he decided that the threat was from a low-cost player.

"I've seen that before," he said. "We build Ferraris. All of our chips were designed for the high end. The best performance, the best triangle rate, and the best polygons. I don't want to let someone come in and be the price leaders, lock me out at the bottom, and climb their way to the top."[2]

He studied the business strategies of other leading companies for inspiration on how to fend off an attack from below. As he looked at Intel's product lineup, he noticed that its Pentium series of CPUs had a range of clock speeds—a key measure of processor performance—but all of the Pentium cores themselves shared the same chip design and theoretically had identical features and capabilities.

"Intel just builds the same damn part. They are selling customers different products based on speed binning," he said, referring to a process in which components that fail quality checks at high speeds can be repurposed to work at lower speeds where they can function properly.

Jensen saw that Nvidia could stop throwing away parts that failed quality tests as a matter of course. True, these parts were not suitable for the company's Ferrari-grade chips. But if they were otherwise functional at lower speeds, Nvidia could repackage them into a less capable (and therefore cheaper) version of the company's mainline products. This would increase the number of usable parts manufactured from every wafer of silicon and improve the company's yields—an industry measure of production efficiency.

At an executive staff meeting, Jensen asked his operations manager, "How much does it cost us to package, test, and assemble a part?"

The answer was $1.32, a small number in the expensive world of chip manufacturing.

"That's it?" Jensen replied, incredulous. This looked like a clear opportunity to make something out of nothing. Rejected parts were generating no revenue for Nvidia; they were thrown out. But by spending a bit more to spruce up the rejected parts for use on less intensive chip lines, Nvidia could create a whole new derivative product line that could turn a profit, without the expensive and time-consuming process of research and development. The line would serve as a defense against competitors for whom the low-cost chip was the main product. With the new low-cost parts, Nvidia could easily afford to price its chips down so much that its competitors would be forced to sell at a loss. Nvidia might lose money on its cheaper lines, but sales from its Ferraris would more than compensate. More important, Nvidia would avoid the trap that had ended the company's one-time rival, 3dfx, which had begun spending so much time and money developing new chips that it fell behind in the race to continuously innovate.

The strategy was dubbed "ship the whole cow," a reference to how butchers find ways to use almost every part of a steer carcass, from nose to tail—not just the prime cuts like the tenderloin and the ribs.

"It became a very powerful tool for us and allowed us to fine-tune our offering," Jeff Fisher said. "We could build a low-yield part at the high end and create four or five different products in the stack. It helped push ASPs (average selling prices) up."[3] It also allowed Nvidia to test the demand for more expensive, top-end products among enthusiast gamers who were willing to pay more for higher performance.

The rest of the graphics industry would soon follow suit, especially as Nvidia's rollout of "ship the whole cow" was responsible for nearly putting another of its competitors, S3 Graphics, out of business.

"'Ship the whole cow' is something the graphics industry takes for granted, but it was an important strategy that made a big difference," Nvidia board member Tench Coxe said.[4] It was a testament to Jensen's strategic forethought and his restless desire to anticipate any threat to Nvidia's future. After all, now that Nvidia was a market leader rather than one start-up among many, Jensen knew that he had a permanent target on his back.

"I don't *think* people are trying to put me out of business," he once said. "I *know* they're trying to."[5]

JENSEN KNEW THAT TECHNICAL SPECIFICATIONS alone did not sell a chip. Marketing and branding mattered almost as much. His competitors all took different approaches to positioning their products in the marketplace. Some went with outlandish, hypermasculine branding that appealed to gamers' self-conceptions: 3dfx's Voodoo Banshee, the ATI Rage Pro, S3 Savage, Righteous Graphics. Others went more technical or industrial-sounding, such as the Matrox G200 or the Verite 2200. Nvidia tended to split the difference, branding its chips with names that both conveyed technical excellence and resonated emotionally, such as the RIVA TNT—RIVA standing for (as we've seen) Real-time Interactive Video and Animation Accelerator, and TNT for TwiN Texels, or the ability for the chip to process two texture elements (texels) at once. But to the average consumer, of course, it was a name "that had something to do with explosions," as one engineer put it.[6]

Yet in a crowded market, Nvidia decided to bend the rules in order to stand out even more. In 1999, it launched the successor to the RIVA TNT2 series, which it called the GeForce 256. It was incontrovertibly true that the GeForce 256 represented a significant advancement in traditional graphics capabilities, which by this point was typical and expected of every new chip generation Nvidia produced. It featured four graphics pipelines, allowing it to process four pixels at the same time. It also integrated a hardware transform and lighting (T&L) engine, which meant it could take on the calculation tasks essential to the moving, rotation, and scaling of 3-D objects. Those tasks were usually handled by the CPU; the GeForce 256 thus took even more computational burden off of the CPU and made the entire computer run faster.

"By putting dedicated hardware to do that, you could suddenly process a lot more geometry and make much more interesting pictures," said former chief scientist David Kirk.

The management team at Nvidia thought that this was far too technical to pitch to customers. The typical in-house naming formula of acronym and number wouldn't work. Nvidia needed something bigger to market its new product.

"We had to find a way to position this product as a much better graphics processor for 3-D graphics than anything out there," said Dan Vivoli. "The chip is big. It has texture and lighting. We've got to charge a lot for it. We need to come up with a way to make sure how great this thing is." He challenged his product-marketing team to come up with something brilliant.

Product manager Sanford Russell got to work on potential ideas. Russell loved bouncing branding, naming, and positioning strategy off his colleagues, including Jensen and Kirk.

"It was never, walk into a room with a PowerPoint and here's the name. It was constant discussion," Russell said. "We were asking them about the technology. What works. What doesn't work."[7]

Russell grabbed Michael Hara for a thirty-minute brainstorm session to figure out how to market the GeForce 256 more effectively, and both executives remember coming out of the room with the notion to call the new chip the first entry in an entirely new product category altogether: a graphics processing unit, or GPU, which would be to graphics rendering what the computer's main central processing unit (CPU) was for all other computational tasks.

The technical specialists at Nvidia knew that their chips were special. The average computer user, though, didn't quite appreciate the complexity or value of a graphics chip. Unlike the CPU, which sounded like the main piece of equipment essential to any computer, graphics cards were just one peripheral among many. A special designation for graphics chips that also drew an explicit comparison to the CPU would, for the first time, make them stand out as truly exceptional.

"My memory has it Mike Hara and I were in the room when we came up with GPU," said Russell. "It didn't seem that important at the time. We were working fourteen-hour days."

He soon told Vivoli the GPU idea, and Vivoli liked it. "Sometimes Dan would take a while to chew on an idea, but GPU rippled through pretty quick."

Within days, the marketing team committed to the GPU designation, which would not only help Nvidia stand out from other graphics chips but also make it easier to command a pricing premium. The world understood that CPUs were supposed to cost hundreds of dollars.

Nvidia chips were sold at wholesale for less than $100 each, even though they were just as complex as, and had more transistors than, CPUs. Once the company started marketing all of its chips as GPUs, the pricing gap narrowed considerably.

Even so, the GPU moniker, when applied first to the GeForce 256, was controversial among Nvidia engineers, who pointed out that a chip could not truly be called a GPU unless it had several features that the GeForce 256 did not. The chip lacked a "state machine," a technical term meaning a dedicated processor that transitions from various states to execute and fetch instructions, in the same manner that a CPU does for programming commands. It was not programmable, meaning that graphics styles and features could not easily be customized by third-party developers. Instead, developers would have to rely on a fixed set of Nvidia-defined hardware functions. Moreover, the GeForce 256 did not have its own programming language.

But the marketing team argued that such features were already planned for the next generation of graphics chips. And even without them, the GeForce 256 delivered a step change in performance that would be obvious to every gamer and computer enthusiast in the world. While not literally a GPU, the GeForce 256 could still be a category-defining product. The chips that would follow—the "true" GPUs that would be fully programmable by outside developers—were coming soon enough.

So Nvidia's marketing team pushed forward with the GPU name over the dissent of Nvidia's engineers. "We don't need anyone's approval," Vivoli told them. He didn't think anyone outside of the industry would really care about the technical definition. Besides, "we knew the next one was going to be programmable. We decided to take a leap, make a stretch that this is a GPU."[8]

When Jensen announced the GeForce 256 in August 1999, he did not shy away from hyperbole. "We are introducing the world's first GPU," he declared in the press release. "The GPU is a major breakthrough for the industry and will fundamentally transform the 3D medium. It will enable a new generation of amazing interactive content that is alive, imaginative, and captivating."

It may have been the first time that the company engaged in significant marketing embellishment for a major launch—and it worked. Vivoli made the decision not to trademark "GPU" because he wanted other companies to use the term, the idea being that Nvidia had pioneered an entirely new category. Hyperbole would become reality: the GPU moniker became an industry standard and helped Nvidia sell hundreds of millions of cards in the ensuing decades.

Vivoli had another idea for the GPU's launch: to actively intimidate rivals. An Nvidia marketer unfurled a banner advertising the GeForce 256 on a highway overpass that led straight to the headquarters of 3dfx (this was before its eventual bankruptcy). The banner announced that the new Nvidia GPU would change the world and crush the competition. The state police quickly removed the banner, which was being displayed illegally, and Nvidia received a formal reprimand. Still, it had served its purpose. "It was *Art of War*. We wanted to demoralize them," Vivoli said. Nvidia was learning how to bend the world to its will.

MODERN GRAPHICS CHIPS ORGANIZE computation through what is called a graphics pipeline, turning geometry data with object coordinates into an image. The first stage of this process, called the geometry stage, involves transforming object vertices, or points, in a virtual 3-D space through scaling and rotation calculations. The second stage, rasterization, determines the position of each object on the screen. The third stage, called the fragment stage, calculates the color and textures. In the final stage, the image is assembled.

Early graphics pipelines involved fixed-function stages each with a handful of hardwired operations. Nvidia and its competitor graphics-card makers each defined how its chips would handle all four stages in the pipeline; third-party developers could not change how the chips rendered anything, meaning that they could only create visual effects and artistic styles from a menu of options set by the chip designers.[9] Because every programmer had to use the same handful of fixed-function operations, every game on the market looked similar—none could stand out through visuals alone.

David Kirk, Nvidia's chief scientist, wanted to change all this by inventing a true GPU. His idea was to introduce a new technology called programmable shaders. These would open up the graphics pipeline to third-party developers, giving them the ability to write their own rendering functions and exert more control over how they presented their games visually. The shaders would allow developers to make visuals in real time that rivaled the best computer-generated graphics in movies. He argued that developers would quickly adopt programmable shaders in their games, as they knew far better than chip designers how to create cutting-edge visuals. This, in turn, would push gamers to Nvidia cards, because they would be the only cards on the market that could support the advanced new graphics. The downside was that programmable shading, and therefore a true GPU, could be enabled only by revising how Nvidia chips were designed. It would be an expensive and time-consuming undertaking, even for an established player.

Kirk knew that the technological upside would be clear to Jensen, who would have the final say. He also knew that Jensen would fixate on cost: how much Nvidia would have to invest to create the technology, whether the market was ready for it, and how much more revenue it would bring in. Although Jensen seemed enthusiastic initially, Kirk didn't know yet whether that was a good sign.

"One of the things that happens with Jensen is right before he's about to kill your project, he will sound optimistic when he's talking to you about it," Kirk said.[10]

To ensure his project's survival, he stoked Jensen's ever-present fear of being outflanked by the competition. He pointed out that Nvidia's lead in fixed-function graphics acceleration would inevitably erode; the fixed-function operations of a traditional graphics chip would someday become miniaturized enough for Intel to include in a section of their CPUs or in a motherboard chip, obviating a separate graphics card entirely. He also said that programmable shaders could one day potentially open up other markets outside of gaming.

"Okay," said Jensen after hearing Kirk's thoughts. "I'll buy that."

In February 2001, Nvidia released the GeForce 3, whose programmable shader technology and support for third-party development of its core graphics functions made it the first true GPU. Kirk's analysis was proved to be correct. The GeForce 3 was a blockbuster success. By the third fiscal quarter of 2001, Nvidia's quarterly revenue reached $370 million—an 87 percent year-over-year increase. It was now generating sales at an annualized run rate of $1 billion, achieving that milestone faster than any other semiconductor company in U.S. history. The previous record holder, Broadcom, had achieved it in thirty-six quarters; Nvidia beat that by nine months. By the end of the year, the stock price had tripled over the prior three quarters. The company was now twenty times more valuable than it had been on IPO day, thanks to a combination of strategic vision, relentless execution, and the paranoia that kept Jensen and his executive team on guard for threats that could come from anywhere, at any time.

THE DRIVE TO CONTINUALLY DIVERSIFY Nvidia's business led the company straight to Apple. Historically, Nvidia had not sold much to Apple, partly because Nvidia optimized its products for Intel-based CPUs, which Apple did not use. But in the early 2000s, Nvidia won a small contract to supply graphics chips for the consumer-oriented iMac G4. The computer was the successor to the colorful all-in-one iMac G3 that marked Steve Jobs's triumphant return to Apple in 1998.

Chris Diskin, who had successfully won Microsoft's Xbox business, was put in charge of the overall sales relationship with Apple. He worked with Dan Vivoli to figure out a strategy to get Nvidia's GeForce chips into more Apple computer products. The key break came thanks to an old, iconic Pixar short film.

By this point, the centerpiece of Nvidia's sales pitch to PC makers was the graphics demo, when it would show off the advanced features and raw computing power of its chips. In the past, the company had used third-party games to wow their audiences. But as Nvidia's cards grew more powerful, older games no longer fully showcased the breadth and depth of a new chip's capabilities. Vivoli decided to put more time and resources into creating better graphics demos for the sales team. He even hired a former colleague from Silicon Graphics named Mark Daly for the specific purpose of enhancing Nvidia's demos.

Vivoli knew that graphics demos would have the most impact if

Nvidia had a thorough understanding of its audience. Earlier demos were targeted at engineers, which is why they showed off the specific features and capabilities of Nvidia's new chips. Like the 3-D cube that Voodoo Graphics impressed the Hambrecht & Quest conference with in 1996, such demos were only impressive if you knew the computations that were occurring "under the hood." A nonengineer wouldn't necessarily know what he or she was looking at. So Vivoli changed the focus of demos away from a cold demonstration of graphics performance—the visual equivalent of reading a list of benchmark metrics—and gave them a sentimental side.

In a brainstorm meeting during the development of the GeForce 3, Daly believed he had come up with the perfect means of showing off Nvidia's new chip. Pixar's two-minute animated short *Luxo Jr.* had been a watershed moment for computer animation. When this film about hopping table lamps was first released in 1986, it demonstrated just what computer-generated imagery (CGI) could do, even at that relatively early stage. But it had taken a huge amount of computational power to produce. Each frame was built on a Cray supercomputer and took three hours to render. At twenty-four frames per second, the computer needed nearly seventy-five hours to generate just a single second of film. Daly thought Nvidia should make a *Luxo Jr.* demo.

Vivoli gave him the green light. "That's a great idea. Go make that demo," he said.

A few months later, Daly reported to Vivoli that the team was making good progress, but there was the fact that *Luxo Jr.* was Pixar's property. If Nvidia used it for a public demonstration, the company ran the risk of infringing on Pixar's copyright.

Vivoli didn't want anything to derail what was shaping up to be an extraordinary showcase for the important GeForce 3 launch. He waved off Daly's concerns.

"That's fine. Don't worry about it. I'll go figure it out," Vivoli said. Both he and David Kirk had contacts at Pixar, and they worked them to get approval for the demo. Their request eventually reached Pixar's chief creative officer, John Lasseter, who had directed *Toy Story, A Bug's Life,* and would later direct *Cars.* Lasseter declined it. He wasn't keen on Pixar's iconic character, which at the time was part of the company's logo and appeared prominently at the start of every Pixar movie, being used to sell graphics chips.

In the meantime, Daly's team had completed the demo, and it looked every bit as impressive as he had envisioned. Vivoli thought, "What if we showed the demo to Steve Jobs?" He believed a real-time rendered version of *Luxo Jr.* would be effective, because it would touch on a landmark moment in Jobs's own career and the development of computers more broadly. It would also show that the new chip was powerful enough to rival the graphics capabilities of a supercomputer, yet precise enough to faithfully reconstruct an important piece of art.

Vivoli and Diskin went to meet with Jobs at Apple's headquarters. During the first part of the demo, the Nvidia team showed off *Luxo Jr.* using similar shots and angles as the original. It was suitably impressive. Jobs said that it "looks good."

Then they ran the demo again, but this time Vivoli started clicking around the demo, which changed the position or the angle of the camera. The camera movements showed that, unlike a static video, Nvidia's chips could render the entire scene in real time. The user could change and watch the scene from any angle with realistic lighting and shadow effects. Now Jobs was blown away. It was impressive enough that Nvidia's GPU could render animations in real time, and with comparable visual fidelity, that had taken Pixar's supercomputers weeks to generate. But on top of that, it offered real-time interactivity. Jobs decided that the Power Mac G4 computer would offer the GeForce 3 as a premium option.

Jobs also asked whether Apple could use the demo at the 2001 Macworld in Tokyo. Vivoli told him about the copyright issue, to which Jobs replied that he would check with the people at Pixar. Diskin and Vivoli later laughed about this moment: Jobs was the CEO of both Apple and Pixar, so he was effectively asking himself for permission.

Jobs ended the meeting after about twenty minutes to head to another. As he prepared to leave, he had some parting advice for the Nvidia team.

"You guys have really got to do some work on mobile because ATI is kicking your ass in laptops," he said, referring to Nvidia's main rival after the demise of 3dfx.

Without hesitating, Diskin responded, "Actually, Steve, I think you're wrong."

The room went quiet. Jobs fixed Diskin with his intense stare and said, "Tell me why?" Diskin got the sense that not many people challenged Steve Jobs, and it was clear he expected a good answer.

Diskin had one. He explained that Nvidia's chips did indeed consume more power—indeed, more power than most laptops could muster—because they offered the higher performance that desktop users required. But their performance and power consumption could easily be lowered to meet laptop specs. In fact, Diskin argued, if Nvidia lowered the clock speed of its chips down to match the speed—and therefore power requirements—of ATI's chips, Nvidia's chips would actually offer better overall performance. It wasn't that ATI was kicking Nvidia's ass in laptops, as Jobs had thought. It was just that Nvidia had not needed to create a chip specifically for a lower-power laptop model, when a throttled-down version of its flagship line would do the job just fine.

"We have more headroom," Diskin said, summarizing his main argument.

Jobs stared at him one more time. "Okay," was all he said. The meeting was over.

Thirty minutes later, Diskin got a call from Apple executive Phil Schiller. "I don't know *what* you told Steve, but we need your entire laptop team in here tomorrow for a full day to review your silicon," he said. Nvidia would go from no presence in Apple laptops to a nearly 85 percent share of Apple's entire computer lineup in a matter of years. Diskin got the chance to prove himself, and Nvidia's chips, thanks not only to his demo but also to his quick thinking and his willingness to challenge one of the most intimidating figures in the tech industry.

NVIDIA WAS GOING FROM STRENGTH to strength. It had added one hundred employees from its vanquished rival 3dfx, won an Xbox gaming-console business deal that would go on to generate $1.8 billion in revenue over its lifetime, and secured contracts to make chips for Apple's Mac computer lines. These achievements led to impressive financial growth and a skyrocketing stock price. But all the new business required attention from management and engineering, drawing focus away from Nvidia's core GPU products—which resulted in one of the worst product launches in the company's history.

In 2000, ATI Technologies acquired the small graphics firm ArtX for $400 million. ArtX specialized in graphics chips for gaming consoles; its founding engineers had worked on the Nintendo 64 console at Silicon Graphics before starting out on their own, and the company had recently secured a contract to develop the graphics chips for the N64's successor, the Nintendo GameCube. ATI's purchase of ArtX gave it instant credibility in the field of console games—and a group of engineers who immediately started working on a chip called the R300. ATI would release the chip on a dedicated graphics card, the Radeon 9700 PRO, which went on sale in August of 2002.

Nvidia, in the meantime, was caught up in a legal dispute with Microsoft. The tech giant had recently revised their vendor agreements around information sharing and intellectual property rights for the Direct3D API. The next major update to Direct3D, called Direct3D 9, would be released in December of 2002, with significant improvements that would be essential to the next generation of chips. There was a catch, though. Chip companies could not get access to Direct3D 9 documentation and could therefore not build around its new features until they signed the new agreement. Nvidia felt that the new language was overly favorable to Microsoft and refused to sign the new contract until it got better terms.

A business problem created an engineering challenge. Nvidia was designing its next chip, which it called the NV30, without access to the upcoming version of Direct3D's technical specifications. "We ended up developing the NV30 without a lot of guidance from Microsoft," David Kirk said. "We had to guess what they were going to do. We made some errors."

Confusion reigned, both from the lack of clear guidelines from

Microsoft and from a lack of coordination between Nvidia's own teams. A former employee remembers an incident when a group of hardware and software engineers were standing in a cubicle and looking at the lackluster performance data from the NV30 during its development phase. One perplexed software engineer said that it was almost as if the hardware fog-shader feature had been removed. The hardware architect replied, "Oh yeah, we took that out. Nobody used that."

The software team was stunned. Fog shaders were still widely used in most games, as they allowed developers to save on graphics computation by blurring object details the further away they were, as though in fog. Nvidia's hardware team did not consult anyone before they removed it, nor did they seem to understand how important it was. All of a sudden, it was as though Nvidia's various teams were siloed— the very kind of organizational structure the company had rejected from the start.

Another Nvidia employee recalls a similar meeting where a hardware engineer was presenting a list of different features in the NV30. One of the developer-relations employees noticed that the list was missing an important feature called multi-sample anti-aliasing (MSAA), the technique to smooth out jagged edges and soften the transitions between an object's line and the background. He asked, "What's up with 4X MSAA? What's going on?"

The hardware engineer replied, "We don't think it's a big deal. It's kind of untested."

The developer-relations employee was aghast. "What are you talking about? ATI is shipping this feature in a product already, and gamers love it." Once again, Nvidia's own engineers seemed to be unaware of what the market wanted. "NV30 was an architectural disaster. It was an architectural tragedy," Jensen later said.[11] "The software team, the architecture team, and the chip-design team hardly communicated with each other."

Nvidia thus failed to ensure that the NV30 met all the benchmarks for the biggest games of the season. New graphics chips were reviewed in the press, and a common feature of reviews was the benchmarking process, wherein independent reviewers test certain metrics, such as frame rate per second, in specific, graphics-intensive games, and under different resolutions. Standard benchmarks give gamers a series of quantitative reference points so that they don't have to rely on subjective analyses of a graphics card's quality (or on marketing by those cards' makers). During the NV30's development, it became clear that the chip would not win many of the benchmarks for the games that consumers then cared most about. For the first time since the NV1, Nvidia was about to release a card that was not at the very top of the market in terms of performance.

ATI, in contrast, had agreed to sign the contract with Microsoft so that it could optimize the R300 with Direct3D 9 from the start. The chip and the new card that housed it, the Radeon 9700 PRO, worked perfectly and was fully compliant with Microsoft's latest release of the API. It ran the latest 3-D games, including *Quake 3* and *Unreal Tournament*, at high resolutions with little trouble. It was able to render pixels in more vibrant 24-bit floating point color, an upgrade from the 16-bit color used in the industry's previous generation of chips. It had far better anti-aliasing capabilities than its competitors, making polygons sharp and lines crisp. And it came out in August 2002 in time for the fall back-to-school rush.

Nvidia's NV30 did none of these things. It didn't work well with Direct3D 9, which meant that new games performed poorly under their highest graphical settings. It had been optimized for 32-bit color, which technically leapfrogged the 24-bit color system on the Radeon 9700 PRO, but Direct3D 9 didn't support 32-bit. Nvidia was forced to tell its graphics-card partners to delay the launch of the company's new products that carried the NV30 by about five months. The delay at least allowed Nvidia to try to make the chip more competitive against the Radeon 9700 PRO but caused Nvidia to miss the critical fall launch window.

Once they compared the NV30-based GeForce FX card with the Radeon 9700 PRO, Nvidia's engineers decided to overhaul the design of their chip to make it more competitive. They created software workarounds to "translate" the new features of DirectX for the NV30. "We had to do backflips to run DirectX 9 calls," Dan Vivoli said. "A call would be made to DirectX, and we'd have to turn it into something else our chip could run."

These "calls," or graphics instructions sent to the DirectX API, required more processing power, which forced Nvidia to turn up the clock speed of the NV30. The excessive heat that resulted led Nvidia to put a big dual-slot fan over the chip, which made a loud, high-pitched noise whenever it activated.

"It was a horrible experience for the gamers who were using the chip because it was so loud," Vivoli said. The fan noise became a constant talking point among customers. The only engineering solution Nvidia could come up with was to write an algorithm to change the timing of the fan's rotation, but that would take time, and it wasn't that effective in the end.

To salvage a small shred of the company's reputation, a member of the marketing team suggested making a spoof video about the fan noise to indicate that it was an intentional feature. "We just fell on our sword. We put together a video where the GeForce FX was on the end of a leaf blower blowing leaves. We showed people cooking off of it because it's so hot," said Vivoli.

This at least partially placated the gaming community, which appreciated Nvidia's ability to poke fun at itself and admit a misstep. It also helped undercut negative mentions of the card. Whenever a competitor tried to point consumers to how loud the GeForce FX was, they found Nvidia's self-critical video.

Although the video was a PR win, it did little to help the chip's fortunes in the market. Compared with the R300, cards based on NV30 were more expensive, ran hotter, ran games slower, and had an excessively loud fan. Sales during the all-important holiday quarter fell 30 percent versus the prior year, and the company's stock price plummeted by 80 percent from its peak just ten months before. Nvidia was reliving the NV1 nightmare all over again. The company's individual teams had lost touch with each other, and the company as a whole had somehow lost touch with its core consumer base.

Jensen was furious at the poor planning and execution on the chip. He called out its engineers at an all-company meeting.

"Let me tell you about the NV30. Is this the piece of shit you intended to build?" he shouted.[12] "The architects did a shitty job putting the product together. How could you not see the leaf blower issue before it happened? Someone should have raised their hand and said, 'We have a design issue here.'"

His criticism didn't end after a single meeting. Later, he invited an executive from Best Buy, which was then the largest electronics retailer in the United States,[13] to speak to Nvidia employees. The executive spent much of the session talking about the NV30's poor performance and customer complaints about the loud fan. Jensen agreed: "He's right. This is crap."

The only thing that saved Nvidia was that its competition did not press its advantage very hard. ATI had decided to peg the price of its R300-based graphics cards at $399, the same price as NV30-based cards. If ATI had cut the price of the R300 aggressively enough, the company could have destroyed demand for the inferior NV30-based cards and likely bankrupted Nvidia. Dwight Diercks said ATI had plenty of profit margin to work with, because its chip had an enormous cost advantage over the poorly designed and bloated NV30. "If Jensen had been running ATI," said Diercks, "he would have put Nvidia out of business."

JENSEN REFLECTED ON THE NV30'S failures. Ultimately, it was his responsibility to ensure that Nvidia's teams collaborated effectively, no matter how large the company got. He now saw that it may have been asking too much to integrate the former 3dfx engineers into Nvidia's culture all at once. "NV30 was the first chip that we built as one company, after we had brought in the 3dfx employees," he concluded many years later.[14] "Organizationally, the harmony wasn't very good."

The Innovator's Dilemma taught Jensen, as it has generations of business leaders, how to protect his company from competition. It helped him understand the threat from low-cost competitors, which is why he launched lines of low-tier and mid-tier Nvidia chips made from parts that were not quite good enough for the top-of-the-line chips. It convinced him to diversify Nvidia's partner portfolio beyond just consumer desktop PCs, into gaming consoles, Mac, and laptops. And it compelled him to made big strategic investments, such as adding programmability to Nvidia chips to make true GPUs.

But one of Christensen's subtler messages escaped Jensen, at least for the first decade of Nvidia's existence. It was not enough to look at external measures of success: revenue, profitability, the price of the stock, or the pace of product launches. A truly sustainable business spent just as much effort looking inward in order to keep its internal culture aligned. As Nvidia established itself as the dominant player in the graphics industry, the company's executives got distracted by its partners, its investors, and its finances. It failed to see the growing problem within its own walls—complacency. And was almost destroyed because of it.

But Jensen is known for following his own rule to not make the same mistake twice. He summoned the same vigilance that he had trained on external threats and turned it toward internal ones. He resolved the contractual disagreement with Microsoft, ensuring that his architects would never have to work in the dark again when it came to Direct3D. He made sure his staff constantly talked to game developers, so the features most important to them, and to gamers, would always be incorporated into Nvidia's chips. He required his teams to ensure the upcoming GPUs would be optimized for the most popular games, with the goal of dominating the benchmark tests in reviews. Most important, he pushed his teams to work with "intellectual honesty"—to always question their own assumptions and embrace their own missteps, so that the company could solve them before they snowballed into a disaster like the NV30.

Nvidia barely survived its first ten years. It had achieved many things: technical wizardry, a blockbuster IPO, and relative longevity in an industry where most competitors last only a few years. It had been humbled by its failures: its near-bankruptcy due to the NV1 and

NV2; the production problems that halted the successful RIVA 128 in its tracks; and, most recently, the NV30 debacle, which signaled a deep organizational problem that the company would need to confront. It had become a large public company, with the same challenges and the same tendency to entropy as any other large public company. Jensen would have to evolve into a different kind of leader for Nvidia to succeed in the coming decade.

PART III

NVIDIA RISING

(2002–2013)

CHAPTER 8

The Era of the GPU

ONE OF THE EARLIEST REFERENCES TO THE TECHNOLOGY that would eventually turn Nvidia into a trillion-dollar company was in a PhD thesis about clouds. Mark Harris, a computer science researcher at the University of North Carolina at Chapel Hill, wanted to find a way to use computers to better simulate complex natural phenomena, such as the movement of fluids or the thermodynamics of atmospheric clouds.

In 2002, Harris observed that an increasing number of computer scientists were using GPUs, such as Nvidia's GeForce 3, for nongraphics applications. Researchers who ran their simulations on computers with GPUs reported significant speed improvements over computers that relied on CPU power only. But to run these simulations required computers to learn how to reframe nongraphics computations in the terms of graphical functions that a GPU could perform. In other words: the researchers had hacked GPUs.

To do so, they utilized the GeForce 3's programmable shader technology, originally designed to paint colors for pixels, to perform matrix multiplication. This function combines two matrices (basically, tables of numbers) to create a new matrix through a series of mathematical calculations. When the matrices are small, it's easy enough to perform matrix multiplication by use of normal computational methods. As matrices get larger, the computational complexity required to multiply them together increases cubically—but so does their ability to explain real-world problems in fields as diverse as physics, chemistry, and engineering.

"Really the modern GPU, we kind of stumbled onto," said Nvidia scientist David Kirk.[1] "We built a super powerful and super flexible giant computation engine to do graphics because graphics is hard. Researchers saw all that floating-point horsepower and the ability to program it a little bit by hiding computation in some graphics algorithm."

Using GPUs for nongraphics purposes, however, required a very specific skill set. Researchers had to rely on programming languages designed exclusively for graphics shading, including OpenGL and Nvidia's Cg (C for graphics), which was introduced in 2002 to run on the GeForce 3. Sufficiently dedicated programmers such as Harris learned how to "translate" their real-world problems into functions that these languages could execute, and they soon figured out how to use GPUs to make progress in understanding protein folding, determining stock-options pricing, and assembling diagnostic images from MRI scans.

The academic world initially referred to the use of GPUs for these kinds of scientific purposes with cumbersome terminology, such as "application of graphics hardware to nongraphics applications" or "exploiting special-purpose hardware for alternative purposes." Harris decided to coin something simpler: "general-purpose computing on GPUs," or "GPGPU." He created a website to promote the term. One year later, he registered the URL GPGPU.org; on the site, he wrote about the budding trend and traded advice with others on the best ways to use GPU programming languages. GPGPU.org quickly became a popular destination for the community of researchers who wanted to harness the power of Nvidia's new devices.

Harris's intense interest in GPUs earned him a job at Nvidia. After he received his PhD from UNC, he moved across the country to Silicon Valley to join the very company whose cards he had learned how to hack. He was surprised to discover that the term he had invented, "GPGPU," was widely used by employees. "People at Nvidia saw potential and were using this silly acronym that I made up," Harris said.

Though he didn't know it, Nvidia had brought him on to help the company make GPGPU much easier. Jensen was quick to grasp that GPGPU had the potential to open up the market for GPUs far beyond mere computer graphics. "Probably the most important influences and early indication that we ought to continue was in medical imaging," he said.[2] Yet the fact that all GPGPU work had to be run through Cg—a language that was proprietary to Nvidia and optimized only for graphical functions—had become a barrier to wider adoption. In order to generate more demand, Nvidia would have to make its cards easier to program.

Harris learned there was a chip team within Nvidia working on a secret project code-named the NV50. Most chip designs were only one or two generations removed from the current architecture. The NV50 was Nvidia's most forward-looking chip under development: it would not be released for several years. It would have its own dedicated compute mode, so that its GPU would be easier to access for nongraphics applications. Instead of Cg, it would utilize extensions to the C programming language, a widely used general-purpose language. And it would enable parallel compute threads with access to addressable memory—in essence, allowing the GPU to perform all the functions of a secondary CPU that might be needed in scientific, technical, or industrial computing.

Nvidia called this programming model for chips the Compute Unified Device Architecture, or CUDA. CUDA made it possible for not only graphics programming specialists but also scientists and engineers to leverage the GPU's computing power. It helped them manage the intricate web of technical instructions that were necessary to execute parallel computations on the GPU's hundreds, and later thousands, of computing cores. Jensen believed it would expand Nvidia's reach into every corner of the tech industry. New software, rather than new hardware, would transform the company.

TWO OF THE MOST IMPORTANT figures in the early development of CUDA were Ian Buck and John Nickolls. Nickolls was the hardware expert. He joined Nvidia in 2003, becoming the hardware architect for the company's early GPU computing effort. He collaborated closely with the chip team to ensure that important features were incorporated into GPUs, such as larger memory caches and different methods for performing floating-point math. Nickolls understood that better performance was necessary if Nvidia hoped to drive adoption of GPU computing. (Nickolls tragically never saw the full success of his work on CUDA. He is considered by many inside Nvidia as an unsung hero for the company. The executive passed away in August 2011 after a battle with cancer. "Without John Nickolls, there'd be no CUDA. He was the most influential of the technologists in our company that ultimately willed CUDA into existence," Jensen said.[3] "He worked on CUDA until his death. He was the one that explained CUDA to me.")

Buck worked on software. He had previously interned at Nvidia but left to pursue a PhD at Stanford. During his studies, Buck developed the BrookGPU programming environment, which provided a language and compiler for GPU-based computing. His work attracted the attention of the Department of Defense's research arm, the Defense Advanced Research Projects Agency (DARPA)—and also that of his former employer, Nvidia, which licensed some of the technology Buck had worked on. In 2004, he was hired by Nvidia.[4]

The early CUDA team was small and tight-knit. Buck's software group consisted of three engineers: Nicholas Wilt and Nolan Goodnight, who worked on the CUDA driver API and implementation, and Norbert Juffa, who wrote the CUDA standard math library. Others focused on hardware compilers, which convert human-readable code into machine-usable code that can be executed by a computer processor. They included Richard Johnson, who designed the Parallel Thread Execution Language (PTX) specification, which served as a virtual hardware compiler target for CUDA; Mike Murphy, who built an Open64 (x86-64 architecture) compiler for CUDA to PTX; and Vinod Grover, who joined in late 2007 and worked on compiler drivers.

It was imperative that both groups work in close harmony. "Any computer architecture has a software side and a hardware side. CUDA is not just a piece of software," said Andy Keane, a former general manager for Nvidia's data-center business. "It's a representation of the machine. It's a way you access the machine, so they have to be designed together."[5]

The original plan was to launch CUDA solely on Nvidia's Quadro GPUs, which were meant for high-end scientific and technical workstations. But this carried some risk. All new technology presents a chicken-or-egg problem. Without developers creating applications that took advantage of the new chips, there would be no reason for users to adopt it. Without a large installed base of users, developers wouldn't want to create software for the new platform. Historically, when a company drives adoption on both fronts, as Arm Holdings did with its ARM chip architecture for mobile phones and as Intel did with its x86 processor for personal computers, the result is usually market dominance for decades. Those companies that fail to drive adoption, such as PowerPC (with its RISC processors) and Digital Equipment (with its Alpha architecture), have found themselves relegated to the dustbin of computer history in the span of a few years.

First impressions matter. If Nvidia initially released CUDA solely for high-end workstations and didn't provide sufficient software support, it might lead developers to pigeonhole it as a tool for a narrow range of technical professions only. "You can't just throw technology over the wall and expect [people] to adopt it," said marketing executive Lee Hirsch. "You can't simply say, 'Here's our new GPU, go crazy.'"

Instead, Nvidia would have to do two things: make CUDA available to everyone, and make it applicable to everything. Jensen insisted that they launch CUDA across Nvidia's entire lineup, including its GeForce line of gaming GPUs, so that it would be widely available for a relatively affordable price. This would ensure that CUDA was synonymous with GPUs, or at least with Nvidia GPUs. Jensen understood the importance not just of launching new technology but also of saturating the market with it. The more people who had CUDA in their hands, the faster the technology would establish itself as a standard.

"We should just push this everywhere and make it a foundational technology," Jensen told the CUDA team.

The move was extremely expensive. Nvidia introduced the NV50, which had been officially rebranded as the G80 for use in its GeForce line of graphics cards, alongside CUDA in November 2006. It would be the company's first GPU chip with a computing function. The G80 boasted 128 CUDA cores, which are extra hardware circuits used to support CUDA functionality. The GPU was able to run up to thousands of computing threads concurrently across those cores by using a hardware multithreading feature. By comparison, Intel's main Core 2 CPU at the time only had up to four computing cores.

Nvidia invested immense amounts of time and money into making the G80. It took four years to develop the GPU computing chip in comparison with the one-year gap between generations of GeForce chips. It cost an astronomical $475 million,[6] or around a third of Nvidia's total research and development budget for those four years.

That was just for one version of CUDA-enabled GPUs. The company invested so much in converting its GPUs for CUDA compatibility that its gross margin, a measure of its profitability, fell from 45.6 percent in the 2008 fiscal year (covering January 2007 to January 2008) to 35.4 percent in the 2010 fiscal year. As Nvidia increased spending on CUDA, the global financial crisis destroyed consumer demand for high-end electronics as well as corporate demand for GPU-powered workstations. The combined pressures caused Nvidia's stock price to fall by more than 80 percent between October 2007 and November 2008.

"CUDA added a ton of cost into our chips," Jensen acknowledged.[7] "We had very few customers for CUDA but we made every chip CUDA compatible. You can go back in history and look at our gross margins. It started out poor and it got worse."[8]

Nevertheless, he believed so strongly in CUDA's market potential that he remained committed to the course he had chosen, even as his investors demanded a strategic course correction. "I believed in CUDA," he said. "We were convinced that accelerated computing would solve problems that normal computers couldn't. We had to make that sacrifice. I had a deep belief in its potential."

Yet upon its release, the G80 failed to gain traction, despite rave reviews from tech publications such as *WIRED* and *Ars Technica*.[9] A year after its launch, about fifty financial analysts arrived at Nvidia's headquarters, now in Santa Clara, to listen to Jensen and the company's investor relations teams present their argument for why Wall Street should continue to believe in Nvidia when all signs pointed to its being on the wrong track.

All morning, management provided details on its plans to expand high-performance GPU computing to new markets such as industrial and medical research applications. The company estimated that the GPU computing market would rise to more than $6 billion in a few years, even though it was near-zero at the time. In particular, Nvidia foresaw a demand for enterprise data centers powered primarily by GPUs and had brought in Andy Keane, who had extensive experience in hardware business development and product marketing at various start-ups, to run a new division dedicated to them. After the morning presentations, it was clear that the analyst group was skeptical about CUDA and saw it mainly in terms of the negative impact it was having on Nvidia's profit margins.

Lunch was held under a tent in the parking lot: a buffet of sandwiches, bottled water, and soda. An analyst from Hudson Square Research named Daniel Ernst got some food and sat at an empty table. He was soon joined by other analysts, and eventually by Jensen as well. The other analysts began peppering the CEO with short-term financial questions; they wanted to know the exact impact of CUDA on the company's profit margins, given that Nvidia was about to transition to a new manufacturing technology for its next generation of chips. It was all material Jensen had covered earlier in the day, and he dutifully reiterated the company's official guidance, which called for an eventual rise in long-term margins after the short-term impact of research and development. This failed to satisfy the analysts, who remained focused on the next few months, not the next few years.

Ernst felt Jensen was growing frustrated and would soon leave the table, so he decided to ask him something different. "Jensen, I have a two-year-old daughter at home. I bought a new Sony A100 DSLR camera and regularly download photos to my Mac to do some light editing in Photoshop. But whenever I do this, my Mac slows down as soon as I open one of these high-resolution images. It's even worse on my ThinkPad. Can a GPU solve this problem?"

Jensen's eyes lit up. "Don't write about this because it's not out yet, but Adobe is a partner of ours. Adobe Photoshop with CUDA can instruct the CPU to off-load the task to the GPU, and make it much faster," he said. "That's exactly what I'm talking about with the coming 'Era of the GPU.'"

Ernst, at least, was impressed. He saw that CUDA was no fad, but could be central to Nvidia's future. He was irritated by the questions from other analysts about the company's financial profile. He was happy Nvidia was willing to sacrifice short-term margin to capture more of CUDA's gigantic upside. The "Era of the GPU" would create so many opportunities that Jensen saw it as his mission to prepare Nvidia to take advantage of it—even if no one could know exactly what those opportunities would be. Everything else, including corporate financial concerns, was entirely secondary.

It would not be easy to match Jensen's vision with market reality. Nvidia had the product and production problems solved, but now Jensen asked his team to figure out ways to create a market for CUDA—to "solve the entire problem," as he put it. This would require a systematic analysis of the needs of every industry, from entertainment to health care to energy, and to not only analyze potential demand but also figure out how to unleash it via special, GPU-centered applications in each field. If developers didn't yet know what to do with CUDA, Nvidia would teach them.

FOR SEVERAL YEARS, NVIDIA'S CHIEF scientist, David Kirk, had been receiving requests from top universities around the country, asking for support from the chip maker.

Nvidia saw a prime opportunity to both help universities and drive adoption of its GPUs. After making several ad hoc donations, Kirk formalized a program with Caltech, the University of Utah, Stanford, the University of North Carolina at Chapel Hill, Brown, and Cornell. Nvidia would provide graphics cards and financial donations to the schools, and in exchange the schools would use Nvidia hardware in graphics programming classes. "It was not entirely selfless," Kirk said. "We wanted them to use our hardware instead of AMD's hardware for their teaching."[10]

The program solved an ongoing issue Nvidia had with its university donation program. Whenever Nvidia made cash donations, universities would charge an overhead or administration fee, thus reducing the donation's impact on actual research. By switching to a more hardware-based donation model, Nvidia was able to ensure that students and not administrators would reap the most benefits from the company's assistance.

Earlier on, Nvidia had established an internship program, where some of the most talented students from the partner schools and others would gain work experience at the corporate office and potentially be evaluated for future employment. This was how CUDA engineer Ian Buck got his first exposure to Nvidia, for example.

Kirk hoped to leverage these same relationships to promote CUDA after its release. He and his colleague David Luebke started a new program they called the CUDA Center of Excellence, offering schools CUDA-capable machines if they committed to teaching a class on the subject. He visited universities, telling students, professors, and department heads they needed to change how they taught computer science because parallel computing was going to become far more important. He gave more than one hundred talks over the course of a year, traveling around the world, sometimes doing multiple talks per day. There were no takers.

"Nobody knew how to program in CUDA, and nobody was devoting effort to it," Kirk said. "Nobody wanted to hear it. I was literally hitting a wall."

Eventually, he found himself pitching Richard Blahut, the head of the Electrical and Computer Engineering Department at the University of Illinois at Urbana-Champaign. Blahut told Kirk it was a really good idea but said that if Kirk was serious about it, he should teach the class himself.

Kirk's initial response was no. At the time, he was living in the mountains in Colorado and didn't have any interest in teaching, let alone in Illinois. But Blahut pressed him, adding the school would match him with one of its top professors, Wen-mei Hwu, who routinely won teaching awards. "You two can teach the class together, and it will be guaranteed to be a success as Hwu can show you how to teach the material," he said. Kirk agreed.

In 2007, Kirk flew from Colorado to Illinois every other week to give his lectures. At the end of the semester, the students carried out CUDA research programming projects and published their work. Other researchers around the country began to request lectures and teaching materials from Kirk and Hwu, so they recorded their classes and made their videos and notes freely available online.

The following year, Nvidia named the University of Illinois at Urbana-Champaign the first CUDA Center of Excellence and provided the school with more than $1 million as well as thirty-two Quadro Plex Model IV systems, each with sixty-four GPUs—the most advanced machines Nvidia made.

"David Kirk and Wen-mei Hwu were the evangelists," said Bill Dally, Kirk's eventual successor as Nvidia's chief scientist. They "taught teacher's courses around the country to basically spread the religion of GPU computing, and it really took off."

Other schools heard about Kirk's class and began to explore how they might also start to teach parallel computing themselves. But because Kirk's was the first course of its kind, there was no common syllabus or set of standards, no textbook to use. So Kirk and Hwu wrote one. Their first edition of *Programming Massively Parallel Processors*, which was published in 2010, sold tens of thousands of copies, was translated into several languages, and was eventually used by hundreds of schools. It was a major inflection point in attracting attention, and talent, to CUDA.

Having built an academic training pipeline for CUDA, Nvidia now moved to drive adoption among nonacademic researchers. In 2010, outside of academic computer science and electrical engineering departments, almost no one used GPUs for scientific research. But gaming provided a glimpse of what was possible. PC games—in particular, first-person shooters—could increasingly produce realistic simulations of physics. When they used GPU processing in its traditional, graphics-acceleration role, these games could calculate the path of a bullet, from the moment it was fired from a gun to the effect of wind on its trajectory to the spalling it produced when it hit a concrete wall. All of these applications relied on various permutations of matrix multiplication—the same math used to solve complex scientific problems.

Nvidia's director of business development for the life-sciences industry, Mark Berger, was responsible for expanding the use of GPUs in chemistry, biology, and materials science. He followed much the same playbook that Oliver Baltuch had used when trying to raise Nvidia's profile among its prospective partners in the tech industry, as we saw in chapter 6.

First, he gave away GPUs to researchers and informed them about Nvidia's substantial investments in creating basic software libraries and tools for CUDA. Although the company might not have been familiar with the esoteric computational problems scientific users might perform, it recognized that those users would rather spend their time designing experiments than building the foundational math libraries they all needed. As a result, the developer tools Berger provided alongside the cards themselves made adoption of CUDA much faster—and helped him establish strong relationships with scientists.

"I got to be Santa Claus and send a ton of GPU boards out to all my developers, and everybody loves Santa Claus," he said.[11]

Second, he started conducting annual two-day technology summits where Nvidia employees could interact with and learn from scientists themselves. Dozens of researchers from the life-sciences industry—chemical engineers, biologists, pharmacologists, as well as the software developers who supported their work—arrived in Santa Clara from across the United States but also from Europe, Japan, and Mexico. On the first day, Nvidia's engineers would tell them about future improvements to CUDA, including software and hardware advances. The scientists and developers would then give their feedback.

"Our engineers aren't clairvoyant," Berger said. "They don't know where the hockey puck is going to be. At one point, I had well over a dozen features that were in CUDA or the hardware because of the input my developers gave."

The scientists and researchers appreciated Nvidia's transparency and willingness to listen, in turn. "They saw us as resources," said Ross

Walker, a biochemistry professor at the University of California, San Diego. "We could go tell them, 'we need this feature,' and they would change the design of the chip or add it to CUDA. There was no way on Earth Intel would have ever done anything like that."

Jensen himself loved attending the summits and sitting down with real-world users of CUDA to get their insights. During one of the first annual meetings, he gave a keynote speech in which he recalled his early days in the industry. When he started in chip design, he had to design the silicon, get it back from the factory, and put it under a microscope to see where the defects were. "He had a real affinity to my guys . . . who were simulating what was going to happen on a molecular level," Berger said.

Jensen then pivoted to explain how simulations had changed the chip industry. He was among the first generation of engineers who were able to do a large amount of virtual debugging of chips before they went out to be manufactured. This was, he argued, the same revolution that CUDA promised to bring to the sciences. Instead of the expensive and manual process of designing and testing new drugs by hand in the lab, they could do it virtually with software. CUDA-powered GPUs could make their research cheaper, faster, and far less prone to human error.

It was new territory for Nvidia. Since his very first meeting with Curtis Priem and Chris Malachowsky at the Denny's in East San Jose, Jensen had always focused on the importance of clearly defining market opportunities and developing new business strategies. Even in 1993, he had to convince himself there was a $50 million annual revenue opportunity in PC graphics if he was going to leave behind steady employment and cofound Nvidia. To survive after the failure of the NV1 and NV2, he had to recalibrate Nvidia's strategy to go after the very top of the market. Here again, the opportunity was clear: although PC graphics was a crowded field, almost no one made truly excellent chips; that would be Nvidia's niche. To avoid the endless cycle of corporate obsolescence, where the top-selling company one year was often leapfrogged in the next year, he had to push his teams to ship three chips per design cycle, instead of just one. And to diversify the company's lines of revenue, so that weak demand in one area would not doom the entire business, he aggressively pushed into new market segments: into console graphics, even when Microsoft originally signed another graphics-chip partner for its Xbox; into Apple's Macintosh series, despite the fact that Nvidia had little experience with the Mac architecture; and even into the professional workstations that it had originally shunned, with its Quadro line that was optimized for computer-aided design.

Now, however, Jensen had overseen the invention of an entirely new computing technology in the GPU and had to build a market for it from scratch. He realized that the opportunity could be astronomically huge—that it could unlock so much potential not in gaming but in business, science, and medicine. To realize that potential and make his market, he would have to develop an entirely new skill set—and teach the company, his investors, and himself the value of patience and persistence in an industry that always expected the next great thing on a very short timeline.

PROFESSOR ROSS WALKER CREATED one of the new-use cases for GPUs in the form of a biotechnology program called Assisted Model Building with Energy Refinement, or AMBER. The program simulates proteins in biological systems and has become one of the most popular applications used by academics and pharmaceutical companies to research new drugs. It was originally designed for high-powered computers, and therefore its reach was limited to only the best-funded research groups in the world. But Walker saw that it could run on little more than a few consumer-grade GPUs working in concert. This has made it one of the most-used tools in the biosciences. The software has more than one thousand university and commercial licenses and is credited in more than fifteen hundred academic publications per year. And it owes its success to its compatibility with Nvidia's CUDA architecture.

Walker received an undergraduate degree in chemistry and a PhD in computational chemistry at Imperial College London. He then worked at the Scripps Research Institute in San Diego as a postdoctoral fellow and as a research scientist investigating computational simulation software focused on enzyme reactions. At a bar one night, he met some employees of the San Diego Supercomputer Center and introduced himself.

"We know you," they said. "Your name is written on our white-board as the person who uses all our computing power."

Walker was offered the lead position in biosciences at the center, which was based at the University of California, San Diego. He accepted. Yet even though he continued his work on AMBER and was appointed a professor, he grew increasingly disillusioned with the academic process—especially when it came to the allocation of precious computing resources.

He sat on a committee that reviewed proposals and awarded time on the center's computers to the winning research teams. At any given session, there were typically fifty proposals to read, and most of the members of the committee would spend only a few minutes discussing each one. It was demoralizing. "I know people spend three months of their lives, their blood, sweat, and tears writing these, and we're spending five minutes deciding their fate," he said. Most proposals were rejected: funding rates hovered in the low single digits.

Even worse, computing capacity on the supercomputers tended to go toward those people and groups who were already successful. Famous scientists such as Klaus Schulten, who developed computer models that could simulate protein and virus structures down to the atomic level, and Greg Voth, who developed "multiscale theory" algorithms that could simulate the behavior of complex biomolecular systems, were given precedence, as Walker saw things.

"But the reason they could do the famous papers was because they were getting the time on supercomputers," Walker said. "Other people who had great ideas never got the time and couldn't make their impact. It wasn't how good your science was, but it was whether you could get access to computing time." It was a catch-22: the only way to get supercomputing resources was to already have gotten supercomputing resources.

Walker remembers once rejecting an application from Schulten to get emergency priority time on the supercomputer to work on molecular dynamics simulations of the H1N1 virus, popularly known as "swine flu," during the 2009 outbreak. He knew any exploratory research would take years to lead to a drug and thus wouldn't change the outcome of the pandemic. But Walker's decision was overruled, and he believed it was because Schulten was able to pull some political strings.

To Walker, it was just another example of how limited resources, along with the politics and bureaucracy of the academic world, had created a bottleneck that restricted progress for the entire field. He was dispirited; he wanted computing power to be available on merit, but there was no way to change the prevailing dynamic, with everything running through a small number of extremely powerful, but extremely expensive, supercomputers. He saw the need for a new kind of technology that could make computing power more accessible. "That was my driving force," Walker said.

He initially looked into commissioning custom-designed application-specific integrated circuits, also known as ASICs, that were optimized specifically for AMBER. But though less expensive than supercomputers, they still cost tens of thousands of dollars apiece—and researchers would have to spend even more to build special computers around them. Even if he could find a designer and fabricator, most researchers could not afford to buy the chips. Those who could probably had easy access to a supercomputer anyway.

Walker next examined gaming consoles and decided his best candidate was the Sony PlayStation series. But he ran into a wall here, too. Although PlayStations were cheap enough, Sony made it difficult to hack into the console's firmware and software. There was no way for Walker to use them for nongaming purposes.

Still, thinking about the PlayStation gave him an idea. Even though he never could successfully hack the console, his investigation into its graphics capabilities convinced him that retail-grade graphics chips were powerful enough to run AMBER. All he needed was an open platform that he could actually program. Then he realized the workstations inside his lab—the ones that his colleagues used to create 3-D visualizations—all had high-end GPUs comparable to the ones in the PlayStation. Although the workstations cost tens of thousands of dollars each, they were a step closer to the consumer-grade hardware that he wanted AMBER to run on. Maybe they could work as a proof of concept.

He first experimented with using the Brook programming language created by Ian Buck. He ran his first tests on graphics cards made for the Radeon series by AMD, Nvidia's primary competitor. But these cards had immature software and were not easily programmable. He then started talking to Nvidia about using their CUDA architecture to run his molecular dynamics models.

It was a perfect match. Walker found CUDA a much easier programming environment to work with, while Nvidia saw an opportunity to extend its reach into the scientific computing world. The company gave Walker technical resources to help redesign AMBER so that it could not only work on CUDA but also use its computing capabilities to the fullest. "We made the decision from day one to move everything onto the GPU, so the CPU would become irrelevant," Walker said.

In 2009, Walker released the first GPU-enabled version of AMBER. It ran up to fifty times faster than the previous version.

Walker had broken the grip of the academic bureaucrats and realized his dream of democratizing computing power. CUDA made it possible for scientists to carry out important experiments on affordable hardware instead of relying on the expensive and scarce supercomputing resources of a few elite universities. For the first time, the tens of thousands of postdoc graduates who used AMBER could do substantial science-computation experiments on their own hardware, at their own pace, and without having to compete with the luminaries of their fields—a competition that they would inevitably lose. Students could outfit a PC with a few Nvidia gaming GeForce cards and have an enormously powerful machine at a reasonable price. "You could buy a $100 CPU and four $500 GeForce cards and have a workstation that was as powerful as a full rack of servers. It was a game changer."

In its 2010 annual report, Nvidia mentioned the success of AMBER at the very top of its discussion of "high-performance computing" products. It appeared above other major announcements, including of its partnerships with Hewlett-Packard, of the launch of a new GPU-powered "seismic software suite" for oil prospecting, and of the use of GPUs by "the investment banking division of a leading European financial institution." To further cement the relationship between Walker and Nvidia, the company appointed him in November 2010 to the CUDA Fellows program, which recognized research and academic leaders for their "exceptional work" in using CUDA within their disciplines and raising awareness of the platform. Just as Jensen had predicted, GPUs were making advanced computing far more accessible and cheaper, which in turn made a program such as AMBER far more accessible. And the widespread adoption of AMBER transformed how the entire field of molecular dynamics conducted research.

THERE WAS ONE ISSUE where Walker and Nvidia diverged, however. Walker was used to dealing with academic institutions, whose main priority was advancing scientific knowledge. Nvidia was a business, with revenue targets to hit and investors to please. And the company's executives had not expected Walker to get AMBER to work so cheaply. Nvidia's high-performance computing division started to recommend that scientists use the company's higher-end Tesla general-purpose graphics cards, which retailed for about $2,000—four times more than the GeForce cards that Walker tended to use. The company claimed that it based this recommendation on the GeForce line's lack of error-correction features, which could leave AMBER outputs vulnerable to the accumulation of small but harmful mathematical errors. The self-detection and self-correction features on the Tesla line were not available on the less expensive GeForce cards.

Walker disagreed. He ran a series of tests that proved the GeForce line's lack of error correction did not result in any issues with AMBER's output. He then set out to prove pretty much the opposite: that the error-correction features on the Tesla line were superfluous, at least for AMBER. He arranged for some of his contacts who worked at the Los Alamos National Lab—one of the Department of Energy's foremost research facilities and where the atomic bomb was developed—to run the same tests with Tesla cards, just to see how many errors the cards actually needed to correct. There was no difference between the performance of the cheaper GeForce cards and the more expensive Tesla cards. Clearly, as he saw it, Nvidia was treating AMBER as an opportunity to up-sell cards as much as an opportunity to advance molecular-simulation technology.

"Nvidia's argument was you can't trust the results. I have the data to prove you can," Walker said. "We ran these simulations for two weeks and did not see a single ECC error. This is like the worst environment, top of the mountain, next to a nuclear lab. Radiation is as high as you can get within the U.S. Still, no errors."

The conflict between Walker and Nvidia escalated. First, Nvidia changed the level of math precision in its gaming cards, which had an imperceptible effect on PC games—but a potentially catastrophic one for research tools that relied on the cards to do advanced calculations. In response, Walker and AMBER developers figured out a way to work around the precision change, so that they could continue to run their simulations on GeForce without any accuracy issues. Then Nvidia began to enforce purchase controls for GeForce cards on its suppliers, making it difficult for people like Walker to buy large quantities of them in a single order. Walker criticized this move on the global mailing list for AMBER users, calling it "a very worrying trend that could hurt us all and have serious repercussions on all of our scientific productivities and the field in general."

He became increasingly frustrated with Nvidia's attempt to wring more money out of him, when he had done so much to make CUDA more than just a niche product for well-resourced developers and academics. The architecture wouldn't have been as successful if Nvidia had restricted its use to cards that cost thousands of dollars; it would have been almost as expensive to use CUDA as it would have been to design a custom ASIC.

"A key to Nvidia's success was allowing CUDA to run on GeForce cards, making it so that poor scientists could do work equivalent to those with multimillion-dollar computers," he told me, years later. "Once it reached a critical mass, they slowly tightened the thumbscrews on GeForce and made it harder to do."

Walker later joined GlaxoSmithKline, the pharmaceutical and biotechnology company, as head of scientific computing. The first thing he did was build a data center cluster by using thousands of GeForce gaming cards that cost only about $800 apiece.

This caught the attention of Nvidia's vice president of health care, Kimberly Powell, who called Walker and said, "You're at GSK now. You need to be buying our enterprise products."

"No," countered Walker. "I should be doing what's best for my employer. That's my job."

JENSEN MADE NO APOLOGIES for Nvidia's aggressive approach to chip sales. In fact, he insisted that salespeople take the same stance with all clients, regardless of size.

Derik Moore was known as one of the best salespeople in the industry when Nvidia poached him from ATI. He remembered getting a call from an Nvidia executive who told him, "You have been kicking my ass for over a year, so we're actually wondering if you would like to come to work for Nvidia?"[12]

Moore managed enterprise sales to large computer companies such as Hewlett-Packard, which bought large quantities of GPUs for its PCs and laptop lines. Nvidia wanted him to bring his book of business with him—and it was willing to pay generously for it. At ATI, he made about $125,000 per year, which in 2004 was well above the mean salary for a sales rep. During the recruitment process, Nvidia offered him almost double that.

He soon learned why. While still working at ATI, he once drove past Nvidia headquarters around 7:00 p.m. and saw that the office was almost entirely full. His manager, who was riding with him, remarked, "Oh, they must be having an evening meeting."

Now that he was on the inside, he realized that "evening meetings" were the norm rather than the exception. He started to regularly work on weekends, something he never did at ATI. He recalls being forced to take part in a conference call on Christmas Eve to discuss a sales shortfall and what the company could do to recover the business. No personal time or day was truly his own. Still, he saw that the commitment expected of him was expected of everyone else, too, all the way up to Jensen, which made the sacrifice easier. "There was a sense of dedication and hard work that resonated through the organization," he said. "The work ethic was contagious."

Hard work was not always enough to shield him from Jensen's critiques. Within a few years of arriving at Nvidia, Moore's work with HP's server division had increased annual sales to HP from $16 million to $250 million. One day, two senior executives from HP's server group came to Nvidia's headquarters. Because they were high ranking, Jensen asked whether he could join the meeting. Moore was delighted to have him there.

The server business was higher stakes than general enterprise sales, as the cards that Nvidia sold for such purposes were often used for mission-critical enterprise applications and thus needed to be more reliable. The customers were also more litigious. The HP executives asked whether Nvidia would give HP unlimited indemnification against lawsuits if something went wrong—basically asking Nvidia to assume all the legal risk if faulty GPUs caused a failure of HP's servers. This was a surprise to Moore, who didn't know the HP executives would start a legal negotiation. He was glad to have Jensen present at the meeting to reply to the unexpected question.

Jensen pointed out the problem with unlimited liability. The graphics chip is a small part of the server, so Nvidia could not indemnify the full value of the server. Doing so would entail a massive and unreasonable financial risk. Instead, he proposed that Nvidia tie indemnity to something more concrete: the amount of annual business the server group did with his company. If HP spent $10 million per year on cards, Nvidia would indemnify them for up to $10 million in the event of component failures. The protection would grow as the business grew. The HP executives accepted the deal on the spot, and Moore walked out of the meeting pleased with the outcome.

Afterward, he went to Jensen. "Thank you for coming to the meeting. I really appreciated it," Moore said.

Jensen, however, saw the meeting differently. "It ended well, but Derik, let me tell you your failure here."

The remark shocked Moore. "It scared the crap out of me," he recalled.

"The failure here was you did not tell us what the company was going to ask in advance," Jensen said. "Nobody likes surprises. Don't *ever* let that happen again."

Jensen referred to his sellers as Nvidia's Green Berets. He needed them to be self-sufficient and aggressive. Moore had failed to match Jensen's expectation for the role—that each seller become the "CEO of your accounts." When they met with their customers, they needed to know more about those customers' businesses than the customers themselves do. They had to anticipate how much customers were willing to pay for Nvidia's superior products. Jensen, for his part, would provide them with whatever resources were necessary: the "reinforcements" behind the elite vanguard.

One such group of "reinforcements" was Nvidia's developer-technology engineers, who acted as consultants and implementation experts for Nvidia products. They would sometimes visit customers to fix problems that came up or figure out how to get a particular program to work better on Nvidia GPUs. These engineers would ensure that as many partners as possible knew how to utilize Nvidia's cards for maximum effect.

All this came at a premium for customers. The company never discounted its chips, not even to match its competitors' pricing, unless it got something in return—a sticker on a partner's computer, a logo on a boot-up splash screen.

"We don't sell on cost. We don't believe our products are commodities," Moore's sales leader told him. "We believe that we bring exceptional value to the customer, and we extract value for our brand."

JENSEN DOESN'T LIKE DESCRIBING the strategy around CUDA as the building of a "moat." He prefers to focus on Nvidia's customers; he talks about how the company has worked to create a strong, self-reinforcing "network" that helps CUDA users. Indeed, CUDA is an incredible success story. Today, there are more than 5 million CUDA developers, 600 AI models, 300 software libraries, and more than 3,700 CUDA GPU-accelerated applications. There are about 500 million CUDA-capable Nvidia GPUs in the market. The platform is also backwards compatible, meaning developers can be confident that any investment in writing software will be usable on future chips. "All the invention of technologies that you build on top of Nvidia accrue," Jensen said. "If you were early there and you were mindful about helping the ecosystem succeed with you, you end up having this network of networks and all these developers and all these customers who built around you."[13]

Nvidia invested heavily in deep learning from the outset, dedicating substantial resources to creating CUDA-enabled frameworks and tools. This proactive approach paid off when artificial intelligence exploded in the early 2020s, because Nvidia was already the preferred choice of AI developers everywhere. Developers want to build AI applications as quickly as possible with minimal technical risk, and Nvidia's platform is far more likely to have fewer technical problems, because the user community has already, over more than a decade, fixed bugs or figured out optimizations. Other AI chip vendors never really had a chance.

"If you have AI applications built on top of CUDA and Nvidia GPUs, it's a huge undertaking to move over to Cerebras, AMD, or whatever," said Leo Tam, head of engineering at Amicus.ai and a former research scientist at Nvidia. "There's more than just putting your programs onto different chips. It's not simple. As a user, I can tell you they never work perfectly. It's not worth it. I'm working on 99 problems for my start-up already. I don't need another problem."

Nvidia had seen the opportunity early on and had seized it. Amir Salek, former Nvidia director of hardware engineering, noted that Nvidia was very quick to integrate important AI software libraries into CUDA, so that developers could easily use the latest innovations in the field without wasting time building or integrating their own software tools.

"If you wanted to write a new AI model or algorithm, CUDA gave you access to library components that are highly optimized and ready to use as opposed to you going all the way down to the nitty gritty details of like moving bits from here to here," Salek said.[14]

For these reasons, and others, it is hard to describe Nvidia's action as anything other than the construction of a competitive moat. Nvidia made a general-purpose GPU that represented the first major leap forward in computational acceleration since the invention of the CPU. The GPU's programmable layer, CUDA, was not only easy to use but also opened up a wide range of functions across scientific, technical, and industrial sectors. As more people learned CUDA, the demand for GPUs increased. By the early 2010s, the market for general-purpose GPUs that had once looked moribund appeared to be on the ascent.

Jensen's strategic brilliance ensured that competitors would have difficulty breaking into a market that Nvidia had created and which was effectively based on its proprietary hardware and software.

Nvidia's current position—among chip designers and in the national and global economies—seems unassailable. As Amir Salek put it: "The moat *is* CUDA."

CHAPTER 9

Tortured into Greatness

THE COMPANY THAT CREATED CUDA AND OPENED THE WAY
to the era of general-purpose computing on GPUs had much in common
with the company founded in a Denny's booth in 1993. It still prized
technical skill and maximum effort above all else. It still made strategic
decisions for the long term rather than try to juice its stock price over
the short term. It still operated with the necessary paranoia of a leading business in a volatile industry, always trying to correct course before
it started down the slope toward irrelevance and obsolescence. And its
CEO still managed the company directly, involving himself deeply in
product decisions, sales negotiations, investor relations, and more.

What had changed, however, was Jensen's relationship with his
employees. Nvidia in 2010 was no longer the start-up with a few dozen
people on the payroll, where he could get as much face time as he wanted
with each one of them, regardless of their level or their job function.
Now, it had 5,700 employees, and although many of them worked at the
headquarters in Santa Clara, it had satellite offices across North America, Europe, and Asia.[1] Jensen had learned that corporate culture tended
to atrophy as more people from more locations joined the company, and
an atrophying culture could hurt product quality—as the company had
learned with the "leaf blower" fan on the NV30-based GeForce FX

5800 Ultra. He had always tried to give direct feedback to his employees as much as possible when the company was small, in order to consistently reinforce his principles and ensure everyone had a clear idea what was expected of them. But in the new, larger Nvidia, he found that it was difficult to reach all the employees on a consistent basis.

Jensen decided to offer Nvidia employees more direct criticism in larger meetings, so that more people could learn from a single mistake.

"I do it right there. I give you feedback in front of everybody," he said. "Feedback is learning. For what reason are you the only person who should learn this? You created the conditions because of some mistake you made or silliness that you brought upon yourself. We should all learn from that opportunity."

Jensen displayed his trademark directness and impatience in all settings. He would often chew people out for fifteen minutes straight, regardless of the venue. "He does it all the time. It's not even at company[-wide] meetings. It's during smaller meetings or alignment meetings," a former Nvidia executive said. "He can't let it go. He just has to make it punitive a little bit."

One well-known example occurred when Nvidia was making one of its first plays in the mobile phone and tablet market, with the Tegra 3 chip. At a company all-hands meeting in 2011, Jensen asked the cameraman to repeatedly zoom in on the project manager of Tegra 3, a man named Mike Rayfield, as Jensen gave him feedback. While everyone in the audience got a good look at Rayfield's face, Jensen launched into him.

"Mike," he said, "you need to get Tegra done. You got to tape Tegra out. Guys, this is an example of how not to run a business."

"It was the most embarrassing, humiliating thing I've ever seen," another former Nvidia employee said. When asked about the incident, Rayfield later said in an e-mail, "That was not the only ass kicking I got [from Jensen]," with a smiley face at the end of his comment. Less than a year after the Tegra chip came out—nearly eight months behind schedule—he left Nvidia. He wasn't pushed out; he resigned voluntarily.

Jensen's at-times harsh approach was a deliberate choice. He knew that people would inevitably fail, especially in a high-pressure industry. He wanted to offer employees more opportunities to prove themselves, believing that they, in every case, are often just one or two epiphanies away from solving their problems themselves.

"I don't like giving up on people," he said. "I'd rather torture them into greatness."

The method is not intended as a means to show off how much smarter he is than his employees. Instead, he sees it as a guard against complacency. Jensen's time, and the time of his employees, is best spent trying to solve the next problem. Praise is a distraction. And the deadliest sin of all is looking back at your past accomplishments as if they will protect you from future threats.

Former sales and marketing executive Dan Vivoli remembers receiving a phone call from Jensen when he was driving to the office a day after Nvidia put on a marketing event for the GeForce 256. Vivoli was proud of the work his team had done.

"How'd the launch go?" Jensen said. Vivoli went on for five minutes about every part of the event he believed was a success. "Uh-huh, uh-huh, uh-huh," Jensen said. Vivoli stopped talking and Jensen asked, "What could you have done better?"

"That's all he said. There was no 'attaboy.' There was no 'great job.' There was none of that. It doesn't matter how well you think you did," Vivoli said. "It's okay to be proud, but the most important thing is trying to improve."[2]

Jensen does not appear to be any less reproachful toward himself. A sales executive named Anthony Medeiros recalled one meeting where Jensen revealed a habit, if not an active practice, of self-criticism.

"I'll never forget this. We had done fantastic. We just blew the doors off the quarter. Then, during our quarterly review meeting, Jensen stood up in front of us."[3]

The first words out of Jensen's mouth were, "I look in the mirror every morning and say, 'you suck.'"

Medeiros was struck by how someone so manifestly successful could still think in such terms. But it was, for better or for worse, the same approach that Jensen wanted everyone else at Nvidia to take toward themselves and their own work. Do your job. Don't be too proud of the past. Focus on the future.

JENSEN'S PREFERENCE FOR THE DIRECT approach also shaped Nvidia's corporate structure as the company grew. Early on, Nvidia nearly drove itself out of business because of a lack of internal alignment. The strategy for a chip did not match what the market wanted, as with the NV1. Or an excellent chip was hamstrung by poor execution on the manufacturing side, as with the RIVA 128. Or a dispute with a key partner created a cascade of technical problems that eventually doomed an entire chip line—the story of the NV30. In all three cases, Jensen placed the failure not on external factors but squarely on Nvidia and its inability to get out of its own way. "When we were a small company," he said, "we were plenty bureaucratic and plenty political."[4]

Over time, Jensen thought about how he would create an ideal organization from scratch. He realized he would choose a much flatter structure, so that employees could act with more independence. He also saw that a flat structure would weed out lower performers who were unaccustomed to thinking for themselves and to acting without being told what to do. "I wanted to create a company that naturally attracts amazing people," he said.[5]

Jensen believed that the traditional corporate pyramid, with an executive suite at the top, multiple layers of middle management in the middle, and a foundation of line workers at the bottom, was antithetical to fostering excellence. Instead of a pyramid, he would remake Nvidia into something that looked more like a computer stack, or a short cylinder.

"The first layer is the senior people. You would think that they need the least amount of management," Jensen said. "They know what they're doing. They're experts in their field." He did not want to spend time on career coaching—because the majority of them had already reached the pinnacle of their careers. As a result, he rarely held one-on-one meetings with his direct reports, at least when it came to such open-ended topics. Instead, he focused on providing them collectively with information from across the organization, as well as with his own strategic guidance. This would ensure that every part of the business was aligned and allow Jensen to manage more executives in a manner that actually added value.

Nvidia's current structure stands in contrast to that of most American companies, whose CEOs have only a handful of direct reports. In the 2010s, Jensen had forty executives on his leadership team, or the "e-staff," each reporting to him. Today the number is more than sixty.[6] He has steadfastly refused to change his management philosophy, even when, for example, new board members joined Nvidia and recommended that he hire a chief operating officer to reduce his administrative burden.

"No, thanks," he would always reply. "This is a great way to make sure everybody knows what's going on," he would add, referring to his direct communication with much of the rest of the company.[7]

The large number of executives in e-staff meetings has fostered a culture of transparency and knowledge sharing. Because there aren't many levels between the e-staff and the most junior person at the company, everyone in the organization can provide assistance on problems and prepare in advance for potential issues.

Oliver Baltuch, a former marketing executive, was impressed by how responsive his Nvidia colleagues were compared with those at his prior jobs. "The biggest difference was you only had to ask somebody once to get something done. It just got done," he said. "You never had to ask a second time."[8]

Andy Keane, a former general manager of Nvidia's data-center business, remembered Jensen explaining the traditional structure of the company's main competitors on a whiteboard, a structure he dubbed "the upside-down V's." This was how most companies were built. "You become a manager and you build your upside-down V. You defend it. Then you become a vice president and you get more upside-down V's of people under you," Jensen said.

Keane said that at other companies, talking to executives one or two levels above your direct manager was frowned upon. "Nobody likes it. It's just insane, right?" he said. "Nvidia was never like that." Keane himself talked to his direct manager once or twice a month but talked with Jensen two to three times a week. "Jensen created a company that he could manage directly," he said. "There is a vast culture difference between Nvidia and other companies."[9]

Keane was also surprised by the sheer openness he found at Nvidia.

He joined at the general-manager level and was allowed to attend every board meeting and off-site board event. When a typical CEO would have eight or nine people in a room for big executive meetings, Jensen would have a packed house. "Everyone could hear what he was telling the executive staff," Keane said. "It kept everybody in sync."

When there is important information to share or an impending change in the direction of the business, Jensen says he tells everybody at Nvidia at the same time and asks for feedback. "It turns out that by having a lot of direct reports, not having one-on-ones, [we] made the company flat, information travels quickly, employees are empowered," Jensen said. "That algorithm was well conceived."

MANY LARGE CORPORATIONS ARE DIVIDED into business units managed by competing executives. These units are locked into long-range strategic plans and must fight among themselves for resources. As a result, most organizations tend to move slowly. There is indecision. Big projects get stuck awaiting approvals from multiple stakeholders and hierarchies across the company. Any decision-maker can unilaterally slow things down by playing internal politics. When things go poorly, companies must shed workers to meet budgetary targets, even if those workers are top performers. All of this contributes to short-term thinking and the hoarding of information at the corporate level. Instead of shaping a company into a single, cohesive team, the usual corporate structure creates the kind of toxic environment that drives good people away.

As Jensen put it, "you want a company that's as large as necessary to do the job well, but to be as small as possible," and not bogged down by overmanagement and processes.

To get there, he decided that rather than rely on a permanent class of professional managers, whose only job was to be in charge of things, he would create a far more fluid system that would orient Nvidia around its business goals. And even as he took the long view, he would get rid of the practice of long-term strategic planning, which would force the company to stick to a particular path even if there were reasons to deviate from it.

"Strategy is not words. Strategy is action," he said. "We don't do a periodic planning system. The reason for that is because the world is a living, breathing thing. We just plan continuously. There's no five-year plan."

He began to tell his employees that their ultimate boss was the mission itself. The idea was to make decisions for the good of the customer, not to boost the career of the executive above them. "The concept of the mission is the boss makes a lot of sense because ultimately we're here to realize a particular mission, not in service of some organization," Jensen said.[10] "It got people thinking about the work and not the organization. The work, not the hierarchy."

Under the "mission is the boss" philosophy, Jensen would start every new project by designating a leader, or a "Pilot in Command" (PIC), who would report directly to Jensen. He found that this created far more accountability—and a far greater incentive to do a job well—than did the standard divisional structure.

"We always have a PIC for every project. Whenever Jensen talks about any project or any deliverables, he always wants the name. Nobody can hide behind, 'such and such a team is working on that,'" former finance executive Simona Jankowski said.[11] "Everything has to have a name attached to it because you have to know who's the PIC, who's accountable."

In exchange for that level of accountability, PICs were granted the weight of Jensen's authority and received priority support throughout the organization. After Jensen organized Nvidia's employees into groups centralized by function—sales, engineering, operations, and so on—they were treated as a general pool of talent and not divided by business units or divisions. This allowed the people with the right skills to be assigned to projects on an ad hoc basis. It also helped mitigate some of the ever-present job insecurity that plagues corporate America.

"Nvidia doesn't constantly fire people and rehire them," said Jay Puri, head of global field operations.[12] "We take people that we have and we are able to redirect them into a new mission." Managers at Nvidia were trained not to get territorial or feel like they "own" their people and instead got used to them moving around between task groups. This practice removed one of the main sources of friction at large companies.

"Managers don't feel like they get power by having large teams," Puri continued. "You get power at Nvidia by doing amazing work."

Jensen found that the changes made Nvidia much faster and much more efficient. Decisions could be made quickly, as employees were empowered to contribute to every decision, regardless of rank. Arguments were decided on the basis of quality of information, data, and merit—not on a leader's need to get promoted or earn a bonus, or that leader's ability to pressure others into going along with him or her.

Most of all, the flat structure freed Jensen to spend his precious time explaining the reasoning behind his decisions at meetings instead of adjudicating turf wars. Not only did he see flatness as key to Nvidia's strategic alignment, keeping everyone focused on the mission; he also saw it as an opportunity to develop his junior employees by showing them how a senior leader should think through a problem. "Let me reason through this. Let me explain why I did that," Jensen said. "How do we compare and contrast these ideas? That process of management is really empowering."

Of course, employees' constant exposure to Jensen and his decision-making process included his public dressings-down of executives and PICs. He justified those potentially painful moments as an efficiency gain for the company: offering private one-on-one feedback behind closed doors would slow him and the company down by requiring the scheduling of separate meetings, but it also deprived junior employees of a learning opportunity.

"I don't take people aside," he said. "We're not optimizing for not embarrassing somebody. We're optimizing for the company learning from our mistakes. If a leader can't handle the slight embarrassment, they can come talk to me. But it's never happened."[13]

NOT EVERYTHING CAN BE COMMUNICATED in meetings. With such a large and distributed organization, Jensen needed to somehow keep tabs on what was going on inside Nvidia in order to make sure everyone had the right priorities. At other companies, an executive would rely on a formal status update from those under him or her. But Nvidia management believed that formal status reports tended to consist of information that had been sanitized so thoroughly that it was useless. Anything smacking of controversy—current problems, expected roadblocks, personnel issues—would be removed in favor of presenting a cheerful picture of harmony to those in charge.

So Jensen asked employees at every level of the organization to send an e-mail to their immediate team and to executives that detailed the top five things they were working on and what they had recently observed in their markets, including customer pain points, competitor activities, technology developments, and the potential for project delays. "The ideal top five e-mail is five bullet points where the first word is an action word. It has to be something like finalize, build, or secure," said early employee Robert Csongor.[14]

To make it easier for himself to filter these e-mails, Jensen had each department tag them by topic in the subject line: cloud service provider, OEM, health care, or retail. That way, if he wanted to get all of his recent e-mails on, say, hyperscaler accounts, he could easily find them through a keyword search.

The "Top 5" e-mails became a crucial feedback channel for Jensen. They enabled him to get ahead of changes in the market that were obvious to junior employees but not yet to him or his e-staff. "I'm looking to detect the weak signals," he would tell his employees when asked why he liked the Top 5 process. "It's easy to pick up the strong signals, but I want to intercept them when they are weak." To his e-staff, he was a little more pointed.

"Don't take this the wrong way, but you may not have the brainpower or the wherewithal to detect something I think is pretty significant."[15]

Every day, he would read about a hundred Top 5 e-mails to get a snapshot of what was happening within the company. On Sundays, he would dedicate an even longer session to Top 5's, usually accompanied by a glass of his favorite single-malt Highland Park scotch whiskey. It was the thing he did for fun: "I drink a scotch, and I do e-mails."

Top 5 e-mails became a source of new market insights. When Jensen got interested in a new market, he used the e-mails to shape his strategic thinking in near real-time. For example, after reading several Top 5 e-mails from employees that discussed machine-learning trends, Jensen decided that the company wasn't moving fast enough to take advantage of that market. "I keep seeing this. I don't think we have enough invested in this technique called RAPIDS," former executive Michael Douglas recalls. Jensen promptly told his staff to add more software engineers to the development of a RAPIDS CUDA library, which became an important resource for accelerating data-science and machine-learning workloads on GPUs.

Driven by Jensen, Nvidia's e-mail culture was and remains unrelenting. "One thing I learned pretty quickly is if you got an e-mail from him, you acted on it," Douglas said.[16] "Nothing stays. Nothing festers. You answer and move on it," former head of human resources John McSorley said.[17] Jensen would often respond to e-mails within minutes of receiving them and wanted a response from an employee within twenty-four hours at most. The responses had to be thoughtful and backed by hard data. Those that fell short of his high standards would get a typically sarcastic response: "Oh, is that right?"

Because of Jensen's lightning-quick reactions, employees learned to time their Top 5 e-mails strategically. "You always have to be concerned if you send it on Friday night because Jensen will respond to you late Friday," a former employee said.[18] "It would wreck your weekend." As a result, most employees sent their Top 5 late on Sunday night, about the time that Jensen would be settling in at his home office with scotch in hand. They could then start working on his directives at the beginning of the work week.

Former life-sciences alliance manager Mark Berger unwittingly triggered all of Jensen's pet peeves around Top 5 e-mails when he sent one of his first ones, which attempted to forecast GPU sales in his market. Jensen thought Nvidia hadn't made sufficient progress in the life sciences and now perceived a lack of rigor in Berger's analysis. The chief executive asked him whether he had bothered to talk to research professor Ross Walker, who had built a lab of scientists at the San Diego Supercomputer Center at UC San Diego.

Berger admitted he hadn't consulted with Walker, believing that the academic would not know the specifics of how GPUs were used in research labs. Jensen unleashed a tirade and challenged Berger to figure out a way to gather more information.

The experience rattled Berger—and made him a better employee. "The one thing with Jensen is you don't bullshit him," he recalled years later. "You bullshit him and your credibility is dead. The appropriate answer is, 'I don't know, Jensen, but I'll find out.' "[19]

Sufficiently chastened, Berger got in touch with Walker right away. The two men designed a survey for other life-sciences academics who did work with GPUs. The survey took thirty minutes to complete, but Berger incentivized scientists to complete it by offering them an entry in a raffle for a gaming GPU. Berger and Walker received comprehensive responses from three hundred fifty scientists on what software they had installed, the size of their modeling projects, what features they wanted from Nvidia, and their backgrounds. It was a treasure trove of data, and when Berger presented it in a follow-up meeting, Jensen was finally satisfied that he had done his due diligence on his market.

JENSEN HAS ALWAYS BEEN TRYING to achieve the closest thing possible to the Vulcan mind meld from *Star Trek*—the complete fusion of his employees' minds with his own. As we saw in the Introduction, perhaps his favorite tool for showing the rest of the company his thought process is the whiteboard.

Jensen's preference for whiteboarding runs counter to the way that the rest of corporate America talks to itself—through PowerPoint presentations where a speaker goes through a series of slides presenting information that is usually accepted by the audience at face value. He has always hated how static such meetings are, with little opportunity to work together or discuss topics in depth.

At the whiteboard, Jensen will sketch out how to organize a particular market, how to accelerate growth of a particular product, and the software or hardware technical stacks involved in a particular case. His whiteboarding creates a specific kind of meeting, one dedicated to solving problems, not reviewing things that have already been done. "When Jensen gets into a meeting, he wants to prioritize what the important issues are, then starts with the top one and works toward solving that problem," said Jay Puri.[20]

Unlike Top 5 e-mails, whiteboarding has been a common practice at Nvidia from the start. The company designed its two current main headquarters buildings, Endeavor and Voyager, built in 2017 and 2022, respectively, to encourage collaboration. Each building has a fully open working space and wall-to-wall whiteboards in dozens of conference rooms. Employees at every level are expected to use those whiteboards as much as possible.

Every quarter, for example, Jensen convenes a meeting with a few hundred of Nvidia's leaders in a big conference room. Each general manager had to go up in front of the room and discuss his or her business. The general managers are expected to use the whiteboard to talk through their business story, explain what they do, and face challenges to their underlying assumptions. Jensen sits in the first row, next to some other senior executives, and asks detailed questions of the person at the whiteboard—questions that often required further whiteboarding.

"It wasn't really a business review, but something forward-looking," recalled Andy Keane. Jensen looked at quarterly results as the final scorecard of decisions made and implemented months or years ago. He wanted everyone to constantly reflect on how they could have made better decisions then, and how they would use those lessons to make better ones now and in the future—especially when it came to allocating resources and deciding on strategy. Even when the numbers were good, he wanted people to remain aggressive. "It was always about how to do better. There was this constant push, push, push," Keane said.

The whiteboarding process helped executives distill what was essential. They all started with an empty board; they had to forget the past and focus on what was important now. "Every meeting was all about the whiteboard," former Nvidia executive David Ragones said.[21] "It's a give and take. While you are whiteboarding, he'd jump up to another whiteboard and write his thoughts there. He wanted to see your understanding and how you're thinking through the issues and then develop his own thinking."

At the conclusion of a meeting, Jensen would summarize the new ideas the group had developed on the whiteboard. That way, he could ensure that there would be no misunderstanding on direction or responsibilities.

His subordinates found that he expected them to be ready to white-board, even when they were traveling. Whenever Michael Douglas went on a business trip with Jensen, he would make sure there was a big white-board at each of their destinations—even if he had to arrange to rent or buy one on-location. "If five people are forced to carry that whiteboard in, that's the right size," Douglas said. "He needs all that whiteboard real estate."[22]

Besides good scotch, one of Jensen's few indulgences is his preferred brand of whiteboard marker. He insists on twelve-millimeter-wide, chisel-tip markers that are sold only in Taiwan. He wants employees sitting in the back to be able to see his writing and diagrams. Nvidia employees must keep a ready stock of these markers handy at all times.

Jensen is nonchalant about the prevalence of whiteboarding culture at Nvidia, almost as if it was a fallback option. "We have to use a white-board because I don't have a projector. I don't have a TV and I don't like slides, so we just talk and draw," he said with a shrug.[23]

But there is more to it than that suggests. Whiteboarding forces peo-ple to be both rigorous and transparent. It requires them to start from scratch every time they step up to the board, and therefore to lay out their thinking as thoroughly and clearly as possible. It becomes imme-diately apparent when someone hasn't thought something through or bases their logic on faulty assumptions, unlike with a slide deck, where you can hide incomplete thoughts in pretty formatting and misleading text. At the whiteboard, there is no place to hide. And when you finish, no matter how brilliant your thoughts are, you must always wipe them away and start anew.

NVIDIA BECAME A MATURE COMPANY not as a result of the size of its revenues, the refinement of its internal structure, or the collective brain power of its employees. Rather, it became mature when Jensen learned how to consistently turn the organization away from inter-nal political dysfunction and disorder. Through mechanisms such as direct public feedback, the Top 5 e-mail, and the requirement to present ideas on a whiteboard rather than as a static PowerPoint, Nvidia equips its workforce with powerful weapons in the constant struggle for accuracy and rigor and against groupthink and inertia. It is these operational principles that have allowed Nvidia to move quickly to take advantage of new opportunities.

If Nvidia had not evolved from its early, more conventional form, it would not have invented the GPU or designed CUDA; it probably wouldn't have survived into a second decade, even with Jensen in charge. But the organizational dynamic he eventually created—one that represents the exact opposite of the "best practices" in most of the rest of corporate America—has made it possible for the company to withstand, and thrive amid, the pressures of an eternally unforgiving market.

CHAPTER 10

The Engineer's Mind

EARLY IN MY WORKING LIFE, I SWITCHED CAREERS, LEAVING consulting to join a small technology fund as a stock analyst. I recall the first time I attended a major Wall Street investment conference, where I looked forward to the breakout Q&A sessions with CEOs that followed their main presentations. At a session with the late Gerald Levin, the CEO of the newly merged AOL Time Warner, I asked a basic, somewhat skeptical strategy question about how the conglomerate planned to use AOL's technology and platform. Levin's response stunned me. Instead of providing a cogent answer, he launched into a lecture on the power and capabilities of AOL Instant Messenger, speaking in such a jumble of buzzwords that I struggled to make sense of it.

As a technology enthusiast who had built several computers and spent considerable time on the then-nascent Internet, it was clear to me that Levin had little understanding of how AOL's products actually worked. I found myself wondering how a business executive with such limited technical knowledge could find himself running one of the largest media and technology companies in the world.

Yet as I learned soon enough, Levin was not an outlier. Activist investor Carl Icahn has a theory that much of corporate America mismanages the succession process in choosing new CEOs. He calls it anti-Darwinian—the very antithesis of the ruthless process of natural selection that allows only the best equipped of a species to survive and reproduce.[1]

Icahn observed that competent executives often get sidelined in favor of more likeable but less capable ones because of behavioral incentives inside companies. The personalities who ascend the corporate ranks resemble college fraternity presidents. They become friendly with the board of directors and are not threatening to the current CEO. They're not prodigies, but they're affable, always available for a drink when you are feeling down. As Icahn put it, these figures (they are mostly men) are "not the smartest, not the brightest, not the best, but likeable and sort of reliable."

CEOs want to survive. Naturally, then, they prefer not to oversee a direct subordinate who is brighter and could potentially replace them. They tend to opt for someone slightly less astute than they themselves are. But when the CEO eventually departs, the glad-handing executive who is now on good terms with the board of directors frequently gets elevated, perpetuating the "survival of the un-fittest" as the new CEO starts a similar cycle.

Over the past few decades, I've seen several examples of the congenial, nontechnical executive with a business background becoming the CEO of major technology companies. As with Gerald Levin and AOL Time Warner, the outcomes have been mediocre or worse.

Microsoft's Steve Ballmer is the classic example. Ballmer started his career as a marketing manager at Procter & Gamble, then began studies toward an MBA from Stanford before joining Microsoft in 1980. He was the first business manager hired by Bill Gates; he held positions in operations, sales, and upper management but had little hands-on experience with technology.

He had a poor reputation in the tech sector. Walt Mossberg, a former columnist for the *Wall Street Journal*, once recounted an interaction with Steve Jobs at Apple.[2] Mossberg was sitting down to interview Jobs when the Apple CEO asked him about his recent trip to Microsoft. Jobs seemed particularly interested to know whether Ballmer remained firmly in control of the software giant. When Mossberg confirmed that he was, Jobs paused, then pumped his arms and yelped, "Yes!" Moss-berg elaborated that while Jobs held Gates in high regard, he had little respect for Ballmer.

Jobs was right. Under Ballmer, Microsoft missed the shift to mobile computing and also made a series of terrible acquisitions, including aQuantive and Nokia. Microsoft's stock price fell more than 30 percent during Ballmer's fourteen years as CEO.

Apple had previously faced its own challenges under a chief executive with more of a business than technical background. Jobs was famously ousted by Apple's board of directors in 1985, who replaced him with John Sculley, a former marketing specialist at PepsiCo. Sculley met with some initial success, including with his strategy of selling incrementally better computers at higher and higher prices. He then made several misguided technology-product decisions, such as introducing the New-ton personal digital assistant and selecting PowerPC processors for the Mac in the early 1990s. The stagnation in technical innovation brought Apple to the brink of bankruptcy later in the decade.

While Ballmer and Sculley could sell different versions of Windows or expensive PowerBook laptops better than anyone, they couldn't pre-dict where technology was going next. Apple wasn't able to upgrade its operating system to modern standards until it acquired Jobs's NeXT Computer, whose technology became the foundation for Mac OS X.

Intel offers another example. Bob Swan joined the chip maker as its chief financial officer in 2016 and rose to the position of CEO two years later. Swan had a primarily financial background; he had previ-ously held CFO roles at eBay and Electronic Data Systems, the company founded by former IBM salesman H. Ross Perot. Under Swan's leader-ship, Intel suffered from repeated delays in moving to more advanced chip-manufacturing technologies and its next generations of processors, falling behind its main CPU competitor, Advanced Micro Devices. Worse, it seemed Swan was mainly focused on executing a substantial multibillion-dollar stock buyback program and issuing billions in div-idends to lift the company's stock price, which siphoned money away from R&D investments. Intel floundered so badly that it lost signifi-cant market share across its businesses and yielded pole position in the technology of CPUs to AMD, which was then led by Lisa Su, who, in contrast to Swan, had a strong engineering pedigree.

Swan also proved a poor manager and allocator of Intel's resources. Like Nvidia, in the late 2010s Intel invested heavily in AI. In 2016, the company acquired deep-learning start-up Nervana Systems for $408 million to develop AI chips. The next year, Intel hired Raja Koduri, the former head of AMD's graphics-chip unit, to lead its GPU efforts. As CEO, Swan further expanded Intel's AI portfolio by acquiring Israel-based Habana Labs for $2 billion in 2019. But Intel had no coherent strategy; it pursued multiple, independent, AI-related chip projects that divided both resources and attention.

This was largely the result of Swan's unfamiliarity with the technical aspects of the business he ran. He lacked the knowledge to make informed decisions about where the company should focus its time and to know who should really be in charge of making those decisions. Instead, he was too easily influenced by whoever could put together the best presentation—even if, according to one former Intel executive, that presentation had no basis in reality.

Under Swan, Intel made a string of poor product decisions. On the AI front, it shut down Nervana Systems, even though the start-up had a promising product that was nearly ready. Instead, the company restarted its AI efforts with Habana, effectively negating the prior several years of development time.

Nvidia's head of GPU engineering, Jonah Alben, commented on Intel's AI plans after the company acquired Habana. "Intel's AI strategy is like throwing darts. They don't know what to do but feel like they need to buy something, so they are buying everything," he said.[3]

In 2021, Swan resigned as Intel's CEO and was replaced by Pat Gelsinger, who came with an impressive background in engineering. One of his first decisions was to halt the stock buybacks.

NVIDIA WAS ABLE TO AVOID similar pitfalls because it had a technical CEO in Jensen. "When you meet Jensen Huang, even with dozens of other graphics companies, you realize this is a guy you want to do business with," said Tench Coxe, one of Nvidia's early investors, who continues to serve on its board today. "What made him great is he is an engineer and he is a computer scientist."[4]

Former product manager Ali Simnad recalled working on a Wi-Fi product that was never released, in part because of Jensen's intense diligence.

"Jensen was very scary," he said.[5] "You would go to a meeting and he would know more about the product than you do." During the product meeting, Jensen made clear that he understood all the technical details of the various Wi-Fi standards. The product wasn't crucial to Nvidia's strategy, but Jensen still made the time to master the technology and specifications. "He knew everything. In every meeting we attended, he was probably the most prepared person."

Jensen is known for being active on numerous internal Nvidia topical e-mail discussion groups to keep up with trends and expand his knowledge. On the "deep learning" list, where engineers discuss the latest technology developments in AI, Jensen has a habit of forwarding articles of interest. "You very much knew what Jensen was thinking about," former Nvidia senior research scientist Leo Tam said.[6]

Former marketing executive Kevin Krewell recalls meeting Jensen on the street outside the NeurIPS conference in Barcelona, Spain, in 2016. NeurIPS is an academic conference held in December, where machine-learning and neuroscience experts present their latest findings. It's not like a SIGGRAPH or GDC, which are known to portions of the general public—NeurIPS is more hardcore.

Krewell knew Jensen wasn't scheduled to speak and asked him what he was doing at the conference. Jensen replied, "I'm here to learn."[7]

Nvidia's CEO had not assigned someone to attend and take notes on his behalf. He had shown up himself so he could absorb the recent developments in artificial intelligence. He wanted to be deeply involved in the space, attending sessions and talking with presenters, students, and professors. Later on, he began hiring many of the people he met at the conference.

Jensen has said many times that he could not do his job effectively without in-depth familiarity with the technology itself. "It's essential we understand the underpinnings of the technology so you have an intuition for how the industry is going to change," he once remarked.[8] "Our ability to extrapolate and see down the road is really vital because technology is changing fast, but it still takes us several years to build a great solution." Only with domain expertise can he decide which projects to support, estimate how long they will take, and then allocate resources properly to generate the best long-term returns.[9]

There can be a downside to being so in the weeds: it can cause decision paralysis. A good leader must make decisions, even when lacking total precision. This was a lesson Jensen learned early on in an engineering class taught by Professor Donald Amort at Oregon State. In his lessons, Amort always used round numbers.

"I hated that," said Jensen. "We were working with exponents and numbers from the real world accurate to three decimal points."[10] Yet Amort rejected such precision if it slowed him down too much; he would round up 0.68 to 0.7, for example. He was teaching his students to not lose sight of the big picture. "It used to drive me crazy. But I learned over the years that false accuracy is pointless."

Jensen applied the round-number rule at Nvidia. His employees call it "CEO math," half-jokingly and half-affectionately. It allows him to do big-picture strategic thinking without getting bogged down. He can determine the size of a new market and its potential to drive profit for Nvidia quickly, and then spend more mental energy on the more complex and intuitive tasks of analyzing the competitive landscape and developing an entry strategy. As Tench Coxe noted, "It's easy to make a spreadsheet tell you whatever you want to see, but Jensen getting comfortable using CEO math was a great growth for him."[11]

Jensen's approach to math—direct, clipped, and oriented toward the big picture—is also how he communicates with Nvidia's employees more generally. Because everything at Nvidia is under his purview, he has to be efficient with his outbound messages. According to former sales executive Jeff Fisher, "His e-mails are short and sweet. Sometimes too short."[12]

"Like a haiku," agrees Bryan Catanzaro.[13]

The comparison is an apt one. The three-line Japanese poems can often be impenetrable or ambiguous—and it can be a challenge for new

Nvidia employees to get used to the brevity of Jensen's e-mail communications. Even veterans can often spend hours debating what a particular e-mail from the CEO means, and when they can't decide among themselves, they will check back with him to get clarification.

But that is, on one level, what he wants. Most senior leaders at Nvidia agree that Jensen relies on his people to exercise their good judgment on interpreting his directions. He doesn't want to control every decision; in fact, being overly prescriptive can stifle the very independence and bias toward action that he seeks to cultivate. Rather, he wants to make sure that they have done their diligence and considered all possible effects of their decisions. Catanzaro emphasized that Jensen's approach is not merely about his personal preferences.

"We're all busy," he says. "We all have way more e-mail than we can read. The message is you should have empathy for the people you're presenting your work [to]. Don't just dump everything on them. Give it to them in a way that piques their interest, so if they want to, they can ask for more details. Jensen is trying to help us be a more effective company and be careful how we use each other's attention. If you want to be impactful in a large organization, don't waste other people's time."

THE PUREST EXPRESSION OF Jensen's engineering background is his seemingly limitless capacity for work. In business, as he sees it, work ethic may well be more important than intelligence. "It doesn't matter how smart you are because there is always someone smarter than you," he said. And in a global world, "your competition doesn't go to sleep."[14]

Neither does Jensen. Although he has changed and matured as a leader—in, for instance, his strategic vision, his understanding of graphics and accelerated computing, and his ability to run an organization—the one constant in his three-decade tenure as CEO has been his commitment to long hours and maximum effort.

An operations executive claimed that Nvidia isn't a 24/7 company, but a 25/8 one. "I'm not kidding. I wake up at 4:30 a.m., and I'm on the phone until 10:00 p.m.," she said. "It's my choice. It's not for everybody."

Another product manager noted that many employees don't want to embrace the grind and end up leaving after a few years. He himself tended to arrive at the office before 9:00 a.m. and rarely left before 7:00 p.m. Once home, he had to log on from 10:00 p.m. to 11:30 p.m. every night to talk to partners in Taiwan. "On weekends, if you could not reply to an e-mail within two hours, you had to let the team know the reason why you wouldn't be able to respond," he said. When he reviewed his calendar, he discovered that he had been either traveling for work or at the office for almost half of his weekends over the past year.

Nvidia's extreme work culture stems from the chief executive himself, who lives and breathes his job and looks down on anyone who isn't as committed. "I don't actually know anybody who is incredibly successful who just approaches business like, 'This is just business. This is what I do from 8 to 5, and I'm going home, and at 5:01, I'm shutting it down,'" Jensen has said.[15] "I've never known anybody who is incredibly successful like that. You have to allow yourself to be obsessed with your work."

Employees dread whenever Jensen goes on a rare vacation because he tends to sit in his hotel and write more e-mails, giving them even more work than usual. During Nvidia's early days, Michael Hara and Dan Vivoli tried to stage an intervention. They called Jensen: "Dude, what are you doing? You are on vacation."

Jensen replied, "I'm sitting here on the balcony watching my kids playing in the sand and writing e-mails."

"Go out and play with your kids!" his subordinates insisted.

"No, no, no," Jensen refused. "This is when I can get a lot of work done."

When he goes to the movies, Jensen says he never remembers the film because he spends the entire time thinking about work. "I work every day. There's not a day that goes by I don't work. If I'm not working, I'm thinking about working," Jensen said. "Working is relaxing for me."[16]

He lacks sympathy for anyone who works less than he does, and he does not believe that he has missed out on anything in life by giving himself so completely to Nvidia. When *60 Minutes* interviewed Jensen in 2024 and asked about employees who said working for him was demanding, that he was a perfectionist and not easy to work for, he simply agreed.

"It should be like that. If you want to do extraordinary things, it shouldn't be easy."

In all my years covering business, as a consultant, an analyst, and now as a business writer, I have never met anyone quite like Jensen. In the field of graphics, he is a pioneer. In the harsh technology market, he is a survivor. And he has been a CEO for more than thirty years—making him, as of this writing, the fourth-longest currently-serving CEO in the S&P 500, after only Warren Buffett of Berkshire Hathaway, Stephen Schwarzman of Blackstone, and Leonard Schleifer of Regeneron. Within the tech sector, his tenure at Nvidia has been longer than Jeff Bezos's twenty-seven years at Amazon, Bill Gates's twenty-five years at Microsoft, and Steve Jobs's fourteen-year second term at Apple—and none of them are still in charge. He is closing in on the overall record in tech set by Larry Ellison, who cofounded Oracle and spent thirty-seven years as its CEO before stepping back to the CTO position in 2014.

What separates Jensen from almost all of his competitors is easy to understand yet hard to implement. He challenges the division of the executive world between those CEO-founders who are technically oriented but naïve in the world of business and those who are business-minded operators but who have no technical acumen. He shows it is possible that one person can serve both roles; in fact, in the highly technical semiconductor industry, his ambidextrousness may be a key to success. This is also why he has an almost symbiotic relationship with Nvidia. In many ways, he *is* Nvidia, and the company *is* Jensen, stretched to the proportions of a multinational corporation with tens of thousands of employees and billions of dollars in revenue.

Of course, this reality raises a question that most likely won't be answered for some time: What happens when he and the company part ways, as they inevitably will?

THE STAKES COULD NOT BE higher. Jensen always reminds Nvidia employees that the company is just one bad decision away from taking the road to obsolescence. The history of Intel, Nvidia's sometimes-partner and sometimes-rival, illustrates this risk all too clearly.

In 1981, IBM introduced the IBM PC, revolutionizing the world of computing. The computer manufacturer made two critical choices for the PC that would define the industry. The first was choosing an Intel 8088 chip as the PC's processor. The second was deciding on MS-DOS, from a small software start-up called Microsoft, as the PC's operating system. IBM made an important strategic error, though. At the time, the company was so confident in its size and distribution might that it didn't secure exclusivity on Intel's and Microsoft's offerings. Soon, "PC-compatible" clones with identical hardware but lower prices flooded the market. PC makers such as Dell and HP priced IBM out of the very product category it had created, and IBM sold its PC division to Lenovo in 2005.

But one consequence of IBM's error was the close association of Microsoft and Intel. For the past four decades, the two companies have dominated the computer industry. The business partnership was eventually dubbed "WinTel," a neologism combining Windows, the name of the operating system Microsoft would later develop, and Intel.

WinTel is an instance of what analysts call "lock-in." Corporations built more of their business processes around custom applications that ran on Microsoft Windows PCs and servers powered by Intel x86 processors. Once this happened, it was too difficult to switch to another operating or computing system, such as Apple's Mac ecosystem. Enterprises can't just take millions of lines of code written for Windows and put them on another chip architecture. Rewriting software dependent on specialized Windows libraries and utilities would have been an enormous task that CIOs deemed too complicated and not worth the technical risks.

However, the fortunes of Microsoft and Intel diverged as each one reacted to disruptive new technology. After Satya Nadella took over as CEO of Microsoft in 2014, the company pivoted and bet aggressively on the rise of cloud subscription software and cloud computing, earning itself a strong number-two position behind Amazon Web Services in the latter category.

Intel, by contrast, missed a pair of generational opportunities: the arrival of smartphone processors and the rise of AI software. In 2006, Steve Jobs asked Intel CEO Paul Otellini whether the chip maker

184 ■ NVIDIA RISING

would be willing to supply processors for the upcoming iPhone. In a fateful decision that would prevent Intel from participating in the future of the smartphone chip market, Otellini declined. "There was a chip that they were interested in, that they [Apple] wanted to pay a certain price for and not a nickel more, and that price was below our forecasted cost. I couldn't see it," he said in a 2013 interview with *The Atlantic*. "The world would have been a lot different if we'd done it."[17]

Also in 2006, Intel sold its XScale unit, which was developing power-efficient ARM-based processors for mobile devices, to Marvell Technology for $600 million. This left the company without important expertise just before the smartphone market came to be dominated by such processors. (Arm Holdings, which returned to public markets in 2023, licenses its power-efficient chip-architecture designs, well suited for mobile devices, to semiconductor companies and hardware makers, including Apple and Qualcomm.)

Compounding matters, Intel made a series of missteps in its core business. It was slow to purchase and introduce new chip-manufacturing equipment from the Netherlands-based company ASML, which uses the advanced chip-manufacturing technology called extreme ultraviolet (EUV) lithography, and it underinvested in production techniques that are based on EUV lithography. As a result, Intel fell behind TSMC in its ability to produce more advanced chips at high volume. In 2020, when Intel announced another round of delays in the transition to seven-nanometer manufacturing, many customers abandoned it for competitors such as Advanced Micro Devices, which designs semiconductors and pays TSMC to make them. And in the same year, Apple started to replace Intel as a Mac processor supplier with its internally designed chips that are based on the ARM-chip architecture that powers the iPhone and which are now used across its entire Mac lineup.

As for GPUs, current Intel CEO Pat Gelsinger laments that the company failed to break into the category with its own in-house product that would have competed with Nvidia's.

"I had a project called Larrabee that, when I was pushed out of Intel, got killed shortly thereafter," he said. "The world would be different today had that not occurred."[18]

Gelsinger had been an executive champion of the project and headed the enterprise-computing division at Intel before he left in 2009 for the data-storage company EMC. The Larrabee GPU was canceled in 2010, and Intel did not restart its GPU efforts until 2018.

While Intel made error after error, Nvidia was intensely focused on inaugurating the era of the GPU. Under Jensen's leadership, the company invested so much in CUDA that it became a foundational ecosystem for AI developers. Nvidia also made smart acquisitions, including the high-speed networking leader Mellanox, to fill out the company's data-center-computing product offering. Nvidia took these decisions in the face of demands from Wall Street to reduce costs and increase profits—exactly the kind of strategy that Intel adopted when it declined to pursue ARM architecture and GPUs. It was an instance of the innovator's dilemma: Intel, as the incumbent, failed to capitalize on new technology, allowing the more agile Nvidia to undercut its entire business model.

So far, every major computing era has seen technology favor the big players who can develop a market-leading platform—a "winner take most" dynamic. WinTel's dominance in PCs is a model for Nvidia's leadership in AI hardware and software. In an August 2023 report, Jefferies analyst Mark Lipacis estimated that WinTel generated an incredible 80 percent of the operating profit of the PC industry era.[19] With the rise of the internet, Google captured 90 percent of the search market.[20] And Apple has been able to generate nearly 80 percent of the profits of the smartphone industry era.

This history may suggest that most of the spoils of the AI era will accrue to Nvidia. The combination of CUDA and Nvidia's GPUs, which are the only chips that can run the platform, is comparable to the "lock-in" power Microsoft's Windows operating system and Intel's x86 processors achieved during the PC boom. Just as corporations built on top of Windows and its libraries, AI model makers and enterprises are building on top of CUDA software libraries.

Of course, Nvidia could falter and miss new computing waves, just as IBM and Intel did. If it hopes to continue to remain relevant, it will have to remain vigilant. Gelsinger commended Jensen for never giving up on his vision for accelerated computing. "I have a lot of respect for Jensen because he stayed true to his mission," he said. But this is not just a question of strategic vision. Nvidia continues to operate like a technology company, not an investment vehicle. It does not focus on margins and profit-taking at the expense of developing new innovations, even when those innovations can drag on Nvidia's bottom line.

"We can only continue to be relevant if we invest," Jensen once said. "In my business, if you don't invest, you'll be out of business soon."

He believes, in other words, that in the highly technical chip industry, innovative engineering matters far more than financial metrics. That belief is perhaps the single thing that most differentiates Jensen from his peers.

INTO THE FUTURE

(2013–PRESENT)

CHAPTER 11

The Road to AI

BY 2005, NVIDIA'S CHIEF SCIENTIST, DAVID KIRK, WAS CON-
sidering a change. He had joined Nvidia in early 1997 during the development of the RIVA 128 chip, which had saved the company. Since then,
he had overseen the launch of several chip architectures and witnessed
Nvidia oscillate between near-death experiences and market-defining
successes. He needed a break from the long hours and the stresses of the
job, but this required finding a worthy successor. Kirk knew of no one in
the industry who could meet his—and Jensen's—high standards for the
role of chief scientist at Nvidia. But Kirk did have an eye on an academic
who had an impressive pedigree. The question was, how would the company lure him away from his current post?

Professor Bill Dally had nothing left to prove in the field of computer science. He was a living legend: after earning his bachelor's degree
in electrical engineering in 1980 from Virginia Tech, he went to work
at Bell Labs on some of the earliest microprocessors ever invented. In
1981, while working at Bell, he got his master's in electrical engineering from Stanford, and then in 1983 he enrolled in the computer science PhD program at Caltech.[1] Dally wrote his dissertation—Richard
Feynman, the Nobel Prize–winning theoretical physicist and pioneer in
quantum mechanics, sat on his committee—on the topic of concurrent

data structures, a technique for structuring information on a computer so that it can be used by multiple computing threads simultaneously. Today, this is known as parallel computing, and Nvidia relies on the technique for its entire line of advanced processors.

After receiving his PhD, Dally taught at MIT, where he worked on both cutting-edge supercomputers and cheaper machines that used off-the-shelf parts. After eleven years in Cambridge, he returned to Stanford to chair its computer science department and eventually was named to one of the university's coveted endowed professorships, becoming the Willard R. and Inez Kerr Bell Professor of Engineering.

Kirk took note of Dally's work in the early 2000s and invited him to consult on the Tesla chip architecture that eventually powered the GeForce 8 series. This was Nvidia's fifth-generation "true" GPU after the first, programmable GeForce 3, but one of its first to really take advantage of parallel computing. It was the first move in what would become a six-year courtship.

"It was a long, slow hire. Once we hooked him, we just reeled him in slowly," Kirk said. "Bill was another essential piece because he's like a master of parallel computing. That's what he's been doing his whole career . . . he had a vision of how parallel computing should work."[2]

In 2008, Dally took a sabbatical to consider his next move. The next year, Kirk finally won, convincing him to make the switch to industry. Dally resigned from his post at Stanford and joined Nvidia full-time, aiming to bring his theoretical work to commercial applications.

Kirk hired Dally not only to succeed him as chief scientist, an important position with many duties across the company. He also knew that Dally could accelerate Nvidia's development of GPU technology.

For the first fifty years of computing history, the most important chip inside the computer was the central processing unit, or CPU. The CPU is a generalist, capable of performing a wide variety of tasks. It moves from task to task with great speed and can dedicate significant processing power to each operation. Nevertheless, it can handle only a few operations simultaneously because of its limited number of cores, which process only a few computation threads at once.

The GPU, in contrast, is optimized for volume over complexity. It contains hundreds or thousands of tiny processing cores, enabling it to break down tasks into numerous simpler operations executed in parallel. While a GPU is less versatile than a CPU, it can vastly outperform a CPU in processing speed for many applications.[3] The secret to a GPU's success is parallel computing—the field Bill Dally had pioneered.

At Nvision 08—a conference held in San Jose aimed not at industry insiders but at graphics enthusiasts—Jamie Hyneman and Adam Savage of the TV show *Mythbusters* put on a presentation at the request of Nvidia. They said that Nvidia had asked them to come up with a practical demonstration of the differences between a CPU and a GPU— "kind of a science lesson," as Savage put it, "about how a GPU works."[4] They brought on stage two machines that were designed to perform the same task—paint a picture—in two different ways. The first machine was called Leonardo, a remote-controlled robot that consisted of a paintball gun on a swiveling arm that was mounted on a pair of tank-like treads. Hyneman piloted the robot across the stage to a point in front of a blank canvas, where it began to shoot paintballs according to a preprogrammed algorithm. Over the course of thirty seconds, Leonardo produced a clearly legible smiley-face image in a single color, blue. This, Savage explained, was how CPUs might perform a task: "as a series of discrete actions performed sequentially, one after the other."

The second machine, Leonardo 2, was more like a GPU. It was a hulking rack of eleven hundred identical tubes, each of which was loaded with a single paintball. The tubes were connected to one of two giant compressed-air tanks, which would launch the entire complement of paintballs simultaneously. Whereas Leonardo took nearly half a minute to paint its simple smiley face, Leonardo 2 took less than a tenth of a second to splatter an entire canvas with a full-color image that was a recognizable approximation of the *Mona Lisa*. "Kind of like a parallel processor," said Hyneman in his trademark deadpan.

Rendering computer graphics is a computationally intensive task, but it is far less complex than, say, recalculating every math formula in a million-cell spreadsheet. As a result, the most efficient way to make a computer better at rendering graphics is to give it access to many more specialized cores that can process more software threads in parallel, all optimized for the small set of tasks related to graphics processing. To be more proficient at what it was designed to do, a GPU doesn't need more flexibility or more brute-force power; it simply needs more throughput.

Over time, the distinction between CPU and GPU has blurred, especially as the kind of matrix math that GPUs can perform has been found to be applicable in fields as diverse as computer vision, physics simulation, and artificial intelligence. The GPU has become more of a general-purpose chip.

SOON AFTER HE STARTED AT NVIDIA, Dally began to redeploy the company's research teams to work on parallel computing. One of the first big projects he had a hand in involved internet cat photos.

One of Dally's former colleagues at Stanford, the computer science professor Andrew Ng, was collaborating with Google Brain—one of Alphabet's AI research labs that would later merge into Google Deep-Mind—to find better ways to conduct deep learning through neural networks. Unlike early neural networks, which required humans to "teach" the networks what they were looking at, deep-learning neural networks were entirely self-directed. Ng's team, for example, fed their deep-learning net a random sampling of 10 million still images taken from YouTube and let it decide which patterns occurred frequently enough for the net to "remember" them. The model was exposed to so many videos of cats that it independently developed a composite image of a cat's face without human intervention. From then on, it could reliably identify cats in images that were not a part of its training set.[5]

To computer science veterans such as Dally, this was a tipping point. "There are really three things that are needed to make deep learning work," he said.[6] "Number one, the core algorithms have been around since the '80s. There have been improvements like transformers, but by and large, around for decades. Number two, datasets. You need a lot of data . . . labeled datasets were interesting things [that] started to emerge in the early 2000s. And then Fei-Fei Li put together the ImageNet dataset. And those were a huge public service because having that big dataset [and] making it public made it available for a lot of people to do very interesting things."

Ng's work had shown the power of applying well-known and well-understood algorithms to sufficiently huge datasets. Although his deep-learning model's ability to recognize cats captured the headlines, it was able to do far more. With more than 1 billion parameters, the Google Brain neural network could identify tens of thousands of different shapes, objects, and even faces.[7] Ng had needed Google, which gave him access to a rich dataset for deep learning, a dataset that just happened to be one of the largest content libraries in the world: YouTube, which Google has owned since 2006. Even his home institution of Stanford, with its large research budget, could not provide him that kind of training material. (Google was not acting out of altruism: in exchange for access to its data, it retained the rights to commercialize anything that Ng developed using that data.)

But the third thing "needed to make deep learning work," according to Dally, was the hardware, and this was proving more difficult to solve. Ng had used one of Google's data centers, building his own deep-learning server by chaining together more than two thousand CPUs, with sixteen thousand computing cores between them.[8] Ng's feat was impressive, to be sure. But he now faced the same challenge that Ross Walker had faced at the San Diego Supercomputing Center: as exciting as his proof-of-concept work might have been, it still put the promise of deep learning far beyond the reach of most organizations. Even well-funded research groups would not be able to purchase thousands of expensive CPUs, let alone rent space at a data center that could store, power, and cool such a massive computing system. In order to truly unlock the potential of deep learning, the hardware would have to become much more affordable.

After leaving Stanford to join Nvidia, Dally kept in touch with Ng. They got together over breakfast one morning, and Ng revealed his work with Google Brain. He described successfully demonstrating how deep-learning theory could be applied to a real-world problem: the automated recognition of objects in photos, without human tagging or intervention. Ng detailed his approach of combining the extensive dataset of YouTube clips with the raw power of tens of thousands of traditional processors.

Dally was impressed. "That's really interesting," he said. Then he made an observation that would change the trajectory of artificial intelligence. "I bet GPUs would be much better at doing that."[9]

He assigned his Nvidia colleague Bryan Catanzaro, who had a PhD in electrical engineering and computer science from the University of California, Berkeley, to help Ng's team use GPUs for deep learning. Dally and Catanzaro were confident that the computational tasks involved could be broken down into smaller, less complex operations that a GPU could execute more efficiently. They developed a series of tests that conclusively proved their case—in theory. The challenge, in practice, was that deep-learning models were too large to run on a single GPU, which could handle only models that had 250 million parameters, a fraction of the size of Ng's Google Brain model. While it was possible to get up to four GPUs on a single server, "chaining" multiple GPU servers together to increase their collective processing power had not been attempted before.[10]

Using Nvidia's CUDA language, Catanzaro's team wrote a new optimized routine to enable the distribution of computation across many GPUs and manage the communication among them. The optimizations allowed Ng and Catanzaro to consolidate the work once performed by two thousand CPUs across a mere twelve Nvidia GPUs.[11]

Catanzaro had demonstrated that with some skilled software work, GPUs could provide "the spark that ignited the AI revolution," according to Dally.[12] "If you think of the fuel as building the algorithms and the air as being the datasets, once you have the GPUs, it makes it possible to apply those to each other. Without that, it just wasn't feasible."

Catanzaro's CUDA optimizations also brought him into direct contact with Jensen for the first time. "All of a sudden, he got really interested in the work that I was doing. He was e-mailing me to ask me questions about what I was trying to do, what deep learning was, how did it work," Catanzaro recalled. "Also, of course, what the role of GPUs could potentially be in bringing that to pass."[13]

Jensen wanted to sell more GPUs, of course. But in order to do that, he would need to find the "killer app" that drove GPU adoption. Deep learning had the potential to be just that—but only if someone could show its use beyond identifying house pets.

IN THE SAME PERIOD WHEN Catanzaro was working to help Ng develop his deep-learning neural network project, a University of Toronto research team showed that such networks could outperform the best human-created software in solving the most challenging computer-vision problems.

The milestone had its roots back in 2007, when a newly minted professor of computer science at Princeton named Fei-Fei Li (whom Dally referenced in a quotation above) began working on a new project. At the time, the field of computer vision was intent on developing the best models and algorithms, because the assumption was that whoever designed the best algorithm would necessarily get the most accurate results. Li turned that assumption on its head, proposing that whoever trained on the best data would get the best results, even if they hadn't designed the most refined algorithm.[14] To give her fellow researchers a head start on the monumental task of collecting the necessary data, she began compiling a catalog of images, each of which was manually tagged based on its content. After two years of work, the database had grown to more than 3 million images with one thousand different and mutually exclusive categories, which ranged from the specific (magpie, barometer, power drill) to the broad (honeycomb, television, church). She christened her database ImageNet and announced it to the academic world in the form of a research paper. At first, no one read the paper or paid much attention to the other ways she tried to draw attention to her research. So she contacted the University of Oxford, which maintained a database similar to hers and sponsored an annual competition in Europe for computer-vision researchers. She asked whether Oxford might be willing to cosponsor something similar in the United States, using ImageNet. The university agreed to do so, and in 2010 the first ImageNet Large Scale Visual Recognition Challenge took place.[15]

The rules were simple: the competing models would get fed random images from ImageNet and would have to correctly assign them to categories. For the first two contests in 2010 and 2011, the results were not very good. During the inaugural competition, one model misclassified almost every single image, and no team scored better than 75 percent correct.[16] In the second year, the teams did better on average—the worst performer got around half of the images correct—but once again, no one correctly categorized more than 75 percent of the images.

In the third contest, which occurred in 2012, University of Toronto professor Gary Hinton and two of his students, Ilya Sutskever and Alex Krizhevsky, put forward an entry they called AlexNet. Unlike the rest of the field, which had started developing algorithms and models before optimizing them for use on ImageNet, the AlexNet team took the opposite approach. They used Nvidia GPUs to support a small-scale deep-learning neural network that was fed ImageNet content and which then "learned" how to build relationships between images and their associated tags. The team did not set out to write the best computer-vision algorithm possible; in fact, they did not write a single line of computer-vision code themselves. Instead, they wrote the best deep-learning model they could—and trusted it to figure out the computer-vision problem on its own.

"GPUs starting around the Fermi generation, they were powerful enough that, you know, you could do an interesting-sized neural network and an interesting-sized amount of data in a reasonable amount of time," said Dally, referring to the chip architecture that powered the GeForce 500 series, which was first released in 2010. "So AlexNet was trained in two weeks."[17]

The results were astounding. Once again, the 75 percent barrier held for most competitors. But AlexNet categorized almost 85 percent of the images correctly—and it had done so on its own, through the power of deep learning. AlexNet's win gave Nvidia a huge PR boost, as Hinton and his students had needed only a pair of off-the-shelf, consumer-grade GPUs that cost a few hundred dollars apiece. AlexNet forever associated the company with what is still considered one of the most important events in the history of artificial intelligence.

"When Alex Krizhevsky and Illya Sutskever published their Image-Net paper, [it] really took the world by storm," said Catanzaro. "One of the things that people often forget is that it's primarily a systems paper.

That paper is not about a fancy new mathematical concept of how to think about artificial intelligence. Instead, what they did was they used accelerated computing to dramatically expand the dataset and the model that they were applying to this particular problem. And that ended up yielding some great results."[18]

Alex Krizhevsky and Illya Sutskever's work stoked Jensen's interest in artificial intelligence. He started talking frequently with Bill Dally and was focused on how much of an opportunity deep learning, and specifically GPU-powered deep learning, would be for Nvidia. There was considerable debate within the executive team on the topic. Several of Jensen's key lieutenants were against investing more in deep learning, in the belief that it was just a passing fad. But the CEO overruled them.

"Deep learning is going to be really big," he said at an executive team meeting in 2013. "We should go all in on it."

THOUGH HE DIDN'T QUITE REALIZE IT, Jensen had spent the first twenty years of Nvidia's history preparing the company for this moment. He had staffed Nvidia with the best talent he could find, including by poaching from rivals and partners alike. He had created a culture that prized technical brilliance, maximum effort, and, above all, a total commitment to the company. He had built a company in the image of his own focused yet far-ranging mind. Now, he would pull every lever at his disposal to navigate Nvidia to the very center of the tech industry—as the company whose hardware could bring about the AI-powered future.

The first step was to assign significantly more personnel and funding to AI. Catanzaro estimated that there had been only a handful of people working on AI-related projects. But as Jensen began to grasp the size of the opportunity before Nvidia, he used the "one team" philosophy to quickly reallocate resources.

"It was definitely not a single day when the entire company changed forever," remembers Catanzaro. "It was a period of several months where Jensen was increasingly interested and started asking increasingly deep questions and then started encouraging the company to swarm to machine learning."[19]

After the "swarming," Nvidia released a torrent of new features designed specifically for the AI market. Jensen had already taken the big and expensive decision to make the company's entire hardware lineup compatible with CUDA, so that researchers and engineers could program Nvidia GPUs for their specific needs. Now, he asked Dally to come up with AI-focused improvements.

Jensen announced the change in strategic focus in a company all-hands meeting. "We need to consider this work as our highest priority," he said.[20] He explained that Nvidia had to get the right people working on AI. If they were currently assigned to something else, they would change focus and work on AI, because it was going to be more important than anything else they could possibly be doing.[21]

Catanzaro turned his GPU-optimization work into a software library Nvidia called CUDA Deep Neural Network, or cuDNN. This became the company's first AI-optimized library. It would evolve into a must-have for AI developers. It worked with all leading AI frameworks and allowed users to automatically employ the most efficient algorithms for whatever GPU task they needed. "Jensen was excited," said Catanzaro. "He wanted to get that productized and shipped as soon as possible."

Another promising path was to modify the level of precision of the math that Nvidia's GPUs could perform. At the time, the company's GPUs supported 32-bit (single float, or FP32) or 64-bit (double float, or FP64) mathematical precision; either math type was a requirement for many scientific and technical fields. But deep-learning models didn't need to be that precise. Models only required the GPUs to perform 16-bit floating-point calculations, because the networks were resistant to calculation errors during training. In other words, Nvidia GPUs did math that was *overly* precise—and therefore much slower—for deep-learning models. To make the GPUs run faster and allow these models to run more efficiently, in 2016 Dally implemented FP16 support on all Nvidia GPUs.

But the real task was making bespoke hardware circuits that were optimized for AI. When Nvidia pivoted to AI, its architects were already working on the next generation of GPUs, called Volta. The new line was several years into development; making even a small change to the chip design at that point would be costly and difficult. But Dally realized, with some prodding from Jensen, that if the company did not try to make AI-optimized chips now, it might not get another opportunity for years.

"The entire team—the GPU group, Jensen, and myself—agreed to incorporate significantly more support" for AI despite how late in the development process they were, said Dally. That "support" included the development of an entirely new type of tiny processor, called the Tensor Core, which was integrated into Volta. In machine learning, a tensor is a type of data container that encodes multiple dimensions of information, especially for complex content types such as images and videos. Because of their richness, tensor-based calculations require large amounts of processing power. And the most interesting forms of deep learning—image recognition, language generation, and autonomous driving—required the use of ever-larger and ever-more-complex tensors.

In much the same way that traditional GPUs marked an improvement over CPU-based computation because of their ability to handle a smaller subset of tasks more efficiently, Tensor Cores were an improvement over traditional GPUs because they were optimized to run an even more specialized subset of tasks at even higher efficiencies. In Dally's words, they were "matrix multiple engines," made for deep learning, and deep learning alone. A Volta-based GPU with Tensor Cores could train a deep-learning model three times faster than the same GPU with standard CUDA cores.[22]

All of these innovations and changes came with an operational cost. Dally and his team made the last tweaks to the Volta line mere months ahead of its schedule for tape-out, the last step before the locked design entered production. It was almost unheard of for a chip maker to do such a thing voluntarily instead of in response to a major defect found at the last minute.

"That was a decision of how much chip area we are going to spend because we think this evolving AI market is going to be a big market," recalled Dally. "It turned out to be a good call. I think that it was a real strength of Nvidia that we could do that."[23]

In a sense, Nvidia was doing what it had always done: spotting a big opportunity and racing to get its products to market before anyone else realized the potential was even there. Jensen came to understand early on in the AI race that it wasn't just about who could make the fastest chip for deep learning. It was just as much about how everything—the hardware and software infrastructure—worked together.

"Having an architecture and an attention mechanism that allowed for scaling of these models really was also a kickstart in the industry," recalled Jensen in 2023.[24]

Dally agreed with Jensen's assessment. "What is more important is building up the whole ecosystem of software early on," he said. Nvidia wanted to produce "all sorts of software to just make it really easy for people to do deep learning efficiently on GPUs" because presenting a ready framework and a library of support software made it all but inevitable that third-party developers, researchers, and engineers would turn to Nvidia first when they thought of AI.

Just as CUDA had made Nvidia's name in the insular world of academic AI researchers, its next generation of hardware would arrive just in time for those same pioneers to try their luck in the commercial market. Soon, the center of gravity in AI would shift away from Stanford, Toronto, and Caltech and move to start-ups and well-established tech companies alike. Geoffrey Hinton and Fei-Fei Li would end up at Google. Andrew Ng worked as the chief scientist at Baidu—originally the largest search engine in China and now a tech conglomerate. And Ilya Sutskever, Hinton's student and one of the three researchers who made the AlexNet breakthrough, would cofound a deep-learning start-up called OpenAI that would bring the AI revolution to public consciousness.

The one thing all of them had in common was that in their academic lives, they had used Nvidia GPUs to do their groundbreaking research. And Nvidia would continue to be their preferred choice as they transformed AI from an obscure academic field into a global obsession that created a huge appetite for new chips, AI servers, and data centers.

The work of Bill Dally and Bryan Catanzaro allowed Jensen to pick up an early signal of the potential of the new technology. Within a decade, Jensen was sure that AI would create "the largest TAM [total addressable market] expansion of software and hardware that we've seen in several decades."[25] He refashioned Nvidia around AI in a matter of years, moving with the "Speed of Light" intensity. In fact, only by taking extreme measures—bucking the industry-wide tendencies toward static organizations, long development timelines, and parsimonious R&D spending—was Jensen able to prepare Nvidia to take advantage of the AI earthquake when it finally occurred. And even then, no one— not even Jensen—knew just how violently the ground was about to shift underneath the entire tech industry.

CHAPTER 12

The "Most Feared" Hedge Fund

THOUGH FEW KNOW IT, THE HISTORIES OF NVIDIA AND Starboard Value, perhaps the most famous activist hedge fund in the world, are intertwined.

Jeff Smith, the founder of Starboard, grew up in the Long Island town of Great Neck. In 1994, he received an economics degree from the University of Pennsylvania's Wharton School and started his career in investment banking. Later, he joined a small hedge fund called Ramius Capital, which merged into Cowen Group.[1] In 2011, Smith and two of his partners spun out Starboard Value as an independent fund, one that would be "focused on unlocking value in underperforming companies for the benefit of all shareholders."[2]

According to a 2014 *Fortune* magazine article, Smith quickly earned a reputation as the "most feared man" in corporate America for his aggressive activist investing.[3] By then the fund had more than $3 billion in assets under management, generating strong returns of 15.5 percent per year. It had replaced more than eighty directors on thirty different corporate boards; the boards it shaped included those of the biotech company SurModics and of the hair salon company Regis. It had experienced a rare loss in a proxy fight to add directors to AOL's board in 2012 but continued to set its sights on ever-larger targets.

In late 2013, Starboard Value made its highest-profile move to date: the fund announced that it had accumulated a 5.6 percent stake in the largest owner of full-service chain restaurants in the country, Darden Restaurants, the owner and operator of Olive Garden, Red Lobster, LongHorn Steakhouse, and other national chains. Darden's sales had been falling for years, and the company had decided to divest from Red Lobster entirely, citing the increasing costs of seafood.[4] Smith disagreed with the decision; he blamed Darden's struggles on mismanagement and argued that Darden divesting itself of Red Lobster would actually destroy value for shareholders, not create it. Starboard believed that Darden already had everything it needed to survive, except good leadership.

In September 2014, Starboard released its proposal to turn Darden around in the form of a PowerPoint presentation that ran to almost three hundred slides. The presentation deck generated significant attention in the national media; business journalists noted the plan's especially pointed tone ("Darden has been mismanaged for years and . . . is in desperate need of a turnaround"), while others made light of some of its cost-saving suggestions, such as asking waiters to be less generous in handing out unlimited breadsticks.[5] But Starboard's plan was both comprehensive and logical—even the breadsticks suggestion, which was intended to increase the number of touch points between staff and guests. And Starboard suggested that it genuinely cared about Darden's brands for more than just financial reasons: "Olive Garden has a special place in our hearts," one slide said.[6] The hedge fund's combination of sentimentality and rigor won over Darden's shareholders; Starboard secured a proxy vote victory and replaced the company's entire twelve-person board. Darden's CEO soon resigned, and the company implemented the Starboard-approved turnaround. Smith's victory cemented his reputation for being both thorough and tough.

A year before Starboard's widely chronicled victory over Darden, Smith had made a less publicized move on Nvidia.

Early in 2013, Nvidia's shareholders were getting restless. The stock price had been roughly flat for four years, and the financial performance

204 INTO THE FUTURE

was mixed. In its latest quarter ending in January, sales were up 7 per-cent year-over-year, but earnings were down 2 percent.

Nvidia had a strong balance sheet of about $3 billion in net cash, which was a significant asset when the overall market value of the com-pany was $8 billion total. However, its growth rate was only in the sin-gle digits, which resulted in a price-to-earnings (P/E) multiple of just 14 times earnings. After backing out Nvidia's cash on hand, Starboard believed that the company was severely undervalued, and its core assets had far more room to grow. The fund pounced: according to Securities and Exchange Commission 13F filings, the hedge fund accumulated a stake of 4.4 million shares in Nvidia, worth about $62 million, during the quarter ending in June of 2013.

Some executives at Nvidia weren't excited about having Starboard as an investor. One senior Nvidia executive said the company's board was very worried that the activist fund would force a reorganization of the company, install its own board, and make Nvidia cut back on its investments in CUDA—the kind of drastic reshaping that it would attempt with Darden the following year. Another Nvidia executive said Starboard wanted a board seat, but the board had pushed back.

Still, the relationship never became too antagonistic. "I don't think it ever got to what I would call a crisis stage. You know DEFCON 1?" one Nvidia executive said, referring to the alert system used by the U.S. military for nuclear war. DEFCON 5 indicates peace, while DEFCON 1 means nuclear war is imminent. "It got to DEFCON 3."

The Starboard team met several times with Jensen and other Nvidia leaders to discuss strategy. Looking back on the investment years later, Smith said that Starboard primarily advocated for an aggressive stock buyback program and a de-emphasis on non-GPU projects such as phone processors.[7] Starboard refrained from applying additional pressure after the meetings. The hedge fund eventually got its wish on the buybacks. In November 2013, Nvidia made two announcements: a commitment to buy back $1 billion of stock by fiscal 2015 and the authorization of an additional $1 billion stock buyback. The stock price rallied about 20 percent in the ensuing few months, and Starboard sold its position in Nvidia by March the following year.

Far from a contentious relationship, Nvidia and Starboard seemed to work well together in this brief period.

"We were incredibly impressed with Jensen," said Smith.

For his part, Jensen recalls the meetings with Starboard but doesn't particularly remember what was discussed. Before he knew it, Starboard was no longer an investor. But that wasn't the end of Starboard's influence on the chip industry, and on Nvidia.

A COMPANY CALLED MELLANOX was founded in 1999 by several Israeli technology executives, led by Eyal Waldman, who became its CEO. Mellanox provided high-speed networking products for data centers and supercomputers under the "InfiniBand" standard and soon became an industry leader. It had impressive revenue growth, going from $500 million in 2012 to $858 million in 2016. However, its high research and development spend left it with very thin profit margins.

In January 2017, Starboard bought an 11 percent stake in Mellanox. It sent a letter criticizing Waldman and his team for their disappointing performance over the prior five years. Mellanox's share price had fallen even though the semiconductor industry index had risen in value by 470 percent. Its operating margins were half of the average of its peer companies. "Mellanox has been one of the worst performing semiconductor companies for an extended period of time," read Starboard's letter. "The time for fringe changes and marginal improvements has long passed."[8]

After a long series of discussions with the board, Starboard and Mellanox reached a compromise in June 2018. Mellanox would appoint three Starboard-approved members to its board and give the hedge fund additional future rights if Mellanox didn't meet certain undisclosed financial targets. Even with those concessions in hand, Starboard retained the option of waging a proxy fight to replace Waldman. Alternatively, Mellanox could choose to sell itself to a company that could generate better returns on its assets than it could as an independent company. The groundwork was laid for what would be one of the most consequential transactions in the history of the chip industry.

In September 2018, Mellanox received a nonbinding purchase offer from an outside company at $102 per share—a premium of almost a third over its current stock price of $76.90. Mellanox was now fully in play. It solicited an investment bank to seek other bidders and eventually expanded its list of potential buyers to seven in total.

Jensen wasn't thinking about acquiring Mellanox when it became available, according to another Nvidia executive. But he quickly saw the strategic importance of the asset, decided Nvidia had to win the auction, and joined the hunt in October.

Eventually, the list was narrowed down to three serious bidders: Nvidia, Intel, and Xilinx, which made chips primarily for industrial uses. The three potential buyers got into a multi-month bidding war, with Intel and Xilinx topping out around a bid of $122.50 a share. Nvidia went just a little bit higher, at $125 per share. It won the bidding war on March 7, 2019, for an all-cash offer of $6.9 billion.

Days later, Nvidia and Mellanox made the deal public and held a conference call with analysts and investors.

"Let me tell you why this makes sense for Nvidia and why I'm excited about it," Jensen said. He talked about how the demand for high-performance computing would rise—how workloads including AI, scientific computing, and data analytics required enormous performance increases, which could only be attained through accelerated computing with GPUs and better networking. He explained how AI applications would eventually require tens of thousands of servers connected to one another and working together in concert, and the market-leading networking technology from Mellanox would be critical to make that possible.

"Emerging AI and data-analytics workloads demand data-center-scale optimization," he said. Jensen was predicting that computing would move beyond one device—that the entire data center would become the computer.

JENSEN'S VISION CAME TRUE JUST a few years later. In May 2024, Nvidia disclosed that the portion of the company that was formerly Mellanox had generated $3.2 billion in quarterly revenue, up more than seven times from the final quarter in early 2020 in which

Mellanox reported as a public company. After just four years, the former Mellanox business, which had cost Nvidia a one-time fee of $6.9 billion, was generating more than $12 billion in annualized revenue and growing at triple-digit rates.

"Mellanox was frankly a wonderful thing thrown in our lap by activists," a senior Nvidia executive said. "If you talk to AI start-ups today, InfiniBand, Mellanox's networking technology, is incredibly important to scale the computing power and make everything work."

Brian Venturo, cofounder and CTO of CoreWeave, a leading GPU cloud-computing provider and a customer of Nvidia's, argues that InfiniBand technology still has the best solution to minimize latency, control network congestion, and to make workloads perform efficiently.

Mellanox was a happy accident for Nvidia in some respects. Jensen wasn't on top of it from the start. But once Nvidia identified and understood the opportunity, it made the decision to pursue Mellanox aggressively. It was a great deal, though the outcome depended on Nvidia's ability to execute once the new business became part of the company. In those ways, Mellanox was a typical Nvidia achievement: the company pounced when others didn't, and Mellanox helped power Nvidia's rise to dominance in the AI space.

"It's absolutely going to go down in history as one of the best acquisitions ever," Nvidia's head of global field operations, Jay Puri, said. "Jensen realized that data-center-scale computing requires really good high-performance networking, and Mellanox was the best in the world at that."[9]

After seeing Nvidia achieve all that is has over the past decade, Jeff Smith of Starboard Value had one summarizing thought, too.

"We never should have exited the position."

CHAPTER 13

Lighting the Future

LIGHT IS A FIENDISHLY COMPLEX NATURAL PHENOMENON.
Sometimes it behaves like a particle; sometimes it behaves like a wave.
Sometimes it bounces off objects, sometimes it scatters through them,
and sometimes it is absorbed completely by them. Unlike, say, the movement of an object through space or the deformation of an object on
impact with another, light is not governed by a single set of physical
principles. Yet we are exposed to it from the moment we open our eyes;
we know intuitively how it "works" in real life.

Light may thus be the most important visual element in computer graphics and also the hardest to reproduce. Without good
lighting, images become flat, harsh, or unreal. With good lighting,
images can approximate the work of the Old Masters—conveying
emotion and drama even in simple compositions. It can take a
human artist or photographer a lifetime to control light in his or her
work. For years, it looked like computers might never reach the same
level of skill.

Most early computer graphics failed at creating convincing lighting because the computations were just too difficult for even the most
advanced processors. The best rendering algorithms could only model
the physics of light in simple ways, resulting in flat textures, fuzzy shad-

ows, and unnatural surface reflections. Even after two decades of steady improvement in most other areas of graphics—and even after the invention of the GPU, which made graphics rendering better and more efficient in almost every way—light remained intractable.

Then came David Luebke. In 1998, Luebke received a PhD in computer science from the University of North Carolina at Chapel Hill and wanted to pursue computer graphics as an academic career. He spent eight years as an assistant professor at the University of Virginia but found himself increasingly frustrated by the slow pace of his work. Each time his team invented a new graphics technique for particle rendering or texture mapping onto objects, it would be obsolete by the time the peer-review process for the resulting paper had been completed more than six months later. The reason for the near-immediate obsolescence of Luebke's work was Nvidia, which was constantly releasing new GPU features that were superior to those his team was inventing in the lab. "I was very loose in the socket and thinking about leaving academia entirely," he said.[1]

Then, out of the blue, he got a call from David Kirk, Nvidia's chief scientist, who was familiar with Luebke's work. "We're starting a long-term research group at Nvidia," he said. "Would you be interested?"

Luebke didn't hold a grudge against Nvidia for continually outpacing his own work. On the contrary, he realized that he wanted to join the leading organization in computer graphics—especially if it meant that he would help define where it went next.

In 2006, he became the first hire at a new division called Nvidia Research. In his first weeks on the job, Luebke had lunch with Steve Molnar, a system architect at Nvidia and a long-time friend, and asked him what he thought a research group at Nvidia should do. For instance, should it be organized around pursuing patents? Molnar thought about it for a while and said, "I don't see Nvidia as some kind of IP fortress. Our strength is just outrunning the other guy."

It was a fair observation. Nvidia had remained at the very forefront of innovation primarily through its operational excellence and strategic discipline. It had fast release cycles and a clear sense of what its priorities were—and funding speculative research without a clear commercial end goal had not been one of them. Nvidia Research almost seemed to be at odds with the company's core competencies.

Yet Kirk had championed the new division precisely because he saw that the most complex problems in computer graphics would require sustained research over time, even if commercialization could take a lot more time. Within a few weeks of starting, Luebke had three new coworkers. At their first team lunch with Kirk, they asked where they might start. Kirk was noncommittal: he told them it was up to them to figure out what their job would be. He did offer some basic guidelines, at least. They should work on something important to the company. They should create significant impact with their projects. And they should focus on innovations that would not occur in the regular course of Nvidia's business—inventions that would not be possible without dedicated, long-term work, of the kind that the rest of the company was not set up to do.

RAY TRACING—A TECHNIQUE THAT SIMULATES the behavior of light rays as they bounce off or pass through objects in a virtual scene—was just such a project. In theory, ray tracing would mean far more lifelike illumination effects than what was currently available on the market. In practice, it proved to be so demanding that computing hardware could not handle it.

The conventional wisdom at the time was that CPUs were better than GPUs at ray tracing because they could perform a wider and more diverse set of calculations. Intel's internal research group pushed this notion hard; they argued that, due to the complexity of light's behavior in the real world, only a CPU could accurately model it.

Within six months of the founding of Nvidia Research, the team had conducted experiments that seemed to indicate not only that GPUs had become powerful enough to handle ray-tracing calculations, but also that they could do it faster than the current generation of CPUs. Excited about the potential to both solve and commercialize a long-standing problem in computer graphics, Luebke scheduled Nvidia Research's first meeting with Jensen.

Normally when Jensen attends a presentation, the speakers get only a few minutes of uninterrupted time before it becomes a back-and-forth discussion. In this case, however, Jensen listened for the entire hour-long presentation. "I think he was being very patient with us to let us have our say," Luebke said.

After Luebke finished, Jensen offered him several pieces of feedback. Ray tracing had obvious potential in the gaming market. But the CEO suggested that Luebke and his team shouldn't ignore other fields. For one, ray tracing could be useful to promote Nvidia's Quadro workstation graphics cards, which were low-volume sellers but accounted for nearly 80 percent of the company's profit at the time, because of their high price points. Impressing the professional and technical market might end up being better for the company.

With Jensen convinced that ray tracing was worth pursuing, Luebke next went to an Nvidia GPU engineering team design session. Luebke's team had several ideas for how to realize the computational capabilities needed for ray tracing, including making changes to the processors that lay at the heart of the GPUs themselves. Accustomed to free-wheeling academic discussions, Luebke and his team assumed that the engineers would be open to something similar. "We showed up at a Fermi chip architecture meeting," he said, referring to a generation of chips that was then under development. "We just wanted the ability for a bunch of threads to be running next to each other on the same CUDA core."

Like Jensen, the Fermi GPU architects accommodated their new colleagues and their unorthodox, noncorporate behavior. "This is pretty low cost. I think we can do this," said Jonah Alben, the head of GPU engineering—but there was a catch. "You guys need to understand, we need to make these decisions on data."

The Nvidia Research team received the message and learned an important lesson. It was acceptable to think out loud, but to make significant decisions, the GPU hardware team required evidence to justify committing time and resources. "You can't just say it's obvious, this is a good idea," Luebke said.

For the next year, the researchers devoted themselves to providing that evidence. They worked on proof-of-concept technology and created algorithms to demonstrate that GPUs could be used cost-effectively for ray tracing. It was engrossing, exciting work, and not just for the researchers themselves. Brian Catanzaro, who was an intern at the time, remembered that Jensen attended a ray-tracing research team meeting in 2008. He asked no questions. He didn't bring a computer. He was there just to listen to the team talk about ray tracing for an hour.

David Kirk was so convinced by the team's results that he pushed Nvidia management to move quickly to get Luebke's ideas into production. The first step was acquiring start-ups that had specific expertise in ray tracing. Nvidia pursued and bought two: Mental Images, based in Berlin, and RayScale, in Utah. Luebke and Kirk flew out to Utah to show the RayScale cofounders Pete Shirley and Steve Parker that ray tracing could work much better on GPUs than the CPUs they were using.

Right after RayScale joined Nvidia, its employees worked alongside the Nvidia Research team to create a demo for the 2008 SIGGRAPH conference. This was the same conference where, in 1991, Curtis Priem had debuted his *Aviator* flight simulator to the world and with it showed what was possible with computer graphics. Nvidia attended the conference frequently, and now, after nearly two decades, it was ready to present the next evolution in computer graphics. The team presented a GPU-powered demo of a sleek, shiny sports car driving through a city filled with the kinds of effects that only ray tracing could produce: reflections off of curved surfaces, sharp shadows, distorted reflections, and motion blur.

"It was a pivotal moment for the company. That was the start of something big," remembered Luebke. "The story that GPUs couldn't do ray tracing was completely put to bed with the demo."

There were several Intel employees in attendance for the demo. Afterward, they came up to the Nvidia Research team and asked whether it really was running on a GPU. When Luebke confirmed that it was, he saw them start tapping furiously away on their Blackberries. Intel's research teams never produced another paper about ray tracing on CPUs.

The following year, at SIGGRAPH 2009, Nvidia launched OptiX, a CUDA-based, fully programmable ray-tracing engine for Quadro cards, which would accelerate ray tracing for photorealistic rendering, industrial design, and radiation research. To support the release, Steve Parker and the former RayScale employees were spun out of the research arm and joined Nvidia's main business.

"We always viewed Nvidia Research as an incubator. If something succeeds, we sort of push it out of the nest and it becomes a product," Luebke said.

In just three years, Nvidia Research had transformed from a group that pursued speculative computing projects into a reliable source of new business opportunities for the company. Still, there was a long way to go to make ray tracing accessible to the masses. The demo that Nvidia had shown at SIGGRAPH 2008 was still beyond the capabilities of consumer-grade graphics cards. While OptiX enabled engineers to render ray-traced scenes faster, unless it was a very simple scene the ray tracing couldn't be done in real time, as it was too computationally intensive. The company decided to set aside any thoughts on making progress in ray-tracing applications in gaming.

Years later, in 2013, David Kirk approached Luebke again. "We need to revisit ray tracing," he said. "What would it take to make it the center of graphics?" He thought it was time for real-time ray tracing in games.

Luebke was so excited by the prospect that he sent an e-mail to all Nvidia employees on June 10, 2013, which became known as the ray-tracing moonshot e-mail. "For some time, we've been planning this new initiative around ray tracing," he wrote. "What could we do if ray tracing were a hundred times more efficient and what would it take to do it a hundred times more efficiently?"

Luebke wasn't exaggerating the scale of the problem. Only such an efficiency gain would make real-time ray tracing possible for cheaper consumer graphics cards. Getting to that point would require new algorithms and the creation of new specialized hardware circuits. It would also require new perspectives on just what was possible with GPU technology.

A key contribution came from an Nvidia team located in Helsinki, whom employees in Santa Clara came to call "the Finns." Timo Aila, who joined Nvidia through an acquisition in 2006, was the first employee in Helsinki. Over time, Aila and his colleagues became a kind of internal strike team, assigned to the toughest research questions facing Nvidia. Now, they took on the challenge of research into a new specialized ray-tracing processor core inside GPUs. They were supported by early Nvidia employee and chip architect Erik Lindholm, who flew out to Finland.

"The Finns are this crack research team where just everything they touch turns to gold," Luebke said.

After Nvidia Research presented to the GPU architecture team and gained its support, engineers in the United States were assigned to work with the Finns on the ray-tracing cores in March 2014. In 2015, the Finns traveled to Nvidia headquarters to hash out the remaining issues. By 2016, the project was nearly completed, and Nvidia Research fully turned it over to the company's engineering team. Although the ray-tracing technology was too late to make the launch of the Pascal architecture, which was rolled out later that year, Nvidia prepared to release dedicated ray-tracing cores with the next architecture, which would be called Turing.

"My job throughout all this is protecting this effort, making sure they got the care, feeding, and attention they needed," Luebke said, referring to the Finns.

Jensen would introduce Turing, with its dedicated ray-tracing cores, as part of his keynote address for SIGGRAPH 2018, exactly ten years after Nvidia Research's demo proved in a stroke that ray tracing belonged on GPUs rather than CPUs. Most of his speech was devoted to introducing the Turing architecture, as well as the improved second-generation Tensor core designed to accelerate "deep-learning" neural net workloads. But Jensen wasn't satisfied. He wanted additional material in his speech to captivate the conference audience.

TWO WEEKS BEFORE THE SHOW, he invited Nvidia executives to pitch ideas for his keynote. Nvidia Research's Aaron Lefohn suggested that he demonstrate the new deep-learning anti-aliasing, or DLAA, feature. Powered by Turing's Tensor cores, DLAA used artificial intelligence to enhance image quality, making high-resolution graphics crisp and objects appear sharply defined. Jensen wasn't impressed. He wanted something more exciting. "A better-looking picture is not going to sell many GPUs."

But he found inspiration in the suggestion. Instead of deep-learning anti-aliasing, which improved already great images, what if they could use Tensor cores to make lower-end cards perform as well as the top of the line? For example, Nvidia could use the image-enhancement function to sample and interpolate additional pixels, so that a card designed to render graphics natively at 1,440p resolution, also known as "Quad HD," could produce images at the higher-resolution 4K, "Ultra HD," at a similar frame rate. AI would be used to fill in details to take the lower-resolution 1440p image to a higher-resolution 4K image.

"What would really help," said Jensen, "is if you could do deep-learning super sampling. *That* would be a big deal. Can you do that?"

Lefohn huddled with his team and then told Jensen it could be possible. They needed to research the idea. A week later, just days before the keynote, Lefohn reported back to Jensen that the early results were promising and they would be able to make what came to be known as DLSS. "Put them on the slides," Jensen said.

"No one in the world had ever thought of making a system and a machine-learning model that can infer hundreds of millions of pixels per second on a home computer," Brian Catanzaro said.[2]

Jensen had come up with DLSS on the spot. He had seen the promise inherent in one technology and transformed that promise into a new feature with a better business case. Now, if DLSS worked, the company's entire product lineup, from the low end to the high end, would become more proficient, and thus valuable, allowing Nvidia to charge higher prices. "The researchers had invented this amazing thing, but Jensen saw what it was good for. It wasn't what they had thought," Luebke said. "It shows what a leader Jensen is and how technical and smart he is."

Jensen's keynote address was well received, but the GeForce RTX cards based on the Turing GPU were not. "We launched ray tracing and DLSS to a thud," Jeff Fisher said. The problem was the GeForce RTX offered negligible gains in frame-rate performance over the previous-generation Pascal cards. And when gamers turned on ray tracing, which was supposed to be the killer new feature, the RTX cards suffered a 25 percent drop in frame rate.

DLSS performed marginally better. When enabled, it allowed cards to run about 40 percent faster than Pascal, but at a noticeable loss of image quality. Nvidia also had to fine tune and train DLSS's AI on footage of each game they wanted the technology to work with, which was a painstaking and time-consuming process. Still, by now Nvidia had learned the value of developing and iterating technology over time and of waiting for the market demand to catch up. "You solve the chicken-and-egg problem by bootstrapping," said Bryan Catanzaro. "You can't have amazing AI in hundreds of millions of households without building it first. Both ray tracing and AI were going to change gaming forever. We knew that this was inevitable."

Catanzaro joined the DLSS project after the launch of Turing in 2018. He worked on DLSS 2.0, which was introduced in March 2020 and didn't need to be tuned for each game. It received much better reviews. "We reconceived the problem and got better results without requiring custom training data from every game," Catanzaro said.

The next iteration was even better. Catanzaro left Nvidia for a brief stint at the Chinese search engine and technology company Baidu but returned to work on what became DLSS 3.0. The goal was to use deep learning to create interstitial, AI-generated frames between rendered frames for games. The thinking was that in every successive frame in a video game there were patterns and correlations, and if the AI chip could predict these patterns and correlations, it could take some of the rendering computational load off of the GPU.

It had taken six years of development to build a sufficiently accurate AI model for the frame-generation feature, according to Catanzaro. "While we were working on it, we saw continuous improvement in the quality of results, so we kept working," he said. "Most academics don't have the freedom to work on one project for six years because they need to graduate."

The development of DLSS and real-time ray tracing reveal how Nvidia came to approach innovation. While it would roll out new chips and boards on a very fast schedule, it would now, with Nvidia Research and other groups, pursue "moonshots" at the same time. "When we got to the next-generation Ampere, we had enough momentum for ray tracing and DLSS to make that product a home run," Jeff Fisher said.

It was a further, institutionalized form of protection against the kind of stagnation that Clayton Christensen warned about in *The Innovator's Dilemma*: the inevitable desire to focus on the company's core, profit-generating business at the expense of investing in more exploratory innovations that might not be commercially viable for years.

According to Jon Peddie Research, Nvidia's share of the discrete or add-in board GPU market has stayed at roughly 80 percent over the past decade, as of this writing. Even though AMD offers better price-to-performance based on traditional metrics, gamers keep choosing Nvidia for its ability to innovate. Both ray tracing and DLSS have become must-have features that developers have incorporated into hundreds of games. And the features perform the best on Nvidia graphics cards, making it difficult for AMD to compete effectively.

In the case of ray tracing, the journey from the inception to integration into GPUs had spanned a decade. Similarly, building successive iterations of DLSS, such as frame generation, took six years. "It requires vision and long-term persistence. It requires investment even when the results aren't totally clear," Catanzaro said.

Ultimately, Nvidia Research showed how Jensen's strategic vision has changed over time. In the beginning, when the company was in survival mode, he wanted everyone to focus on concrete projects: delivering the next generation of chips at the "Speed of Light," selling the "whole cow," and beating competitors through sheer execution. As Nvidia got bigger, Jensen realized that survival now meant future-proofing the company in as many ways as possible. Continuous innovation would require a more flexible approach to Nvidia's operations, even if that meant pursuing some bets that a younger Jensen might have dismissed.

This new, more mature Jensen was no longer afraid of making a single wrong move, not least because the company now had some financial cushion. "You can't innovate if you're not willing to take some chances and embarrass yourself," he said.[3] "We don't have an ROI timeline. If you don't have an ROI timeline and you don't have a profitability target, those aren't things we're optimizing for. The only thing we're optimizing for is this: Is it incredibly cool, and are people going to like it?"

One former senior industry executive argues that Nvidia sets itself apart from its rivals in its willingness to experiment and invest over long periods, successfully monetizing its more open-ended efforts. This contrasts with larger technology giants such as Google, which often spend heavily on researching new technologies but have little to show for it commercially. Notably, all eight Google scientists who authored the seminal "Attention Is All You Need" paper on the Transformer deep-learning architecture—which proved foundational for advancements in modern AI large language models (LLMs), including the launch of ChatGPT—soon after left Google to pursue AI entrepreneurship elsewhere. "It's just a side effect of being a big company," said Llion Jones, one of the coauthors of the Transformer paper.[4] "I think the bureaucracy [at Google] had built to the point where I just felt like I couldn't get anything done," he added, expressing frustration with his inability to access resources and data.

Nvidia's second decade began with successful R&D investments in programmable shaders and then progressed to the industry-shaping innovation that is CUDA. Next came Nvidia Research's breakthroughs in ray tracing, DLSS, and AI, all of which proved critical to the company's future. The team is now three hundred researchers strong, led by Chief Scientist Bill Dally. Nvidia appeared not only to have solved the innovator's dilemma but also to have completely overcome it.

CHAPTER 14

The Big Bang

PROFESSIONAL TRADERS ARE A DYING BREED. COMPUTERS, which are faster and generally more effective at placing bets in response to releases of corporate financial results and economic data, have decimated the ranks of human traders over the past two decades.

Connors Manguino is one of the few thousand or so humans who still make a living by trading on news headlines and earnings announcements. Armed with decades of experience and a Bloomberg terminal, he still goes against the algorithms every quarter. He's good enough at it to stay alive and make a living.

He needs to react quickly. A sub-second delay in pressing the buy or sell key could mean the difference between a good entry point and a devastating loss. The running joke among his friends is that Manguino has an inhuman ability to not blink during important news periods.

On Wednesday, May 24, 2023, he was waiting for Nvidia's earnings report, which was scheduled to arrive after the market close. It was one of the most widely anticipated reports in years, and as the minutes ticked down toward the end of the trading day, he found himself staring intently at his terminal.

OpenAI's release of ChatGPT in late 2022 had generated enormous media coverage. The chatbot captivated the public with its ability to create poems, food recipes, and song lyrics on demand. ChatGPT became the fastest-growing consumer app in history, surpassing 100 million monthly active users in just two months. All of a sudden, companies were now trying to use the purported benefits of AI—its speed, its computational power, and above all its ability to process and generate natural-sounding language—any way they could.

Manguino knew that Nvidia was in prime position to take advantage of the AI boom. The question was, how big of a boom would it be, and how much of an effect would the boom have on Nvidia? The company's GPUs were well known in the academic world, thanks largely to David Kirk's efforts to build relationships with top universities. Jensen, for his part, had spent the prior decade working to transform Nvidia's reputation from a graphics company to an AI company. He had achieved some success, with Meta and TikTok using Nvidia's GPUs to make their algorithms more effective in recommending videos and ads. But AI was not a massive driver of Nvidia's earnings. During the company's fiscal year 2023, which ended in January 2023, data-center revenue, which included AI GPUs, accounted for about 55 percent of overall sales. But that figure was primarily due to a 25 percent decline elsewhere, in the company's gaming-card revenue, following a postpandemic slowdown in demand for games overall.

Then everything changed, twenty-one minutes after the stock market's close at 4:00 p.m. Manguino saw the headline flash on his terminal screen.

NVIDIA SEES 2Q REV. $11.00B PLUS OR MINUS 2%, EST. $7.18B

The financial shorthand was, to a seasoned trader, nothing short of extraordinary. Nvidia had crushed Wall Street estimates for its second-quarter revenue outlook—by roughly $4 billion. As he read the earnings print and guidance, Manguino froze. "$4 billion? How could that be real?" he thought to himself. "Holy shit. What a raise!"

By the time he came to his senses, it was too late to take advantage of the gap between the earnings release and the market's reaction. Nvidia shares had already spiked by a double-digit percentage in after-hours trading. As a consolation prize, Manguino bought shares in Advanced Micro Devices, Nvidia's main GPU competitor, hoping that the run on Nvidia stock might also boost its competitors. In this instance, the algorithms had won; unlike him, they did not hesitate in reacting to an earnings report that was better than any he had ever seen.

Other Wall Street analysts had similar reactions. Bernstein's Stacy Rasgon titled his note: "The Big Bang."

"In the 15+ years we have been doing this job, we have never seen a guide like the one Nvidia just put up," he wrote, adding that the company's outlook "was, by all accounts, cosmological." Morgan Stanley analyst Joseph Moore reported that "Nvidia guides to the largest dollar revenue upside in industry history." And former star Fidelity fund manager Gavin Baker, who now has his own technology hedge fund with several billions of dollars under management, compared Nvidia's forward-looking guidance to other seminal financial reports in the history of the tech industry. He was there for Google's first blockbuster report after its 2004 IPO, during which it reported a doubling of revenue and profit after just a single quarter as a public company.[1] He was there for Facebook's second-quarter 2013 earnings, when the company demonstrated for the first time that it could successfully transition its ad business to mobile, beating Wall Street's revenue expectations by $200 million.[2] Nvidia's guidance was better than either. "I have never seen such a large beat at this scale," he said.

The following day, Nvidia shares soared by 24 percent and added $184 billion in market value—more than the entire value of Intel, and one of the largest single-day gains ever for a U.S. public company.

Jensen capitalized on the attention, pressing his advantage the following week when he gave the keynote address at the Computex technology conference in Taiwan. In his speech, he announced Nvidia's new DGX GH200 AI supercomputer, which incorporated 256 GPUs in one system, thirty-two times the number of GPUs that were in the previous model. It meant significantly more computing power for generative artificial intelligence applications, allowing developers to build better language models for AI chatbots, create more complex recommendation algorithms, and develop more effective fraud-detection and data-analysis tools.

But his main message was so simple that even a nontechnical listener could understand it. Nvidia offered far more computing power at a lower cost per GPU. He hammered this home over the course of his remarks, punctuating his readouts of technical specs with a refrain: "The more you buy, the more you save."

More broadly, Nvidia's salespeople had been able to stoke unprecedented demand by arguing to customers that they had to invest aggressively in generative AI or face the existential threat of falling behind their competitors. Jensen himself has called AI a "universal function approximator" that can predict the future with reasonable accuracy. This applies as much in "high-tech" fields such as computer vision, speech recognition, and recommendations systems as it does in "low-tech" tasks such as correcting grammar or analyzing financial data. He believes that eventually it will apply to "almost anything that has structure."

The best way to access this universal function approximator, of course, was through Nvidia technology. And over the next four quarters, the company achieved one of the most incredible revenue ramps in technology history. Its first-quarter data-center business for fiscal 2024 rose by 427 percent from the prior year, to $22.6 billion—driven primarily by artificial-intelligence chip demand. Unlike software, which is easy to scale at essentially no incremental cost, Nvidia is producing and shipping complex high-end AI products and systems, some of which contain up to 35,000 parts. There was no precedent for this level of hardware growth at a technology company the size of Nvidia.

To those outside of the company, Nvidia's meteoric rise seems like a miracle. Those inside it, however, consider it a natural evolution, said Jeff Fisher. Nvidia wasn't lucky; it was able to perceive the wave of demand on the horizon years in advance and had prepared for this very moment. It went to its manufacturing partners—Foxconn, Wistron, TSMC, among others—to help them build out production capacity. Nvidia sent out so-called tiger teams to those partners, doing whatever they could to help them become more efficient: the teams bought equipment, added factory space, automated testing, and sourced advanced chip packaging.

In keeping with Jensen's "rough justice" model, Nvidia was not doing all this just to make its partners more efficient at their current processes. It wanted to produce new chip designs more quickly, transitioning from its previous two-year product cycle to a one-year cadence for its AI chips. In the 1990s, Nvidia shifted to a faster product cadence by releasing a new graphics card every six months. Now, it wanted to do the same for AI chips. "The bigger AI gets, the more solutions that will be needed, and the faster we will meet those goals and expectations," said Nvidia CFO Colette Kress.[3]

Typically, hardware-production plants have average cycle times of fourteen to eighteen weeks between phases of the manufacturing process. Manufacturers build in buffer time between those phases, in case an upstream problem creates issues down the line. This can leave machines, materials, and components idle for days. Nvidia's teams figured out how to add quality controls early in the process to reduce the risk of unforeseen problems and removing the need for buffer time. According to Jeff Fisher, Nvidia's approach involves "no magic." It's just hard work and ruthless efficiency, all in the service of maintaining competitive advantage. And everyone who works with Nvidia must embrace it, not just its internal teams.[4] Everything the tiger teams did was expensive and resulted in a drag on the bottom line. Yet Nvidia has always been willing to use its financial resources to invest in critical parts of the business—even when that has meant other companies' business.

Nvidia has key advantages over other AI chip makers. Similar to Apple's approach with the iPhone, the company employs a "full-stack" model that optimizes the customer's experience across hardware, software, and networking. Most of its rivals just make chips. And Nvidia moves faster than its competitors.

For instance, the core architecture used in modern large language models is the Transformer introduced in the 2017 paper "Attention Is All You Need" by Google scientists. The primary innovation is self-attention, which enables the model to measure the importance of different words in a sentence and measure long-range dependencies on the basis of their context. The attention mechanism empowers the model to focus on the more important information, to train the AI model quicker, and thus to generate higher-quality results compared with prior deep-learning architectures.

Jensen grasped the need to add support for Transformers in Nvidia's AI offerings almost right away. Simona Jankowski, a former finance executive at Nvidia, remembers Jensen getting into a fairly detailed discussion about Transformers on a quarterly earnings call just months after the Google scientists' paper came out.[5] He instructed his GPU software teams to write a special library for Nvidia Tensor Cores that optimizes them for use with Transformer operations; the library was later called the Transformer Engine.[6] It was included for the first time in the Hopper chip architecture, which went into development in the late 2010s and was released in 2022, one month before ChatGPT was launched. According to Nvidia's own testing, GPUs with Transformer Engine could train even the largest models, in a matter of days or even hours, whereas without Transformer Engine those same training runs might take weeks or months.

"The Transformer was a big deal," Jensen said in 2023. "The ability for you to learn patterns and relationships from spatial as well as sequential data must be an architecture that's very effective, right? And so I think on its first principles, you can kind of think Transformer's going to be a big, big deal. Not only that, you could train it in parallel and you can really scale this model up."[7]

When demand for generative AI exploded in 2023, Nvidia was the only hardware manufacturer ready to fully support it. And it was ready only because it was able to spot the early signals, productize them in the form of hardware and software acceleration features, and insert those features into a line of chips that was only months away from arriving on the open market. The breathtaking speed Nvidia demonstrated was a sign that it will be difficult to dethrone, even though several other large technology companies, including Microsoft, Amazon, Google, Intel, and Advanced Micro Devices, are developing their own AI chips. Nvidia has proved, as it enters its fourth decade, that it can still outrun the competition.

Its second, but lesser-known, advantage is pricing power. Nvidia doesn't believe in building commodity products, because commodities are subject to downward pricing pressure as competition increases. Instead, from the very beginning, its pricing has only gone in the opposite direction: up.

"Jensen has always said that we should be doing things that other people cannot. We need to bring unique value to the marketplace, and he feels that by doing work that is cutting edge and revolutionary, it allows the company to attract good people," Nvidia executive Jay Puri said. "We don't have the culture of just going after market share. We would rather create the market."[8]

A former Nvidia executive recalls how Jensen would become upset if any other company tried to negotiate pricing with him. Potential customers would always want to meet him when contract discussions were nearing an end. "We always try to do our best to prepare the customers," the former Nvidia executive said. "Do not discuss price. We are here to close the deal."[9]

Jensen has instilled this mentality across the company. Michael Hara, a former director of marketing, remembers debating with Jensen how to price Nvidia's earliest products. When Hara left S3 to join Nvidia, he was used to a commodity-like pricing strategy; at the time, S3's market-leading 3-D graphics chip sold for $5 (about $11 today). When the RIVA 128 came out in 1997, Hara was worried if they priced it too high, the buyers would balk. Ten dollars at most, he replied. Jensen said, "No, I think that's too cheap. Let's go with $15." The card sold out at that price. The derivative RIVA 128ZX chip that came out the following year was priced at $32. And the next-generation GeForce 256, which came out in 1999, cost $65.

Jensen understood that gamers who buy Nvidia cards are willing to pay for performance. "As long as they look at the screen and can see something radically different than they saw before, they're going to buy it," he said. It was a lesson that has stuck with Hara ever since. When he moved from marketing to investor relations, he made the same case to Nvidia's investors—that Nvidia would be a unique semiconductor company where product ASPs (average selling prices) rise. "We're going to be the only guy where ASPs go up over time, when everybody else's ASPs will go down," he said.

The reason is that computation for 3-D graphics is an infinitely complex problem to solve and thus drives a competition to make better and better hardware. Hardware will never be powerful enough to perfectly reflect reality. Even so, when you purchase the latest 3-D graphics card, you can clearly see an improvement in performance over the past generation—lighting looks better, textures look more realistic, objects move more fluidly.

A similar dynamic problem is playing out right now with deep learning and artificial intelligence. Nvidia's current-generation hardware has enabled AI models to grow exponentially in size and ability in only a few years. Yet the demand for AI computational power is growing even faster, because the problems that AI can solve get ever more complex. There are step-changes in between generations of AI models, because the underlying hardware and software have also improved in tandem with the models. Still, the promise of true general artificial intelligence remains far off: there is plenty more work to be done. By remaining on the cutting edge of technology—and by cleverly positioning itself in highly visible fields where performance increases are immediately obvious—Nvidia is able to increase its pricing power and its ASPs.

Today, Nvidia graphics cards cost more than $2,000 apiece. And those are the consumer-grade prices. In the past decade, the company has started offering AI-server systems equipped with eight GPUs, with each system costing hundreds of thousands of dollars. Ross Walker, who went head-to-head against Nvidia over his use of the cheaper GeForce line to accelerate his molecular dynamics software AMBER (as we saw in chapter 8), remembered that at the time, a top-of-the-line Nvidia GPU server cost as much as a small used car such as a Honda Civic. Now, a similar server might cost as much as a house.

"I was in the audience when Nvidia announced the DGX-1 for $149,000," he said, referring to the first GPU server optimized with Tensor Cores and Transformer Engine for AI research. "There were audible gasps in the audience. I couldn't believe it."[10]

And that's not even close to the most expensive Nvidia product. Nvidia's latest server rack system as of this writing, the Blackwell GB200 series, was specifically designed to train "trillion-parameter" AI models.

It comes with seventy-two GPUs and costs $2 million to $3 million—the most expensive Nvidia machine ever made. The company's top-end-product pricing isn't merely increasing; it is accelerating.

JENSEN DOES NOT POSSESS SPECIAL visionary powers that allowed him to predict exactly when AI would take off. One could argue, in fact, that the company was initially measured in its approach; Nvidia did not allocate many people or resources toward AI development until he saw significant signals indicating what could be possible. Then, he moved with a speed and totality of purpose unmatched by the competition.

Early enough, however, Jensen knew the end game. Consider what Reed Hastings achieved with Netflix, which he cofounded. Hastings knew that someday the world would move to streaming video over the internet. Although he did not know exactly when this would happen, he had the intuitive sense that it would become the ultimate solution. As CEO, he managed the DVD-by-mail business only until the technology advanced enough to make streaming possible, and he made the transition forcefully when the time came.

Jensen did something similar with AI and, before that, with video games. In the early 1990s, he was convinced video games were going to be an enormous market. "We grew up in the video-game generation," he said.[11] "The entertainment value of video games and computer games was very obvious to me." He believed the PC game market would explode soon enough, within five or ten years or fifteen years—which it did, when *GLQuake* was released in 1997.

Jensen is always trying to figure out the next thing and what Nvidia can do to prepare itself to take advantage of it. In early 2023, he was asked by a student to predict what will follow, and build upon, AI. "There's no question," he said. "Digital biology is going to be it."[12]

Though biology is one of the most complex systems, Jensen explained that for the first time in history, it could be digitally engineered. With AI models, scientists can now start to model the structure of biological systems in greater depth than ever before. They can learn how proteins interact with each other and with their environments, and use the vast computing power unlocked by advanced computing to perform computer-aided drug research and discovery. "I'm very proud to say that Nvidia is at the center of all that. We made it possible for some of the breakthroughs to happen," he said. "It's going to be profound."

Jensen sees parallels today between digital biology and almost every major milestone in Nvidia's history. When he cofounded the company, computer-aided semiconductor design was just starting to become feasible. "It was the combination of algorithms, computers that are fast enough, and know-how," he said.[13] When those three things reached a certain stage of development, the semiconductor industry could create larger, more complex chips, because engineers could now design and simulate chips using higher-level abstractions in software without having to physically lay out every signal transistor. The same combination of factors saw Nvidia invent the GPU in the early 2000s and take over the AI space in the late 2010s—the "fuel-air mixture" that Bill Dally spoke of.

Nvidia's vice president of health care, Kimberly Powell, has said that computer-aided drug discovery will do for drug design what computer-aided design and electronic design automation did for chip design. Companies will become more consistent and efficient in finding drugs to treat diseases and even personalize them for individual people. It will "go beyond discovery and evolve into design, helping create the conditions to no longer be a hit-or-miss industry," she said.[14]

Generate:Biomedicines is one of the start-ups using AI and Nvidia GPUs to develop new molecular structures and protein-based drugs that do not form from natural processes. The biotech company has studied millions of proteins by using machine-learning algorithms to arrive at a more in-depth picture of how nature functions, a picture it then uses to create new drugs. Gevorg Grigoryan, the company's cofounder and chief technology officer, was previously a professor at Dartmouth College, where he studied statistical patterns of proteins and tried to better design and model proteins by using computing power.

"Using very simple statistics, I was seeing that the patterns in the data were generalizable. We were finding principles that would go beyond the dataset," he said. "It was very clear the next step was to use AI, machine learning, and large-scale data generation."[15] Grigoryan couldn't do that in academia because purchasing the required computing power would be beyond his institution's reach. He saw the commercial potential of a new way of designing molecules, and soon enough, Generate:Biomedicines was born.

Starting in the early 2000s, Grigoryan observed that many scientists who ran molecular-dynamics simulations were buying Nvidia gaming GPUs and coercing them into performing nongraphics computations. He appreciated how the company catered to and collaborated with the research community, even though the cards were supposed to be used for video games. "That was really the beginning of this beautiful marriage between Nvidia and molecular science," he said.

When he started to use machine learning himself, it was natural for him to rely on PyTorch, a free, open-source machine-learning library created by Meta in 2016, now under the purview of the Linux Foundation. "PyTorch was something that was very well developed, had a huge community, and had tons of support from Nvidia," Grigoryan said. "It was not even a choice of what type of GPU we'd go with. PyTorch works well with CUDA, CUDA is Nvidia's creation. By default, we always used Nvidia hardware without even thinking too much about it."

Structural prediction and protein design, once considered impossible problems, are now solvable. Grigoryan explains that the complexity of a protein and its possible states surpasses the number of atoms in the universe. "Those numbers are extremely challenging for any computational tools to deal with," he said. But he believes a skilled protein biophysicist can examine a particular molecular structure and deduce its potential functions, suggesting there may be learnable general principles in nature—exactly the sort of operation that a "universal prediction engine" such as AI should be able to figure out.

Generate:Biomedicines has applied AI to examine and map molecules at the cell level, and Grigoryan sees the potential to extend the same technique to the entire human body. Simulating how the human body will react is orders of magnitude more complicated, but Grigoryan thinks it will be possible. "Once you see it working, it's hard to imagine it doesn't just continue," he said, referring to the power of AI.

While it may sound like science fiction, Grigoryan and his team are already building generative models that optimize molecule functions inside cells. The ultimate dream is to make drug discovery a software question, where an AI model can take a disease, including a type of cancer, as input and generate a molecule that cures it. "It's not totally crazy. I think it may even be within our lifetime that we'll be able to see that kind of impact," he said. "Science always surprises us, but man, what a time to be alive, right?"

THERE IS AN ENORMOUS REPOSITORY of data inside corporations that remains untouched and unstructured by AI: e-mails, memos, proprietary internal documents, and presentations. Because the consumer internet has already been mined to near-exhaustion by chatbots such as ChatGPT, the next significant opportunity lies within enterprises, where customized AI models can enable employees to access knowledge currently siloed across a company.

Jensen has said AI will completely change how employees interact and work with information. Traditional IT systems have relied on a static file-retrieval system, requiring explicitly written technical searches pointed at a specific storage device. These requests often do not work because of the fragile and brittle nature of the query format.

Current AI models can now understand requests via context and because they can grasp natural conversational language. It is a major breakthrough. "The core of generative AI is the ability for software to understand the meaning of data," Jensen said.[16] He believes that companies will "vectorize" their databases, indexing and capturing representations of information and connecting it to a large language model, enabling users to "talk to their data."

This use case makes obvious sense to me. My first job after college was in management consulting. The worst part of the role was manually sifting through file directories on servers, searching PowerPoint or Word documents for specific pieces of information a partner asked for from years past. Sometimes it would take hours or even days to find the document. Large language models powered by AI applications such as Nvidia's ChatRTX now allow users to receive contextually relevant answers instantly from private files on computers. It increases productivity dramatically. What was a tedious, repetitive task that took significant time now takes seconds and gives employees more space for more critical, high-level work. Employees will have a virtual assistant, almost like a brilliant intern with near-perfect memory, capable of instantly recalling any piece of knowledge stored on computers and the internet. Instead of simple file retrieval, the models can generate smarter insights drawn from the entire pool of a company's internal data.

In a late 2023 report, Goldman Sachs predicted generative AI-driven cost reductions could total more than $3 trillion over the next decade across industries. Nvidia management has repeatedly stated that the $1 trillion that has been invested in global data-center computer infrastructure over the years, which is currently powered by traditional CPU servers, will eventually transition to GPUs capable of the parallel computations necessary for AI. That transition represents a gold mine for Nvidia. In mid-2024, J.P. Morgan published survey results from 166 chief information officers, who are responsible for $123 billion in annual enterprise tech spending. The report revealed that CIOs plan to increase their AI compute hardware spending by more than 40 percent annually over the next three years, going from 5 percent of total IT budgets to more than 14 percent in 2027. One-third of CIOs also said they will defund other IT projects in order to support the new AI investments. The three biggest categories slated for defunding included legacy system upgrades, infrastructure, and internal app development.

Jensen believes that increased expenditure on AI will benefit more than just executives and investors. "I believe that artificial intelligence is the technology industry's single greatest contribution to social elevation, to lift all of the people that have historically been left behind," Jensen said at an event at Oregon State University in 2024.[17] He does not often venture into social commentary, but Nvidia's size and prominence now almost require him to offer such opinions.

The only thing that might hinder Nvidia are the so-called AI scaling laws. There are three components of these laws: model size, computing power, and data. Large technology companies and start-ups are confident that the capabilities of AI models will continue to improve in the near term and are aggressively increasing their AI infrastructure spending into 2025. Yet as companies keep increasing model size, adding more computing power from Nvidia GPUs, and incorporating larger datasets, they will eventually encounter diminishing returns. This would lead to an air pocket in demand for Nvidia, as the majority of its data-center revenue is related to model training. In early 2024, Nvidia said about 60 percent of its data-center GPUs were sold to train AI models, while the other 40 percent of its data-center GPUs were purchased for inferencing, or the process of generating answers from AI models.

No one knows when this AI slowdown will happen, whether it is in 2026, 2028, or more than five years from now. But history shows Nvidia will be prepared for the challenge. It will also be ready to adapt to the next big computing trend, regardless of what it may be.

CONCLUSION

The Nvidia Way

EVEN AFTER THIRTY-ONE YEARS LEADING NVIDIA, JENSEN Huang refuses to work in a private office. Instead, he stakes out the Metropolis conference room in Nvidia's Endeavor headquarters building, where he hosts group meetings throughout the day. For smaller meetings, he'll move to a five-person room called Mind Meld, a reference to the ability of the Vulcans in *Star Trek* to telepathically combine their thoughts with those of other beings. It's an apt metaphor, if a little on the nose, for how Jensen has designed Nvidia—as an extension of his own formidable intellect.

Jensen is a technical founder and CEO, which is part of Nvidia's advantage over some of its competitors. But to call him a mere technologist is to undersell his skill at hiring and developing people who are good fits for Nvidia's particular culture. He gives his employees a high degree of independence over their individual projects, but only if they can keep those projects perfectly aligned with the company's core objectives. To reduce ambiguity, Jensen spends a great deal of his time communicating with his employees and ensures that everyone at the company knows the overall strategy and vision. He offers a level of visibility most companies don't share outside of the C-suite.

A former senior executive at a large software company said that he was always struck by how you could talk to multiple Nvidia employees and they would never contradict one another. The message from the top was consistent, and Nvidia staff learned it and made it their own. He drew a contrast with almost every other company he'd ever worked with, whose representatives sometimes argued with each other in front of external clients.

"Ultimately, my e-staff is something that I have to know how to work with. The company's organization is like a race car. It has to be a machine that the CEO knows how to drive," Jensen said.

Hiring raw talent is the first essential component of the Nvidia Way. Y Combinator cofounder Paul Graham, who once worked for Yahoo, noticed that once Yahoo started losing the war for the best engineers to Google and Microsoft, the company began slouching toward mediocrity. "Good programmers want to work with other good programmers. So once the quality of programmers at your company starts to drop, you enter a death spiral from which there is no recovery," he wrote. "In technology, once you have bad programmers, you're doomed."[1]

Much of the time, that talent finds Nvidia first. Or Nvidia proactively finds the best people: more than a third of new hires are referred by current employees.[2]

When Nvidia sees an opportunity to poach talent from its rivals, it moves with aggression and speed. Hock Leow, former chief technology officer of Creative Labs, witnessed an Nvidia approach first-hand. In 2002, Creative Labs acquired a company called 3Dlabs, which had an office for graphics-chip engineers in Huntsville, Alabama. Three years later, Creative announced that it was going to shut down 3Dlabs and the Huntsville location altogether.

Intel moved quickly, more quickly than Nvidia at first, attempting to lure away the former 3Dlabs employees in Huntsville. But the offers it produced were contingent on relocation to another of Intel's sites, all of them located far away from Alabama. Many of the workers were reluctant to uproot their families or to move to a place with a higher cost of living.

Jensen, upon learning of Intel's interest, promptly sent his executives to make offers to the 3Dlabs team that did not include a relocation demand. In fact, he instructed the executives to open a new office in Huntsville to accommodate the new team members. "Nvidia moves very fast," Leow said. "They aggressively accumulate human and technology assets to win. Speed of execution and decision-making is an Nvidia trademark." Nvidia maintains an office in Huntsville to this day.

Former Nvidia executive Ben de Waal recounted a similar experience. In 2005, he and his boss, head of software engineering Dwight Diercks, traveled to Pune, India, to evaluate a potential acquisition: a roughly fifty-person video-encoder-software company. Upon arriving, they discovered the owners had gathered the employees in a hotel ballroom to announce the company's dissolution. The company had tax problems and was in financial trouble. "It was rough and emotional. People were crying. They put their hearts and souls into this company," de Waal said. "I wondered why we were even there."[3]

Diercks knew that to return to California with nothing would be a missed opportunity. Nvidia needed larger software teams for new projects, and these workers were excellent. He had been to India nine times that year on scouting trips and had identified this specific company as the best available prospect.

He had an idea: why not hire the employees directly instead of acquiring the company? He pitched it to Jensen, who approved it right away. "We changed our trip from an acquisition mode to a hiring mode," Diercks said. "We spent all night in the run-down hotel business center printing out about fifty offer packages, which in India is more complex than a U.S. standard package."[4]

By the end of the first day, fifty-one out of fifty-four employees had accepted Nvidia's offers. They became the core of a new Nvidia office in Pune, which would eventually grow into an essential engineering operation with more than fourteen hundred employees.

"You always need the best people," Diercks said, adding that Nvidia saw hiring talent in bunches as a strategy.

Occasionally, Nvidia will go for the most direct approach possible. Its executives have no qualms telling top technical architects at other companies that they are going to lose, so they might as well join the winner. This was how Nvidia poached Walt Donovan, the chief architect of Rendition, after they demonstrated the RIVA 128 chip to him at a conference in 1997.

"Walt was the first chief architect from a rival company who wanted to be part of the Nvidia team rather than trying to compete with us," Kirk said. "It gave me the idea that if we hire the best person from every other company, we can do so much more and do so much better."[5]

David Kirk, Nvidia's former chief scientist, became particularly skilled at poaching. He would ask around to find out who the crucial employee at a company was, and then call that person with his pitch. "Hey, how's life? How's your job? I heard your name. I have a lot of respect for you," he recalled asking his targets. "You guys have been making some great products. How many architects do you have working on this stuff?"

Usually, the number was one or two architects per company. This was standard and on one level made sense: an architect usually oversaw an entire family of chips, and most companies had a handful of chip families in production at a time. Not at Nvidia, however. Kirk would explain that Nvidia had twenty architects, and that each was working on groundbreaking projects and had all the resources they could possibly need. Kirk would say that he needed people like the person on the other end of the line. "Maybe you want to come in and do this project with us. It'd be really fun, and we'll probably make a lot of money together too, instead of just working by yourself there. That's probably not as much fun."

In later years, Nvidia employees were impressed by how the company was able to poach and retain so many accomplished architects, who are known for their egos. But because Nvidia's chips had become so complex, they needed as many high-level chip designers as possible. There was more than enough work to go around. And Kirk was deliberate in his choice of who to pursue, preferring to hire for complementary skill sets rather than just whoever came along. Some were leaders and managers, while others were hired to handle specific areas such as math and graphics algorithms.

"It wasn't like you could just draw a diagram on the back of an envelope and have a couple of engineers design a chip together anymore," Kirk said.

One example of the emphasis on complementarity was Nvidia's most famous hire, Silicon Graphics' John Montrym, who had developed SGI's high-end RealityEngine 3-D graphics hardware. He was brought on to work alongside Donovan, who had joined the company just a few months earlier. Kirk said Montrym was talented as an overall system architect, in that he saw how all the components fit together, and Donovan was an expert at graphics textures and texture filtering—"our pixel quality god" according to one Nvidia employee. Both would remain at Nvidia for decades.

"We built the all-star team of architects," said Kirk. "Executives were bitter we were stealing their good people."

Diercks's own arrival at Nvidia in 1994 demonstrated Jensen's persistence when it comes to important, but difficult, hires. Before Nvidia, Diercks had worked at a graphics start-up company called Pellucid, which was acquired by Media Vision—a company that later faced allegations of financial fraud. His former Pellucid colleague Scott Sellers, who later cofounded 3dfx, had originally talked with Jensen about joining Nvidia, but nothing came of it. During the interview, however, Sellers was asked about talent at Pellucid, and he said the two members on the software team, Diercks and his direct boss, were exceptional. Jensen made a mental note.

Later, Jensen called up Diercks's boss and said, "I hear you're one of the smartest guys in the Valley. You should come and talk to us." Diercks's boss agreed and jumped ship for Nvidia.

Not long afterward, Diercks decided he wanted to leave as well, because the situation with Media Vision was deteriorating. His former boss reached out and told him to meet Jensen. After talking with Diercks, Jensen, clearly impressed, told the former boss: "Dwight is a warrior. If I send you and Dwight to Vietnam, you would come back on his back."

Diercks was excited. He resigned the next day and told Pellucid's top executive he was going to Nvidia. The executive was livid.

"You can't go there," he shouted. "I'm going to sue you and Nvidia. You'll never work in the Valley again." He told Diercks that a legal threat would scare Nvidia away—the company was only a year old at the time and had limited funds.

But when he told Jensen about the threat, the CEO wasn't fazed.

"Bring it on," he replied. This, Diercks realized, was the type of boss he wanted to work for. He accepted Nvidia's offer and has remained at the company for more than thirty years.

THE COMPANY'S HIRING METHODS are just one component of the Nvidia Way. Its emphasis on retention is another. Jensen rewards performance by using stock grants, which are distributed on the basis of how important an employee is considered to the company.

"Jensen looks at stock like his blood," said former head of human resources John McSorley. "He pores over the stock-allocation reports."

Equity compensation occurs through stock grants called restricted stock units (RSUs). When an individual starts at the company, that employee receives a brokerage account. At the end of the first year, the employee vests and receives one-quarter of his or her initial stock grant in a lump sum; if the total package was one thousand shares, the employee would get two hundred fifty. Subsequently, the employee receives one-quarter of his or her annual grant every quarter.

To avoid the "equity cliff" (when engineers depart after their stock packages have fully vested over the industry-standard four years), Nvidia offers annual refresher grants. If an employee receives an "outperform" rating from his or her manager, that employee may be awarded an additional three hundred shares that vest over the next four years. In theory, employees can receive these refresher grants every year—more and more reasons to remain with the company.

Another wrinkle is the TC, or "top contributor," designation. Managers can refer an employee for special consideration to senior executives. Jensen will review the list of TC candidates and give out special one-off grants that also vest over a four-year period.

Once such a grant is approved, the employee receives an e-mail from a senior executive, with Jensen copied. The subject line says "Special Grant," authorizing the RSU grant "in recognition of your extraordinary contributions," with a clear description of the rationale behind the award.

Jensen can also reach down into the organization at any time and award stock directly, without waiting for an annual compensation review. This allows him to ensure that people who are doing great work feel appreciated in the moment. It is yet another sign of his interest in every aspect, and level, of the company.

Former senior director of sales and marketing Chris Diskin, who played an important role in closing the Xbox partnership with Microsoft in 2000, said Jensen doubled his stock grant within months of him joining Nvidia. Diskin thanked Jensen but pressed for more, saying, "If you're really impressed, you'd more than double it." When he saw his grant, it had indeed more than doubled.

Nvidia's merit-based, adaptive, and agile compensation philosophy has played a role in keeping turnover exceptionally low. In fiscal 2024, Nvidia reported a turnover rate of under 3 percent in an industry where 13 percent is the average, according to LinkedIn. It helps that the stock's price keeps going up, giving anyone with unvested stock more reason to stay.

"The company treats people extremely well, not only in terms of salaries and benefits but also by treating people as human beings rather than fungible engineers," a former Nvidia employee said. "There are many opportunities for advancement." This person mentioned Nvidia offering flexibility on remote work when a family member received a cancer diagnosis or providing ex gratia payments when an employee's house burned down.

"People tend to be loyal to a company that supports them," he said.

Another senior executive spoke about a time when his spouse had a major health event. He told Jensen he had to move across the country to be close to family. "Don't worry about it," Jensen said. "Go and call me when you're ready to work again." The employee was kept on the payroll even though he wasn't able to work full-time.

A COMPANY CAN RETAIN PEOPLE not only with compensation but also through a culture of excellence—the third component of the Nvidia Way. No employee wants to spend years working on products or technologies that get shuttered or set aside or rendered obsolete. At Nvidia, engineers work alongside industry luminaries who have deep technical knowledge and experience while making products that may well reshape the world.

Many senior executives and engineers tend to stay at Nvidia for the long haul, even more so than at other major technology companies. Head of software engineering Dwight Diercks, PC business executive Jeff Fisher, and head of GPU architecture Jonah Alben have all worked at the company for nearly three decades. Few senior executives have left for competitors or attempted to strike out on their own in the start-up world. (Of course, they may also be intimidated by the prospect of competing with Nvidia.)

For employees at every level, the focus on excellence in one's work, rather than on internal politics, is reason enough to commit to the company. The type of person who jockeys for position more than he or she contributes to the broader good will struggle at Nvidia. "Some companies will prefer these kinds of people, but not Nvidia," former GPU architect Li-Yi Wei said. "You can be 100 percent focused on the technology side without worrying about everything else."[6]

In fact, Nvidia actively resists the emergence of the kind of cutthroat culture that most other organizations foster, intentionally or not. Employees are encouraged to ask for help if they are struggling to meet a target or are facing a technical challenge.

"If we're going to lose, it's not going to be because you didn't have help. We're going to work together. No one loses alone," Jensen regularly advises Nvidia employees.[7]

For example, if you are a sales executive working in a particular region and you are falling behind in meeting your quota, you are expected to inform your team early on so they can assist you. Other resources across the company, from Jensen to senior engineering staff, may be brought in to solve the issue.

" 'No one loses alone' is particularly pertinent in the sales organization," said Jay Puri, head of global field operations. Referring to the head count on his sales team, he added that "We are so small compared to our competitors that when something important is happening, we all need to come together."[8]

Sales executive Anthony Medeiros saw a different mentality when he worked at Sun Microsystems. He and his peers were expected to fig- ure it out on their own and justify their salaries; asking for help was seen as weakness.

"It is critical you speak up," is how he described the culture at Nvidia. "You would get in more trouble if you didn't."[9]

IN EXCHANGE FOR THE SUPPORT and the high compensation, Nvidia demands much of its people. Extreme commitment is critical to the Nvidia Way. Sixty-hour workweeks are expected as the bare min- imum, even at junior positions. The workweek can stretch to eighty hours or more during critical periods in chip development—especially for hardware engineers—or as the result of a major and sudden change in corporate strategy, such as during the pivot to AI.

Transparency is also critical to the Nvidia Way. In addition to the standard reporting lines, Nvidia employees must have a separate line of communication with Jensen himself. Sometimes it takes the form of "Top 5" e-mails. In other instances, it can take the form of a drive-by questioning in a hallway or even in the bathroom.

It is not possible to hide at Nvidia, even at company events. Former developer-technology engineer Peter Young was first introduced to Jen- sen at a party for new hires. Jensen already knew who he was. "You're Peter Young," Jensen said. "You've been here for a year from Sony Play- Station and 3dfx prior to that." He had a similar recall of biographical details for all fifty attendees of the party.

Young was surprised by how much the CEO knew about someone both relatively new and relatively low-level. He mentioned this to his manager, who replied: "That's normal. He's like this with everybody." Young found it inspiring that the CEO of the company with thousands of employees cared enough to put that much time and effort into con- necting with each employee.[10] But it was also a signal that Jensen had his eye on everyone at the company, knew their potential, and expected them to perform accordingly.

He expects them to continuously expand the company's—and Jen- sen's own—knowledge base, as well. His executive staff chuckles about a habit of Jensen that has remained constant over the decades. Whenever one of them returns from a trade show, gaming event, or trip to Taiwan, he corners them and asks, "So, what did you learn?"

"That kind of characterizes Jensen because he always wants to know what's going on out there," Jeff Fisher said. "He just wants to know what's going on out in the world, so he can make better decisions."[11]

When Jensen feels he can't make the best decisions possible, he will get frustrated—which, given Nvidia's culture of transparency, often turns into a public spectacle. Yet at least some employees don't think it is fair to describe Jensen as quick tempered.

"He can show his temper, but you have to screw up badly for him to get to that stage," one employee said. "He wants to be involved and understand what you are doing. Through that process, he's going to be very direct and ask lots of tough questions. If you're not ready for that type of discussion, it can be a little alarming, but there's no malice behind it. It's all about let's get an airtight case before we move forward on something."

Jensen is also ruthless about prioritizing his time. Adobe CEO Shantanu Narayen recalls a breakfast with Jensen where they had a great conversation about business issues, from innovation and strategy to culture.[12] When Narayen checked his watch, Jensen remarked, "Why are you looking at your watch?" Narayen responded, "Jensen, don't you have a calendar?" Jensen replied, "What are you doing? I do what I want." Narayen appreciated the advice. Jensen was telling him to focus on the most important activity at all times and not be beholden to a schedule.

Conversely, when an employee starts rambling, Jensen will say "LUA," which he pronounces like a single word: *Looh-ahh*. Bryan Catanzaro, the Nvidia executive, explained that LUA is a warning sign that Jensen's patience is growing thin. When he says it, Jensen wants the employee to stop and do three things: Listen to the question. Understand the question. Answer the question.

"LUA means pay attention because you're talking about something important and you need to do it properly," Catanzaro said. "He does not like it when people put up an abstraction or sort of puffery to deflect an answer to a question. Everyone who works for Jensen has heard LUA."[13]

It's a mantra that Jensen turns on himself, too. Everyone I talked to for this book lists Jensen's extraordinary capacity to listen, understand, and answer any question about advanced computing. Eunhak Bae, a longtime Nvidia investor, values Jensen's ability to "talk through everything, not just from a technology standpoint, but from a business standpoint. When I think of truly well-rounded and deep technology CEOs, Jensen stands out."[14]

JENSEN HUANG IS SURELY THE only person who could have gotten Nvidia to where it is today. He grasps technology and business strategy and also understands the harder work of actually operating a large business, day to day. He personally enforces his own high standards and snuffs out the dysfunction before it can take root. He has structured Nvidia to generate step-change performance, not the slow crawl of incremental improvement. The entire business operates at the speed of light, and if Jensen catches you coasting, he will call you

Curtis Priem, Jensen Huang, and Chris Malachowsky
in front of Endeavor. (NVIDIA)

out in front of everyone. Perhaps the most succinct definition of the Nvidia Way is that it is Jensen's way, or that it is simply Jensen himself.

But this also means Nvidia is almost completely dependent on him; in a sense, he is its single point of failure. As of this writing, he is sixty-one years old. It is hard to imagine that he will retire at sixty-five like many American men do, but there will eventually be a time when he will step back from Nvidia. Who will take his place at the center of the world's most important computer hardware company? Who could possibly run Nvidia as successfully as he has done the past thirty-one years?

In writing the history of Nvidia, I was struck by the times it verged on failure and outright destruction. If things had gone just a little bit differently in a few instances, computing would have taken another course—we would be living in an altered world. Some of Nvidia's success was pure serendipity. Chris Malachowsky might have decided to pursue a career in medicine after taking the MCAT. He might have gone in for that next interview with Digital Equipment instead of accepting the offer from Sun Microsystems, which was supposed to be just a practice run. Curtis Priem might have decided to make the NV1 chip more like everything else on the market, and it might have succeeded. But that would have deprived Nvidia of the chance to learn from its failure and respond with the RIVA 128—the chip that saved the company. "Nvidia would have been a failure if NV1 had not failed," Priem said.[15]

But much of the Nvidia story is a result of Jensen's own efforts. He raised funds to launch Nvidia and then raised new funds when it was the only way to save the company. He licensed the VGA core to get the RIVA 128 out on time. He kept Wall Street at bay during the CUDA years, when everyone wanted him to sacrifice his long-term vision for short-term profit taking. He learned how to set a high bar for performance and talent and to buck conventional wisdom. His bluntness and directness saved time, avoided miscommunication, and accelerated Nvidia's pace at critical moments. And he has distilled his philosophy into a few stock phrases that keep people focused on what's really important. "The mission is the boss." "Speed of Light." "How hard can it be?"

Jensen and the culture he created have kept Nvidia internally aligned despite the near-death experiences and the company's exponential growth in head count and revenue. When I interviewed Jensen, he told me repeatedly that intelligence and genius had little to do with Nvidia's success. Instead, it was hard work and resilience. It didn't have to be this hard, but it was—and it was always going to be. The work demanded one thing out of everyone, including himself: "sheer will."

Nvidia remains the only stand-alone graphics-chip firm to this day, even though hundreds of others have thrown their hats in the ring. Jensen himself is now the technology industry's longest-serving CEO.

We are sometimes told, by various self-help experts and gurus, that we can make more money while working less. Jensen is the antithesis of that notion. There are no shortcuts. The best way to be successful is to take the more difficult route. And the best teacher of all is adversity—something he has become well acquainted with. It is why he still keeps going at a pace that would see most other people, at any age, burn out. It is why he still says, to this day, and without any trace of hesitation or irony or self-doubt: "I love Nvidia."

APPENDIX

Jensen-isms

"As many as needed, as few as possible": Invite only the essential employees, those with relevant knowledge, to meetings, and avoid wasting people's time if their presence is not necessary.

"AMAN, ALAP": As much as needed, as little as possible. Be frugal with employee time and company resources.

"Always hire the best": If you hire smart and capable people, they will be able to solve problems and adapt to new challenges.

"Criticism is a gift": Providing direct feedback leads to continuous improvement.

"Don't worry about the score. Worry about how you play the game": Don't be distracted by stock price volatility. Focus on delivering excellent work and creating value.

"Early indicators of future success": Evidence a new project is starting to get traction.

"Floor sweeping" and "Ship the whole cow": Design chips with redundancy, so that even if there are small manufacturing defects, the chips can still be sold as lower-performance parts, reducing waste.

"Honing the sword": Spirited debate often leads to the best ideas.

"How hard can it be?": A refrain to use to avoid feeling overwhelmed by the amount of work ahead.

"Intellectual honesty": Tell the truth, acknowledge failure, be willing to move forward and learn from past mistakes.

"If you measure it, you can improve it, but you have to measure the right thing!": Don't fall for tracking the wrong metrics. Be data driven in a smart way.

"Is it world class?": Nvidia's products, talent acquisition, and business practices must be benchmarked against the best in the industry.

"Let's go back to first principles": Tackle problems with a clean sheet of paper, not on the basis of how they were approached in the past.

"LUA": Listen to the question, understand the question, and answer the question. A warning sign Jensen is getting frustrated about a long-winded response.

"The mission is the boss": Decisions are made on the basis of the end goal of serving the customer, not internal politics.

"No one loses alone": If you are falling behind, inform your team promptly, so they can help.

"Nvidia can execute": Nvidia wins with superior technology and execution.

"Pilot-in-Command": Jensen's designated leader for an important project who should receive priority support from the entire company.

"Second place is the first loser": The goal and expectation is to win every time.

"Small steps, big vision": Prioritize actionable items and complete the most important first task to the best of your ability.

"Speed of Light": Strive to improve performance to the absolute limit of what's possible according to the laws of physics rather than comparing results against previous ones.

"Strategy is about the things you give up": Sort through everything, pick the most important thing, and then do that and leave the others aside.

"We don't steal market share, we create markets": Nvidia wants to be the market leader in a new area rather than fight over an existing business.

"You got to believe, what you got to believe": If you believe in something, go invest in it. Go do it. Put all your energy there.

"Your strength is your weakness": Being overly kind and tactful can hinder progress.

ACKNOWLEDGMENTS

THE ORIGIN OF THIS BOOK STARTED WITH A COLD E-MAIL. ON May 10, 2023, I received a message with the subject header: "Hello from W. W. Norton—a book on Nvidia?" It came from an editor, Dan Gerstle. He reached out at the suggestion of one of his authors (thanks, Matthew Ball), who thought I could write a book on Nvidia.

I thought there must be several books on Nvidia, as every other major technology company had at least half a dozen. After searching, I found none. At that moment, I realized I wanted to write this book.

From there, life moved quickly. I met with Dan at Bryant Park Café in Manhattan. At the end of the meeting, he said I needed a book agent. On the recommendation of friends, I met with Pilar Queen, who agreed to represent me. A month after receiving the first e-mail, I had secured a book deal.

The past year has been a whirlwind. I'm indebted to Dan and Pilar for taking a chance on a new author and providing invaluable advice and guidance. I also want to thank my freelance editor, Darryl Campbell, who worked tirelessly, editing and offering great feedback on the manuscript.

I want to thank Jensen. Although Nvidia was initially hesitant about cooperating with this book, maybe due to some of my prior unfavorable coverage, he never discouraged sources from speaking with me. I also want to thank Curtis Priem and Chris Malachowsky for their contributions, as well as the Nvidia team: Stephanie, Bob, Mylene, Ken, and Hector.

Finally, I extend my heartfelt gratitude to my sources for taking time out of their busy lives to share their experiences. Gathering their accounts of the early decades of computer history, many of which were documented for the first time, has been an honor. Their generosity enriched this book and made it possible.

NOTES

Introduction

1. Hendrik Bessembinder, "Which U.S. Stocks Generated the Highest Long-Term Returns?," S&P Global Market Intelligence Research Paper Series, July 16, 2024. http://dx.doi.org/10.2139/ssrn.4897069.

Chapter 1: Pain and Suffering

1. Lizzy Gurdus, "Nvidia CEO: My Mom Taught Me English," CNBC, May 6, 2018.
2. Matthew Yi, "Nvidia Founder Learned Key Lesson in Pingpong," *San Francisco Chronicle*, February 21, 2005.
3. "A Conversation with Nvidia's Jensen Huang," Stripe, May 21, 2024, video, 10:02.
4. Maggie Shiels, "Nvidia's Jen-Hsun Huang," BBC News, January 14, 2010.
5. Brian Dumaine, "The Man Who Came Back from the Dead Again," *Fortune*, September 1, 2001.
6. Interview with Judy Hoarfrost, 2024.
7. "19th Hole: The Readers Take Over," *Sports Illustrated*, January 30, 1978.
8. Yi, "Nvidia Founder Learned Key Lesson."
9. "2021 SIA Awards Dinner," SIAAmerica, February 11, 2022, video. https://www.youtube.com/watch?v=5yvN_T8xaw8.
10. "The Moment with Ryan Patel: Featuring NVIDIA CEO Jensen Huang | HP," HP, October 26, 2023, video, 1:47.
11. "Jen-Hsun Huang," *Charlie Rose*, February 5, 2009.
12. Interview with Jensen Huang, 2024.
13. "2021 SIA Awards Dinner," SIAAmerica, 1:04:00.
14. "The Moment with Ryan Patel," HP, 3:07.
15. "Jen-Hsun Huang, NVIDIA Co-Founder, Invests in the Next Generation of Stanford Engineers," School News, Stanford Engineering, October 1, 2010.
16. Gurdus, "Nvidia CEO."
17. "Jensen Huang," Stanford Institute for Economic Policy Research, March 7, 2024, video, 38:00.

Chapter 2: The Graphics Revolution
1. Frederick Van Veen, *The General Radio Story* (self-pub., 2011), 153.
2. Van Veen, *General Radio Story*, 171–75.
3. Interview with Chris Malachowsky, 2023.
4. Interview with Curtis Priem, 2024.
5. Van Hook was a graphics pioneer in his own right, however. He would later design the graphics architecture of the Nintendo 64.
6. Interview with Chris Malachowsky, 2023.

Chapter 3: The Birth of Nvidia
1. "Jensen Huang," Sequoia Capital, November 30, 2023, video, 5:13.
2. "Jen-Hsun Huang, NVIDIA Co-Founder, Invests in the Next Generation of Stanford Engineers," School News, Stanford Engineering, October 1, 2010.
3. "2021 SIA Awards Dinner," SIAAmerica, February 11, 2022, video, 1:11:09. https://www.youtube.com/watch?v=5yvN_T8xaw8.
4. "Jen-Hsun Huang," Stanford Online, June 23, 2011, video, 9:25.
5. National Science Board, "Science and Engineering Indicators–2002," NSB-02-01 (Arlington, VA: National Science Foundation, 2002). https://www.nsf.gov/publications/pub_summ.jsp?ods_key=nsb0201.
6. Interview with Jensen Huang, 2024.
7. "Jensen Huang," Sequoia Capital.
8. Interview with Mark Stevens, 2024.

Chapter 4: All In
1. "Jen-Hsun Huang," Stanford Online, June 23, 2011, video, 45:37.
2. Interview with Pat Gelsinger, 2023.
3. Interview with Dwight Diercks, 2024.
4. Jon Peddie, *The History of the GPU: Steps to Invention* (Cham, Switzerland: Springer, 2022), 278.
5. Peddie, *History of the GPU*, 278.
6. Interview with Curtis Priem, 2024.
7. Interview with Michael Hara, 2024.
8. "Jen-Hsun Huang, NVIDIA Co-Founder, Invests in the Next Generation of Stanford Engineers," School News, Stanford Engineering, October 1, 2010.
9. "Jensen Huang," Sequoia Capital, November 30, 2023, video, 13:57.
10. Jon Stokes, "Nvidia Cofounder Chris Malachowsky Speaks," *Ars Technica*, September 3, 2008.
11. "Dean's Speaker Series | Jensen Huang Founder, President & CEO, NVIDIA," Berkeley Haas, January 31, 2023, video, 32:09.
12. Interview with former Nvidia employee, 2023.
13. "3dfx Oral History Panel," Computer History Museum, July 29, 2013, video.
14. Orchid Technology, "Orchid Ships Righteous 3D," press release, October 7, 1996.
15. "3dfx Oral History Panel," Computer History Museum.
16. Interview with Scott Sellers, 2023.

17. Interview with Dwight Diercks, 2024.
18. "Jen-Hsun Huang," Oregon State University, February 22, 2013, video, 37:20.
19. Interview with former Nvidia employee, 2023.
20. "Jen-Hsun Huang," Oregon State University, 30:28.
21. Interview with Curtis Priem, 2024.
22. Interview with Dwight Diercks, 2024.
23. Interview with Henry Levin, 2023.
24. Interview with Chris Malachowsky, 2023.
25. Interview with Jensen Huang, 2024.
26. Interview with Eric Christenson, 2023.
27. Personal e-mail from Sutter Hill CFO Chris Basso.
28. Nvidia, "Upstart Nvidia Ships Over One Million Performance 3D Processors," press release, January 12, 1998.
29. Interview with Jensen Huang, 2024.

Chapter 5: Ultra-Aggressive
1. Interview with Caroline Landry, 2024.
2. Interview with Michael Hara, 2024.
3. Interviews with Tench Coxe and other former Nvidia employees, 2023.
4. Interview with Robert Csongor, 2023.
5. Interview with Jeff Fisher, 2024.
6. Interview with Geoff Ribar, 2023.
7. Interview with John McSorley, 2023.
8. Interview with Andrew Logan, 2024.
9. Interview with Kenneth Hurley, 2024.
10. Interview with Caroline Landry, 2024.
11. Interview with Sanford Russell, 2024.
12. Interview with Andrew Logan, 2024.
13. Interview with Jeff Fisher, 2024.
14. "Morris Chang, in Conversation with Jen-Hsun Huang," Computer History Museum, October 17, 2007, video, 23:00.
15. Interview with Chris Malachowsky, 2023.
16. Interview with Curtis Priem, 2024.
17. Interview with Geoff Ribar, 2023.
18. Interview with Michael Hara, 2024.
19. Interview with Michael Hara, 2024.
20. Interview with Jeff Fisher, 2024.
21. Interview with Curtis Priem, 2024.
22. Interview with Nick Triantos, 2023.

Chapter 6: Just Go Win
1. Interview with Ross Smith, 2023.
2. Interview with Scott Sellers, 2023.
3. Interview with Dwight Diercks, 2024.

4. Interview with Michael Hara, 2024.
5. Interview with David Kirk, 2024.
6. Interview with Curtis Priem, 2024.
7. Interview with Dwight Diercks, 2024.
8. Interview with Dwight Diercks, 2024.
9. Interview with Rick Tsai, 2024.
10. Dean Takahashi, "Shares of Nvidia Surge 64% after Initial Public Offering," *Wall Street Journal*, January 25, 1999.
11. Interview with Kenneth Hurley, 2024.
12. Takahashi, "Shares of Nvidia Surge."
13. Dean Takahashi, *Opening the Xbox: Inside Microsoft's Plan to Unleash an Entertainment Revolution* (Roseville, CA: Prima Publishing, 2002), 230.
14. Interview with Oliver Baltuch, 2023.
15. Takahashi, *Opening the Xbox*, 202.
16. Interview with George Haber, 2023.
17. Interview with Chris Diskin, 2024.
18. Interview with George Haber, 2023.
19. Interview with Curtis Priem, 2024
20. Interview with Michael Hara, 2024.

Chapter 7: GeForce and the Innovator's Dilemma

1. Clayton Christensen, *The Innovator's Dilemma: When New Technologies Cause Great Firms to Fail* (Boston, MA: Harvard Business School Press, 1997), 47.
2. Interview with Michael Hara, 2024.
3. Interview with Jeff Fisher, 2024.
4. Interview with Tench Coxe, 2023.
5. "Jensen Huang of Nvidia on the Future of A.I. | DealBook Summit 2023," *New York Times*, November 30, 2023, video, 19:54.
6. Interview with Nvidia employee, 2023.
7. Interview with Sanford Russell, 2024.
8. Interview with Dan Vivoli, 2024.
9. John D. Owens et al., "A Survey of General-Purpose Computation on Graphics Hardware," State of the Art Reports, Eurographics 2005, August 1, 2005. https://doi.org/10.2312/egst.20051043.
10. Interview with David Kirk, 2024.
11. Interview with Jensen Huang, 2024.
12. Interview with two former Nvidia employees, 2023.
13. "Best Buy Named in Suit over Sam Goody Performance," *New York Times*, November 27, 2003.
14. Interview with Jensen Huang, 2024.

Chapter 8: The Era of the GPU
1. Interview with David Kirk, 2024.
2. Interview with Jensen Huang, 2024.
3. Interview with Jensen Huang, 2024.
4. Ian Buck et al., "Brook for GPUs: Stream Computing on Graphics Hardware," *ACM Transactions on Graphics* 23, no. 3 (August 2004): 777–86.
5. Interview with Andy Keane, 2024.
6. Anand Lal Shimpi, "Nvidia's GeForce 8800," *Anandtech*, November 8, 2006.
7. "A Conversation with Nvidia's Jensen Huang," Stripe Sessions 2024, April 24, 2024, video, 01:04:49.
8. "No Priors Ep. 13 | With Jensen Huang, Founder & CEO of NVIDIA," No Priors: AI, Machine Learning, Tech, & Startups, April 25, 2023, video. https://www.youtube.com/watch?v=ZFtW3g1dbUU.
9. Rob Beschizza, "nVidia G80 Poked and Prodded. Verdict: Fast as Hell," *WIRED*, November 3, 2006; Jon Stokes, "NVIDIA Rethinks the GPU with the New GeForce 8800," *Ars Technica*, November 8, 2006.
10. Interview with David Kirk, 2024.
11. Interview with Mark Berger, 2024.
12. Interview with Derik Moore, 2024.
13. "NVIDIA CEO Jensen Huang," Acquired, October 15, 2023, video, 49:42.
14. Interview with Amir Salek, 2023.

Chapter 9: Tortured into Greatness
1. Nvidia Corporation, "Letter to Stockholders: Notice of 2010 Annual Meeting" (Santa Clara, CA: Nvidia, April 2010).
2. Interview with Dan Vivoli, 2023.
3. Interview with Anthony Medeiros, 2024.
4. Interview with Jensen Huang, 2024.
5. "In Conversation | Jensen Huang and Joel Hellermark," Sana AI Summit, June 29, 2023, video, 32:10.
6. "A Conversation with Nvidia's Jensen Huang," Stripe, May 21, 2024, video, 11:06.
7. Interview with Tench Coxe, 2023.
8. Interview with Oliver Baltuch, 2023.
9. Interview with Andy Keane, 2024.
10. Interview with Jensen Huang, 2024.
11. Interview with Simona Jankowski, 2024.
12. Interview with Jay Puri, 2024.
13. Interview with Jensen Huang, 2024.
14. Interview with Robert Csongor, 2023.
15. Interview with Michael Douglas, 2024.
16. Interview with Michael Douglas, 2023.
17. Interview with John McSorley, 2023.
18. Interview with former Nvidia employee, 2024.
19. Interview with Mark Berger, 2024.

20. Interview with Jay Puri, 2024.

21. Interview with David Ragones, 2024.

22. Interview with Michael Douglas, 2024.

23. Interview with Jensen Huang, 2024.

Chapter 10: The Engineer's Mind

1. Carl Icahn, "Beyond Passive Investing," Founder's Council program, Greenwich Roundtable, April 12, 2005.

2. Walt Mossberg, "On Steve Jobs the Man, the Myth, the Movie," Ctrl-Walt-Delete Podcast, October 22, 2015.

3. Interview with former Nvidia employee, 2024.

4. Interview with Tench Coxe, 2023.

5. Interview with Ali Simnad, 2024.

6. Interview with Leo Tam, 2023.

7. Interview with Kevin Krewell, 2024.

8. "In Conversation | Jensen Huang and Joel Hellermark," Sana AI Summit, June 29, 2023, video, 29:20.

9. "Jen-Hsun Huang," Stanford Online, June 23, 2011, video, 32:41.

10. "Jen-Hsun Huang," Oregon State University, February 22, 2013, video, 1:15:58.

11. Interview with Tench Coxe, 2023.

12. Interview with Jeff Fisher, 2023.

13. Interview with Bryan Catanzaro, 2024.

14. Maggie Shiels, "Nvidia's Jen-Hsun Huang," BBC, January 14, 2010.

15. "Saturday's Panel: A Conversation with Jen-Hsun Huang (5/7)," Committee of 100, May 18, 2007, video, 5:43.

16. "Jensen Huang—CEO of NVIDIA | Podcast | In Good Company | Norges Bank Investment Management," Norges Bank, November 19, 2023, video, 44:50.

17. Alexis C. Madrigal, "Paul Otellini's Intel: Can the Company That Built the Future Survive It?," *The Atlantic*, May 16, 2013.

18. Interview with Pat Gelsinger, 2023.

19. Mark Lipacis, "NVDA Deep-Dive Presentation," Jefferies Equity Research, August 17, 2023.

20. "Search Engine Market Share Worldwide," Statcounter. https://gs.statcounter.com/search-engine-market-share (accessed August 9, 2024).

Chapter 11: The Road to AI

1. William James Dally, "A VLSI Architecture for Concurrent Data Structures," PhD diss., California Institute of Technology, 1986.

2. Interview with David Kirk, 2024.

3. Brian Caulfield, "What's the Difference Between a CPU and a GPU?," Nvidia Blog, December 16, 2009.

4. "NVIDIA: Adam and Jamie Explain Parallel Processing on GPU's," Artmaze1974, September 15, 2008, video.

5. John Markoff, "How Many Computers to Identify a Cat? 16,000," *New York Times*, June 26, 2012.

6. Interview with Bill Dally, 2024.

7. Adam Coates et al., "Deep Learning with COTS HPC Systems," in *Proceedings of the 30th International Conference on Machine Learning*, Proceedings of Machine Learning Research, vol. 28, cycle 3, ed. Sanjoy Dasgupta and David McAllester (Atlanta, GA: PMLR, 2013), 1337–45.

8. Jensen Huang, "Accelerating AI with GPUs: A New Computing Model," Nvidia Blog, January 12, 2016.

9. Interview with Bill Dally, 2024.

10. Coates et al., "Deep Learning with COTS HPC Systems," 1338.

11. Coates et al., "Deep Learning with COTS HPC Systems," 1345.

12. Interview with Bill Dally, 2024.

13. Interview with Bryan Catanzaro, 2024.

14. Dave Gershgorn, "The Data That Transformed AI Research—and Possibly the World," *Quartz*, July 26, 2017.

15. Jessi Hempel, "Fei-Fei Li's Quest to Make AI Better for Humanity," *WIRED*, November 13, 2018.

16. Gershgorn, "The Data That Transformed AI Research."

17. Interview with Bill Dally, 2024.

18. Interview with Bryan Catanzaro, 2024.

19. Interview with Bryan Catanzaro, 2024.

20. Interview with Bryan Catanzaro, 2024.

21. Interview with Bryan Catanzaro, 2024.

22. "NVIDIA Tesla V100: The First Tensor Core GPU," Nvidia. https://www.nvidia.com/en-gb/data-center/tesla-v100/ (accessed August 13, 2024).

23. Interview with Bill Dally, 2024.

24. "No Priors Ep. 13 | With Jensen Huang, Founder & CEO of NVIDIA," No Priors: AI, Machine Learning, Tech, & Startups, April 25, 2023, video, 16:19. https://www.youtube.com/watch?v=ZFtW3g1dbUU.

25. "Q3 2024 Earnings Call," Nvidia, November 21, 2023.

Chapter 12: The "Most Feared" Hedge Fund

1. Michael J. de la Merced, "A Primer on Starboard, the Activist That Pushed for a Staples-Office Depot Merger," *New York Times*, February 4, 2015.

2. "Transforming Darden Restaurants," Starboard Value, PowerPoint presentation, September 11, 2014.

3. William D. Cohan, "Starboard Value's Jeff Smith: The Investor CEOs Fear Most," *Fortunate*, December 3, 2014.

4. Darden Restaurants, "Darden Addresses Inaccurate and Misleading Statements by Starboard and Provides the Facts on Value Achieved with Red Lobster Sale," press release, August 4, 2014.

5. Myles Udland and Elena Holodny, "Hedge Fund Manager Publishes Dizzying

294-Slide Presentation Exposing How Olive Garden Wastes Money and Fails Customers," *Business Insider*, September 12, 2014.
6. "Transforming Darden Restaurants," Starboard Value, 6–7.
7. Interview with Jeff Smith, 2024.
8. Starboard Value letter to Mellanox Technologies, Ltd., January 8, 2017.
9. Interview with Jay Puri, 2024.

Chapter 13: Lighting the Future
1. Interview with David Luebke, 2024.
2. Interview with Bryan Catanzaro, 2024.
3. Interview with Jensen Huang, 2024.
4. Jordan Novet, "Google A.I. Researcher Says He Left to Build a Startup after Encountering 'Big Company-itis,'" CNBC, August 17, 2023.

Chapter 14: The Big Bang
1. John Markoff, "At Google, Earnings Soar, and Share Price Follows," *New York Times*, October 22, 2004.
2. Ben Popper, "Facebook's Q2 2013 Earnings Beat Expectations," *The Verge*, July 24, 2013.
3. Interview with Colette Kress, 2023.
4. Interview with Jeff Fisher, 2024.
5. Interview with Simona Jankowski, 2024.
6. Dave Salvator, "H100 Transformer Engine Supercharges AI Training, Delivering Up to 6x Higher Performance without Losing Accuracy," Nvidia Blog, March 22, 2022.
7. "No Priors Ep. 13 | With Jensen Huang, Founder & CEO of NVIDIA," No Priors: AI, Machine Learning, Tech, & Startups, video, 16:51. https://www.youtube.com/watch?v=ZFtW3g1dbUU.
8. Interview with Jay Puri, 2024.
9. Interview with former Nvidia executive, 2024.
10. Interview with Ross Walker, 2024.
11. "Jen-Hsun Huang," Stanford Online, June 23, 2011, video, 9:25.
12. "Dean's Speaker Series | Jensen Huang Founder, President & CEO, NVIDIA," Berkeley Haas, January 31, 2023, video, 49:25.
13. "Download Day 2024 — Fireside Chat: NVIDIA Founder & CEO Jensen Huang and Recursion's Chris Gibson," Recursion, June 24, 2024, video, 1:32.
14. Kimberly Powell Q&A interview by analyst Harlan Sur, 42nd Annual J.P. Morgan Healthcare Conference, San Francisco, CA, January 8, 2024.
15. Interview with Gevorg Grigoryan, 2024.
16. "Nvidia CEO," HBR IdeaCast, November 14, 2023.
17. Brian Caulfield, "AI Is Tech's 'Greatest Contribution to Social Elevation,' NVIDIA CEO Tells Oregon State Students," Nvidia Blog, April 15, 2024.

Conclusion: The Nvidia Way

1. Paul Graham, "What Happened to Yahoo," PaulGraham.com, August 2010.
2. Nvidia Corporation, "NVIDIA Corporate Responsibility Report Fiscal Year 2023" (Santa Clara, CA: Nvidia), 16.
3. Interview with Ben de Waal, 2023.
4. Interview with Dwight Diercks, 2024.
5. Interview with David Kirk, 2024.
6. Interview with Li-Yi Wei, 2024.
7. Interview with Anthony Medeiros, 2024.
8. Interview with Jay Puri, 2024.
9. Interview with Anthony Medeiros, 2024.
10. Interview with Peter Young, 2024.
11. Interview with Jeff Fisher, 2024.
12. Interview with Shantanu Narayen, 2024.
13. Interview with Bryan Catanzaro, 2024.
14. Interview with Jeff Fisher, 2024.
15. Interview with Curtis Priem, 2024.